HOSTAGES
NO MORE

HOSTAGES NO MORE

THE FIGHT FOR EDUCATION FREEDOM
AND THE
FUTURE OF THE AMERICAN CHILD

Betsy DeVos

CENTER
STREET®

NASHVILLE   NEW YORK

Copyright © 2022 by Betsy DeVos

Jacket image Shutterstock

Cover copyright © 2022 by Hachette Book Group, Inc.

Hachette Book Group supports the right to free expression and the value of copyright. The purpose of copyright is to encourage writers and artists to produce the creative works that enrich our culture.

The scanning, uploading, and distribution of this book without permission is a theft of the author's intellectual property. If you would like permission to use material from the book (other than for review purposes), please contact permissions@hbgusa.com. Thank you for your support of the author's rights.

Center Street
Hachette Book Group
1290 Avenue of the Americas, New York, NY 10104
centerstreet.com
twitter.com/centerstreet

First Edition: June 2022

Center Street is a division of Hachette Book Group, Inc.
The Center Street name and logo are trademarks of Hachette Book Group, Inc.

The publisher is not responsible for websites (or their content) that are not owned by the publisher.

The Hachette Speakers Bureau provides a wide range of authors for speaking events. To find out more, go to www.hachettespeakersbureau.com or call (866) 376-6591.

Library of Congress Cataloging-in-Publication Data has been applied for.

Interior book design by Timothy Shaner, NightandDayDesign.biz

ISBNs: 9781546002017 (Hardcover), 9781668602782 (Audiobook), 9781546002031 (E-Book)

Printed in the United States of America

LSC-C

Printing 1, 2022

To Dick,
my beloved husband
and a truly great man

CONTENTS

THE QUIET PART OUT LOUD

I n the fall of 2021, a politician told the truth and started a movement.

Glenn Youngkin, the underdog candidate for Virginia governor, defended parental control over children's education in a debate. To which Terry McAuliffe, the front-runner, replied: "I don't think parents should be telling schools what they should teach."

Some called it a "gaffe"—a mistake. But mistakes don't inspire a million angry social media comments. Mistakes don't upend elections. Mistakes don't spark a prairie fire of parental dissatisfaction.

Only the truth does that.

Terry McAuliffe meant what he said. And parents across America knew he did. *That's* what started the movement. *He said the quiet part out loud.*

Parents were patient at first when COVID-19 hit. They cooperated when schools were closed, doing their part to "stop the spread." But as schools remained closed for months and months—well after it was clear that children could safely go back—the mood among Americans began to shift. I heard echoes of it repeatedly when I met with parents. They were frustrated. More importantly, their children were suffering. And the children suffering the *most* were the children who could *least* afford to be out of school: the poor and the disadvantaged.

In other words, the very children the people who run our public schools *claim* to care about the most. In an egregious display of hypocrisy and ruthlessness, the school union bosses and public education establishment made every excuse to not open schools. They shifted goalposts. They made endless demands—few of them related to the pandemic or public health in any way—before they would even think about allowing children to return to the classroom.

They treated our children like bargaining chips. Like hostages. Pawns in a fight for power and resources—and ideology.

But the Terry McAuliffes of the world miscalculated. History will judge the prolonged closure of American schools as one of the biggest public health failures of our lifetime. It also opened parents' eyes. When children started to "learn" remotely from their homes, parents saw firsthand what their children were being taught in America's classrooms. Suddenly it was right there, on computer screens resting on kitchen tables. Far too many parents saw their kids learning very little at all, beyond how to mute and unmute a Zoom conference. Many awakened to all the things their children should have been learning, but *didn't*. At worst, parents saw their children being taught to hate their country, and even to hate themselves. They saw lesson plans labeling the foundation of the American dream—of hard work and achievement—as a racist conspiracy, purposefully designed to oppress certain people. COVID-19 laid bare the failings of the system. What parents saw when their children were sent home fed the movement.

As 2021 went on, upset parents at school board meetings would be the subject of countless viral videos, news reports, and campaign commercials. Parents were feeling disempowered when it came to their children's education—and they showed it. The object of their frustration morphed from school closings to mask mandates to critical race theory. But the central power disparity on display at every school board meeting remained unchanged: Parents stood behind microphones and begged public school officials to think about their children. And officials sat opposite them on daises and pondered what their price would be.

Horace Mann, the creator of America's industrial-style public education system, once wrote: "We who are engaged in the sacred cause of education are entitled to look upon all parents as having given hostages to our cause."

Mann argued that parents could not be trusted to raise their children appropriately, and thus the children must be sent to compulsory public schooling. The school system he created—one that emulated the model of rigid, mass education developed in eighteenth-century Prussia—was intended to enforce conformity. Everyone learning to do the same things, the same way, to prepare them to populate America's factories. It was a system where trained educators, not parents, knew best.[1]

Mann was open about students being held "hostage" to his statist vision of education. Today the school union bosses and the education establishment are still using our kids as hostages to a cause, but they're not as open about just what that cause is. Most parents take them at their word that they are dedicated to educating children, which many, many teachers are. But teachers are not the ones who hold the power in education. The real cause for which the education *establishment* has been willing to sacrifice the education of so many American children has little to do with educating students and empowering parents and much to do with enriching and placating adults. The jobs, the pay, the bloat, the power of the education *system* is their cause. The students are merely the means to that end.

The growing awareness of parental powerlessness in the face of the public education establishment has brought us to a pivotal time. Suburban parents have learned what urban parents have long known—even the "good" schools care more about the people who run them than the children and teachers within.

Those parents who can afford to have begun voting with their feet. They have moved to different cities or switched their children to private schools that they know will be reliably open. Others have opted to homeschool their kids because of the poisonous messages being taught in public schools. School choice, long demonized by the education establishment, is being transformed in the public's eye from an interesting experiment to an absolute necessity. And more and more parents are wondering why education freedom, by which I mean the ability for a family to choose when, where, and how their child is educated, isn't the norm for all kids instead of the privilege of the wealthy.

This age of parental enlightenment couldn't have come at a worse time for the public school establishment. It's not just that they kept schools needlessly shuttered and kids needlessly masked during the pandemic. It's not even the fact that they were caught trying to supplant academics with racially charged indoctrination. Even before COVID-19—before critical race theory—America's schools were failing, and American students were falling further and further behind. The system has become a giant albatross for families nationwide.

The Nation's Report Card, which lists the results of the only nationally administered assessment of student learning, showed the first recorded decline in math and reading scores for thirteen-year-olds in the fifty-year history of the assessment *before the pandemic*.[2] Some examples of just how bad things are:

- The lowest-performing 10 percent of thirteen-year-olds saw their math scores fall by 13 points since 2012. Their scores are the same now as they were in 1982.
- The lowest-performing 10 percent of nine-year-olds saw their reading scores fall by 7 points since 2012.

• Thirteen-year-old black students saw their math scores fall 8 points, while Hispanic students saw a decline of 4 points, further widening the gap with their white peers.

Not even high-performing students saw any measurable achievement gains pre-pandemic. There wasn't a single bright spot to be found *anywhere* in the data. No student group, of any age, of any ethnicity, saw their performance improve since 2012. Most saw declines.

Again, this was *before* COVID-19 shut down schools and learning.

Some say the solution is more money, but the data tells a different story. Per-pupil spending has nearly tripled in constant dollars since the 1960s. Today the United States spends, on average, 37 percent more per pupil than every other major developed nation.[3] Yet math and science test scores aren't improving. According to the 2018 Program for International Student Assessment (PISA), American students rank thirty-seventh in the world in math.[4] We rank in the teens in reading and science. In fact, the United States does not rank in the top ten globally on *any* subject tested.

Doing the same thing—and more of it—won't bring about new results. Albert Einstein famously called such an approach the definition of insanity.

I made a long journey—thirty-plus years of working in the states to promote school choice, advise governors, and drive reforms—to come to Washington to champion a different approach: freedom.

Freedom defines the United States. But for most of the people on the daises at school board meetings, education freedom is an unthinkable concept. The establishment is organized against freedom because powerful groups are threatened by it. Overcoming these forces on behalf of America's schoolchildren has always been a titanic struggle. Now the moms, the civil rights activists, the religious educators, and the visionaries who have fought this fight have gained potent new allies: the millions of American parents who are fed up with being considered nuisances and dismissed by the public school establishment.

Americans have never been as receptive to fundamental change in our education system as they are today. But decades-long experience in the education freedom trenches has taught me that this new receptivity must translate into political will—bipartisan political will. That means Democrats have to rethink their role as the political arm of the school union bosses. And many Republicans have to reevaluate their reluctance to act boldly to advance school choice.

The time has come for a truly new approach. We tried throwing truckloads of money at schools. That didn't make them open any sooner during the pandemic. We tried banning poisonous ideologies like critical race theory, but that hasn't—and won't—stop the tendency to indoctrinate our children in government-run schools.

The answer is education freedom. It means empowering families to choose how and where the education dollars already designated for their children are spent—to fund students, not systems or buildings. It means giving teachers freedom to innovate and grow in their profession. It means reempowering the parents behind the podiums at school board meetings.

We have a rare opportunity to change the balance of power in our schools. And we can't act quickly enough.

In late September 2021, the National School Boards Association (NSBA) wrote a letter to President Joe Biden likening vocal parents demanding better for their children to perpetrators of "domestic terrorism." But the NSBA wasn't acting on its own. It had been coordinating with the Biden White House. Five days after the letter was sent, the Department of Justice (DOJ) issued a memo directing federal law enforcement—the FBI—to investigate perceived threats to school boards. American parents found themselves in the crosshairs of federal authorities for the "crime" of advocating for their children. The school board group later retracted the letter and issued an apology—albeit in the same disingenuous way a child apologizes for raiding the cookie jar after he gets caught. The DOJ, critically, did not retract its memo.

It was a truly frightening episode. Americans have been generally aware of collusion between the Democratic Party and the school union bosses to enforce union prerogatives in schools. But collusion between federal law enforcement and the education establishment to smother free speech is a new low that fundamentally threatens our freedoms. It compels us, as a nation, to act to restore the rights of parents in our schools.

In my decades working to help students, I have never before seen the kind of momentum for change we've seen in the last couple of years. The seeds we planted in state capitals in West Virginia, Kentucky, Florida, Arizona, Indiana, South Dakota, and Oklahoma—just to name a few—are bearing fruit with new or expanded state school choice programs.

This momentum is both a shot across the bow for politicians and a beacon of hope for millions of American parents. Our education system is controlled by adults who are using our children as hostages to their cause, be it more regulations on teachers, shutting down competition from charter schools, or the promotion of "woke" ideology. It's long past time to affirm the obvious: Education must be about students, and not the special interests that control the system.

This is our movement. This is our moment. While the chapters that follow tell my story of fighting for education freedom, this is really a story of *our* cause: the cause of ensuring that every single child in America has equal access to a world-class education.

The cause of ensuring that our children are *hostages no more*.

CHAPTER ONE

THE OPPORTUNITY OF
A LIFETIME

I woke up the morning after election day 2016 not knowing who was president-elect. I had gone to bed around midnight the night before because I had to get up early to go to Indianapolis for meetings with state legislators. My last check of the news on election night showed the contest still undecided. Donald Trump was gaining ground against the heavily favored Hillary Clinton. Trump was winning battlegrounds like Florida, Ohio, Wisconsin, and North Carolina. The networks seemed to be having a hard time accepting what was happening. By bedtime, Hillary Clinton's election was dependent on victories in Pennsylvania and in my home state of Michigan, where the preelection polls had her leading but the voters were telling a different story.

Like the rest of America, I watched that night in amazement. Before the election, the idea of Donald Trump as president was one I had difficulty taking seriously. My family, the extended DeVos family, gets together periodically to make decisions about our businesses and our philanthropy. We had one such family meeting early in the Republican primary process, when Donald Trump was still viewed as little more than a joke by those who were supposedly in the know. At the meeting, my ninety-year-old father-in-law, Rich DeVos—who had an affinity for successful, charismatic businessmen—leaned in and announced, "I think we should all support Trump." My response was, "You've got to be kidding."

Although he would later deny being such a lightweight, my husband, Dick, had also gone to bed early on election night. After I got up, turned on the TV, and saw that Trump was the president-elect, I called to Dick. "You won't believe it!" I said. "Trump won."

There was no mistaking the fact that the political ground had shifted in America. I had been very involved in Republican Party politics since I was in college. I was a "Scatterblitzer," which I will explain later, for hometown favorite Gerald Ford in 1976. I cheered Ronald Reagan's victory in 1980, and again in 1984. I knew and supported George H. W. Bush in 1988. After the Clinton years, I supported Bush's son, George W. I had seen America elect its first African-American president in 2008. But I had never seen anything like Donald Trump's victory in 2016.

Once again, my father-in-law had seen it coming.

The morning after the election, members of the media all had the dazed, battered look of losers in a heavyweight bout. Crowds, soon to be mobs, were forming on the streets of big cities across the country. But there wasn't much time for me to contemplate America's future under a Trump administration. I had to get on a plane to Indianapolis. Indiana was one of the battleground states in the fight to give students—especially low-income students—freedom from a failing education system that cares more about adults than kids. I was huddled on the plane with a colleague from the education policy organization I chaired, going over our pitch to the Indiana legislators, when I noticed one particular email in my inbox. It was from a longtime friend and fellow warrior for education freedom, Jeb Bush. It was one line:

"Would you ever consider being Secretary of Education?"

I laughed and showed it to my colleague. "Look at this," I said. "It's crazy."

I didn't respond to Jeb. Not yet.

"Crazy." That's the word that kept coming to my mind at the thought of going to Washington to be a cabinet secretary. I had spent the last thirty-plus years fighting to diminish Washington's control of education; to take the power and resources heaped on the U.S. Department of Education and give them to parents and children. Now someone was suggesting I run the place? Not to mention the fact that I didn't know Donald Trump. I had never met the man. I had never contributed to his campaign. Jeb had been my first choice for president in 2016.

I hadn't been able to make up my mind on Trump during the campaign. Part of the reason was that, throughout the Republican primaries, education was barely mentioned. I told a reporter that I would be "watching and listening with interest" at the Republican National Convention in Cleveland. There was also the fact that many of the things Trump had said over the course of the campaign gave me great pause. He was a tough sell for me. On the other hand, the alternative—the Democratic nominee, Hillary Clinton—was not an option. I was in limbo.

I went to the convention as a delegate for former Ohio governor John Kasich, not because he was my candidate but because I wanted to be there and the only slot our district had available was designated for Kasich. As promised, I watched and listened with interest. I was pleased to hear Trump's rhetoric begin to change. In his nomination acceptance speech, he called for education choice for parents. He aimed his rhetoric straight at the central problem with our education system: It is designed to serve adults, not kids.

"We will rescue kids from failing schools by helping their parents send them to a safe school of their choice," Trump told the delegates. "My opponent would rather protect bureaucrats than serve American children."

He was singing my song.

Later, Trump put some meat on these bones by announcing a $20 billion block grant to the states that would allow parents to choose their children's schools. The details of the proposal were spot-on. The funds would be directed toward low-income students, precisely the students who are being most damaged by the system. And it would be up to the states to determine exactly how the money would be used—a must for me. I firmly believe American education should *never* be commanded and controlled by the federal government. Power should be as close to parents and students as possible—and that means first with families and then with local communities.

It was all encouraging stuff. The day after the election, Trump's plan was in the back of my mind as I finished my meetings in Indianapolis and flew back home. This was an agenda I would be eager to help make real for American families as the U.S. secretary of education. But was it really feasible I would get that opportunity? I was dubious.

When Dick and I finally had a chance to sit down and talk, I told him about the email I received from Jeb that morning. He chuckled—one of those "are you serious?" chuckles—and asked how I had responded. I told Dick I was waiting to respond to Jeb, but that I thought my answer to being secretary of education should be something like, "That's not something I have ever thought about, but if I ever had the opportunity, how could I not consider it?" Dick replied, "That's exactly what I was thinking you'd say." We both intuitively knew that if I was asked to serve our country in this way, we had to seriously consider it.

This was not my first offer to serve in the federal government. I was asked to be the U.S. ambassador to the Netherlands during the second term of President George W. Bush. It was an honor to have the opportunity, but I turned the ambassadorship down. I was doing work on education freedom in a variety of states, and it was having a real impact.

The opportunity to be education secretary, however, was different. It was a chance to have an impact on a higher level.

Still, I hesitated.

I didn't doubt my passion for education reform. Next to my family, it is the cause of my life. And I didn't doubt my ability to do the job. I had seen education from both the bottom up and the top down—from mentoring at-risk kids and helping Dick start a charter school to leading national organizations and advising candidates and elected officials of all stripes. What I *did* doubt was that the education establishment—the school union bosses, the alphabet soup of lobbying organizations, and the bureaucrats who hold the real power in the system—would ever allow me to serve. I was not, to say the least, a conventional candidate for education secretary. But then again, I thought, we did not have a conventional president-elect.

I emailed Jeb back.

It's tough to articulate how it feels to see yourself being described by strangers in the media. The novelty wears off quickly. And then, in my experience, reading about myself becomes a source of frustration—which is why I mostly avoid it. The media likes to portray heroes and villains; cartoon images of people in a black-and-white world. But life isn't like that and neither am I. I'm not that splashy, and I'm basically an introvert. I don't like talking about myself and I don't like talking trash about other people. My parents taught me to do good and do well, but not necessarily to talk about it. My faith taught me that I am a unique, irreplaceable child of God, and so are all other human beings. And my community taught me that there is great joy and comfort in being part of a larger whole. Real community, I have learned, requires modesty, generosity, and sacrifice.

I am the granddaughter and great-granddaughter of immigrants. My mom's parents came to America from the Netherlands when they were teenagers. My dad's family came a generation earlier. They were both farming families. We found out later that Dad's family had lived less than ten miles away from my mom's family in the Friesland region of the Netherlands. There's no indication that the families knew one another in the homeland. But when they came to America, like so many other Dutch immigrants they settled in West Michigan. And like the first Dutch immigrants of the mid-nineteenth century, they came to West Michigan seeking religious freedom and economic opportunity—a chance at the American dream. They settled in a town less than six miles from Lake Michigan. It's called—you guessed it—Holland.

Both my mom, Elsa Zwiep, and my dad, Edgar Prince, were born and lived their entire lives in Holland. When she was young, my mom lived above the seed store her parents owned. The store backed up to a Christian elementary school. My mom didn't attend the school but she played on its playground whenever she got a chance. One day when she was about four, the school principal saw Elsa playing and asked her why she wasn't in school. She said she wasn't old enough. He replied, "Well, you're here all the time—you may as well be in school." So Mom started school. Her mother never finished high school, but Mom went on to graduate from Calvin College in Grand Rapids. Her senior year, a local public school needed a kindergarten teacher. They reached out to my mom. As soon as she graduated she was responsible for thirty-six kindergartners in the morning class and thirty-seven in the afternoon. When she looks back on it now, she smiles and has only two words to describe the experience: "I survived."

My father's story is less sunny. When he was just twelve years old, his life was forever changed by a family tragedy. His father—my grandfather, Peter Prince—died suddenly of a heart attack while delivering produce, his daily routine. He left behind my grandmother, Edith, to raise three children on her own in the middle of the Great Depression. Edith was proud. She refused to accept help from anyone outside the family. She sewed draperies and curtains in their home while my dad washed cars for a local auto dealership after school and on Saturdays. By fourteen, he drove cars back and forth to Detroit for the dealership. All the while, Dad managed to continue to go to school. He never had the chance to play sports or belong to clubs. When he wasn't in school he was always working. He eventually worked his way through Michigan Technological University and the University of Michigan and graduated with a degree in engineering.

It's impossible to really know my family, Holland, and West Michigan for that matter, without knowing just a little about the Dutch Reformed Church adherents who originally settled there. Like so many things in West Michigan, the church's roots in the Netherlands run deep. Many of its members immigrated to America in the mid-nineteenth century to escape religious persecution and seek economic freedom. They were settlers in a strange land, but they managed to survive and, in many cases, thrive. While membership in the various Reformed churches in America is small in numbers, its members have impacted the world for good in ways too numerous to mention.

Today, Holland is home to many faiths. Immigrants from around the globe have added to our diversity. Holland has been called "city of churches" and its citizens' strong faiths have literally shaped the community. We are a small town of just over thirty thousand residents but we give more of our time and resources to charitable endeavors than most places in the country. And not just for those in need in Holland, but for the poor or suffering all over the world.

The media and popular culture tend to caricature communities of faith as narrow-minded and judgmental. Holland is the opposite.

Its people are warm and welcoming. My hometown is a special place, not in spite of its faith, but because of it.

Like many of my neighbors, I am a follower of Jesus Christ. My faith became "my own" when I was in my late twenties. It was no longer my parents' faith or my community's faith. It was mine. It was personal to me. It has informed just about every aspect of my life.

My faith has encouraged me to be grateful and generous. The Bible verse "To whom much is given, much will be required; and from the one to whom much has been entrusted, even more will be demanded" (Luke 12:48) rings true for me daily. The same firm faith guided my parents and helped them to be grateful optimists. Mom credits her faith with giving her the strength to conquer small challenges like walking in Holland's annual Tulip Time parade with seventy-plus kindergartners. And it gave her the strength to go on after my father's early death.

Mom and Dad met as teenagers through friends in the church. Dad proposed when he was at the University of Michigan. As soon as they were married, Dad's military service took them to live in Denver and then Sumter, South Carolina, for a few years. While Dad analyzed photo intelligence for the Air Force, Mom taught first grade. In South Carolina, she educated both the children of officers and children from very poor homes. She was required to have one of her annual parent-teacher conferences at the home of each student. She remembers some houses that were in such poor condition she had to take care where she walked to avoid falling through the floorboards.

After Dad completed his service, my parents returned to Holland, where Dad began working as an engineer at Buss Machine Works, a company that made die-cast machinery—the huge machines that mold metal into things like car parts. My parents' first house—where they lived when I was born—was on Floral Avenue. We called it "the Little Red House." It had two bedrooms and a white rail fence Dad built around the yard. Mom and Dad painted it. My grandma Prince sewed the drapes. My father made the cherrywood cabinet that held our black-and-white television in the family living room. Some of my earliest memories are of playing in the yard. One sad day, Dad and I buried my beloved goldfish under the sprinkler pump. I also vividly remember getting stung on the cheek by a bee as I climbed on the crossbar of our swing set.

We had one car, which Dad drove to work, so Mom and I were pretty much homebound. When Mom got a stroller, our big outing for the day was walking the three blocks to the Central Park Grocery. This is where we shopped and crossed paths with other neighborhood moms and kids. Don't let the name fool you. Central Park Grocery was and is a convenience-sized market. Like most of the small businesses in Holland, it was owned and operated by patriotic, hardworking people. Today little has changed. The little store is still there. An aging reader board stands atop the front corner that says, "The land of the free because of the brave."

Dad worked a lot, so at first it was often just my mom and me. She was home by choice, and we spent a lot of time talking and reading books while she worked around the house. So many women don't have the choice my mom had, though she and my dad sacrificed for her to be home. I've always understood the need and the desire for many mothers to work outside the home but I consider myself very blessed to have had a mom who was home when I was a young child. The great thing is that she felt the same way. She considered being home with her children to be fun—an opportunity she did not want to miss.

———————

I t was a mostly carefree childhood. I was happy and active in an ordinary middle-class family. Growing up, I was what was commonly referred to as a "tomboy." I loved to play in the woods, climb trees, and build forts. My sisters and I rode bikes and go-carts with neighborhood friends. It was a big deal when we went out as a family for burgers at Russ' Drive-In. I swam competitively each summer, starting around age seven. I rode my bike a couple of miles to and from practice early every morning.

When I was four, my parents built a split-level house on a quiet cul-de-sac about a mile and a half from the Little Red House. Our family was growing. There were eventually three of us girls, each about two years apart. My parents both had the same initials, E.D., for Elsa Doreen and Edgar Dale, so they decided to continue the trend. I was Elisabeth Dee and my sisters were Eileen Dawn and Emilie Dianne. I was almost twelve when my little brother surprised my parents with his appearance. They named him Erik Dean.

About the same time that I started swimming competitively, my family embarked on a new adventure that, while we couldn't predict it at the time, would have a significant impact on our lives later. My dad was the kind of person who always saw a way to improve something or do something better. It didn't matter if he knew much about the product or process; he could still see ways to improve it. After a few years at Buss Machine Works, Dad had built a new die-cast machinery business for the company and made it one of the best around. He designed and made huge machines that in turn made engine blocks and other things, like the iconic Bundt pan. But my father could already see beyond what he could accomplish for someone else. He wanted to venture out on his own, to risk his own time and capital and see what he could do better.

In the mid-1960s, the American auto industry was reaching its peak in Detroit, just 179 miles east. There was opportunity for an enterprising and innovative automobile parts maker. For my dad, capitalizing a new die-cast machine business was a tremendous challenge and undertaking. Some of the machines were as big as a room and would cost millions of dollars today. Dad's former employer at Buss Machine Works said they were crazy to do it, but my parents mortgaged their house and everything they owned to start a new company. Dad also made the rounds, raising money in small amounts from friends and relatives willing to bet on his potential.

Dad built the initial factory and office building on the outskirts of Holland. It was simple, cement block construction, painted a steel blue. I can remember that building and the color as vividly today as then. As a seven-year-old, I was very proud to help my dad paint the walls after school, rolling the paint as high as my young arms were able up the building blocks. It was exciting, not only because I was "working" with my dad, but also because he was building something that was his own. Even as a child, I understood this new project was a big risk. Dad was putting it all on the line. The Prince Manufacturing Company was being born.

My father worked day and night. It was hard on my mom. She knew intellectually why, as the founder and owner, Dad had to work nights and Saturdays, but emotionally it wasn't so easy. Mom felt strongly about having dinner as a family—so strongly, in fact, that she would delay dinner so Dad could join us. I remember being hungry and impatient and going to my mom pleading to just let the rest of us get going with dinner. She would insist on waiting. While it was often late—especially on school nights—we managed to have dinner together pretty regularly. It was never easy for my mom. But taking care of us and making a home mostly on her own was a burden she accepted with grit and a can-do attitude.

With a lot of hard work and a great team drawn from the local Holland community, my dad's die-cast machinery business did well. By the early seventies, he was once again asking himself what he could do better. The business of making these hulking machines was unpredictable. When the economy was bad, the first thing manufacturers cut back on was the purchase of new equipment with high price tags. Dad wanted to manufacture a product that was less dependent on the ups and downs of the economy.

From the beginning, Dad had established a great research and development team at Prince—a rarity for a business that size. He gave his engineers wide latitude to develop products beyond die-cast machines, challenging them to work on products that would solve the cyclical challenge. What became the Prince Corporation went on to make all kinds of auto parts—virtually everything you find inside a car except the seats. But it was his first foray into manufacturing parts for the interior of an automobile that would be the most successful, and it would change our lives forever.

―――――――

It seems hard to believe now, but there was a time when the sun visors that hang above the front seats in cars didn't have mirrors and didn't light up. They were just shades to keep the sun out of the driver's and passenger's eyes. My dad's team, particularly an engineer named Konrad Marcus, changed that in 1971. That was the year they developed a sun visor with a lighted mirror inside of it. It was the first of its kind. The inspiration may have come from Kon's wife complaining that she couldn't see herself when she tried to apply lipstick at night in the car. Maybe. In any case, Dad started manufacturing these visors in a new cement block building just across the parking lot from the die-cast machine building. The numbers were few at first, just one or two visors in the various interior fabrics offered at the time by each of the Big Three in Detroit (Chrysler, Ford, and General Motors). We would send the visors to the car companies and pray they would order them in larger quantities. The first summer the visor plant was in operation, during my junior high school years, I worked the end of the manufacturing line. I inspected (and fixed any flaws when possible), packed, and shipped the visors to Detroit. They made their debut in the 1972 Cadillac Seville.

The business was more successful, but our lives at home didn't change that much. Dad worked a lot so we still didn't travel for family vacations other than an occasional weekend camping trip with family friends. In the summers I swam and worked. During the school year I attended South Side Christian Elementary School, Holland Christian Junior High School, and, later, Holland Christian High School.

I was an "okay" student but I was generally quite bored with most of the classes and subjects.

Still, I had a few favorite teachers. Mrs. Walcott was my second-grade teacher. She often used my cursive penmanship papers as "good" examples for the other kids, which for a left-handed six-year-old was very encouraging. (I was six years old in second grade because I went to kindergarten when I was four.) Then there was Mr. Potthoven, my high school U.S. government teacher. I loved his class, everything about it. I guess it was a foreshadowing of my life to come. Finally, there was Mr. VanderLinde, the Holland Christian Schools band director. Mr. VanderLinde directed *all* the school bands—elementary, junior high, and high school—with much intensity and enthusiasm. I played percussion. Not just drums but every other fun instrument in the percussion section—cymbals, chimes, glockenspiel, wood block, triangle—you name it. Under Mr. VanderLinde's leadership, our marching bands were second to none.

In high school, I worked the third shift at the visor manufacturing plant. As the boss's daughter, I was given the worst job—or at least the worst job I was qualified for. I was a riveter. I would take the plastic core of the visor, hot (literally) off the injection molding machine, attach a rubber edge band around it, add a metal corner plate where it would attach to the car, fold it closed, and rivet it shut in about eight places. Then I put the visors in a box, where they would accumulate before they were moved on to the next step in the manufacturing process. I did this, over and over and over and over, working solo from 11 p.m. until 7 a.m. I had two fifteen-minute breaks. It was monotonous, but I was expected to work. Plus, I didn't really mind the hours (though my family, who tells me I was quite crabby from lack of sleep that summer, did!). I wanted to keep my summer days free for sunning and waterskiing on Lake Macatawa. It was a small miracle I never riveted my fingers to anything.

Holland was and still is a small, down-to-earth community of hardworking people. My family was no different, and my parents made sure us kids never forgot that. My dad's one leisure-time love was being on the water in any kind of boat. On summer weekend afternoons when he wasn't working, our family was often out on Lake Michigan. One of these afternoons when I was young—around eleven or twelve—we were out for a quiet sail when I decided to make an announcement. I said with much certainty that I would never, *ever* pick blueberries in my life.

To this day, I can't remember what put the idea in my head. Holland had—and still has—a number of small, family-owned blueberry farms. Even as a child, I knew picking the berries was hot and scratchy work. Somehow I had concluded I was too good for such work and let my parents know it. Suffice to say, my father quickly disabused me of that notion. He told me in words I can't repeat that I was not above hard work—even the hard work of picking blueberries. And to make sure I never forgot the lesson, he arranged for me to spend the next two weeks picking berries at a local blueberry farm.

Every morning I walked or rode my bike to the farm and spent my day berry picking alongside the seasonal workers. Every night I would come home, sunburnt and scratched up. I resented it at the time, but I've come to view my "punishment" in a different light as an adult. It was my parents' way of teaching me that there was no honest work that I couldn't or wouldn't be expected to do. It wasn't a complex or overthought lesson. It was practical and, importantly, humbling for a too-big-for-her-britches twelve-year-old. To this day it is one of the things I most appreciate having learned from my parents.

From 1965 to 1972, my father worked hard at his business. He wasn't comfortable delegating much, so in those first years, Dad's default was to try to do everything himself. He was at the factory most nights and weekends. The machines ran twenty-four hours a day, so he would get calls in the middle of the night when something had broken down and wasn't working. He would put on his steel-toed shoes and his robe over his pajamas and race to the factory to fix the machine. As the company grew, so did his level of stress. He was operating what these days would be called a "start-up." And the risks he took for himself, for our family, and for all his employees were a tremendous burden on him. He literally bet almost everything we had on the proposition that the car companies would want his products.

Then, one morning in October 1972, my father woke up and said he wasn't feeling well. At forty-one, Dad didn't pay a lot of attention to his health, and he certainly didn't complain about it. He had a meeting in Grand Rapids that day that he was intent on keeping, so he went to work over my mother's objections. As the day went on he felt worse and came home early. Mom insisted he go to the doctor and the doctor sent him immediately to the hospital. He was having a heart attack.

My sisters and I were in school at the time. I remember coming home to a neighbor at the house watching my baby brother Erik. Mom was at the hospital, where she would be for much of the next ten days as my father recuperated. The doctors refused to let anyone else visit him, including his children and especially anyone from work. I remember standing on the lawn outside the hospital with my sisters and waving to Dad through the window as he lay in bed on the second floor. It was as close as we could get to him.

Today, Dad probably would have had bypass surgery or stents implanted. But back in 1972, the cardiothoracic technologies weren't nearly as advanced. Dad was just told his heart was healing itself. He would have to wait for four months before he could go back to work.

Two important things happened when Dad had his first heart attack. First, his financial director smuggled a note into him while he lay in his hospital bed. Prince Corporation was profitable for the first time. It was a huge milestone.

Much more important to my mom, my brother and sisters, and me, however, was the change that came over Dad when he got out of the hospital. He had always been a caring and attentive father. But his heart attack made him keenly aware of how precious his time on earth was and how quickly things can change. He felt blessed to have survived and he resolved to spend more of his time with his family. Looking back on it, my mom also remembers that time as something of a blessing. She says that while she would never wish anyone to be "blessed" by a heart attack, the experience changed my father for the better.

For the first time, my dad blocked out time to travel with our family. The summer after his heart attack, we went to Europe. We visited a great-uncle and great-aunt in the Netherlands. They showed us the little room at the back of their bakery under their home in Haarlem where they had hidden Jewish refugees during World War II. It was something I had never known about our family.

My parents also made the very deliberate decision to take us behind the Iron Curtain, to Czechoslovakia and East Germany. They wanted us to see for ourselves what communism did to the freedom and the quality of life of the people in Eastern Europe. They wanted us to understand how fortunate we were to be Americans.

It was the early 1970s and the differences between western and eastern Europe—between freedom and tyranny—could not have been starker. We crossed from Austria into communist Czechoslovakia and were held at the border for more than an hour while the guards watched a parade in Moscow on their tiny black-and-white

TV. In Prague, destruction from World War II and the Prague Spring uprising of 1968 was still evident in piles of rubble littered throughout the city. A desperate man with a large, muzzled dog approached my very young brother to trade Czechoslovak currency in the shabby hotel coffee shop.

Traveling through Checkpoint Charlie from West Berlin into East Berlin left an indelible mark on me. It was like going from a riot of color to a world of black and white. West Berlin was a modern, bustling city. Meanwhile, the gray and empty landscape of East Berlin was punctuated only by workers hand-rolling patches of asphalt and the occasional two-stroke Trabant bumping along decrepit streets. We visited the Checkpoint Charlie Museum and saw the pictures and read the stories of the East Germans who tried to escape across the Berlin Wall to freedom—including those who were shot by the East German border guards. It was another of my parents' invaluable lessons for us. Even as a teenager, I realized that all people have an innate desire to be free. I couldn't take my freedom for granted.

A couple of years later we took another kind of trip—a tour of the American West. There were six of us in a motor home, rolling from state to state. All the girls—Eileen (whom we nicknamed "Scoob" for reasons lost to history), Emilie, and me—were teenagers. Erik was six. Like lots of little brothers, Erik was precocious. From day one he was curious and adventurous. He would go headlong into anything he thought was interesting. Even with all of his big sisters constantly supervising, Erik ended up in the emergency room for stitches three times before he was a year old. Mom says she could see the Navy SEAL he would become when he was still a little boy.

Dad drove the RV to South Dakota, Wyoming, Montana, British Columbia, Washington, Oregon, Nevada, Arizona, and California. For kids who had spent the vast majority of their lives within a hundred-mile radius of Holland, Michigan, everything out west was a great new adventure.

When we were visiting Los Angeles, Mom suggested I get a haircut. For some unknown reason, she had booked an appointment at a "real" hair salon. I was eighteen years old and I'd never been to a hair salon. I was used to having my hair cut by one of Mom's friends in her basement. So the salon was new and uncharted territory. When the hairdresser asked me to get in the chair to have my hair washed, I climbed in, on my knees, facing the sink so I could put my head over it. It was the posture that made the most sense to me at the time. I'm pretty sure I laughed when I realized my mistake—everyone else in the salon certainly did!

I was in college before Prince Corporation began to really take off. The automakers—and then the auto drivers—loved the lighted visors. The orders for the visors continued to grow and Dad had to expand manufacturing operations. The eventual campus of Prince buildings in Holland housed production for 100,000 lighted mirror visors per week, as well as making instrument panels, overhead systems, consoles, and other assorted interior trim parts. I worked summers at the factory and we still lived in the house we had moved into when I was four—the house I would live in until I got married. But there were some changes in our life as a family. We built a summer cottage on Lake Macatawa. My parents started to travel more.

I'm biased, of course, but to me my dad's success says something important about America and the kind of men and women who built our country. Dad was ambitious and confident, yes, but he was also deeply committed to his community. Like him, the men and women who create family businesses in small and medium-sized towns across America don't just make money, they literally build their communities. They create good jobs so families can stay in their hometowns, raise children, send them off to college or careers, and hopefully have them return. They sponsor Girl Scouts and Little League teams. They contribute to the arts and the annual Fourth of July parade. They are the kind of men and women we should encourage and cherish.

At its peak, Prince Corporation had more than five thousand employees—all based in the Holland area. Dad knew early on that treating his employees well wasn't just the right thing to do, it was good for business. He was successful because he knew how to bring out the best in the people who worked for him. More than once, someone would come in looking for a job when Dad didn't have an opening. But he would see something valuable in that individual—a willingness to work hard or a conscientiousness of spirit. So he would come up with a way to give them a job and keep them in the company.

Dad valued his employees and cared about their families. He bought an indoor tennis club near the company headquarters and turned it into a family and fitness center for employees. It had two doctors on-site offering physical exams, primary health care, and physical therapy. There was an on-site pharmacy. There were tennis and swimming lessons for employees' children. They even offered a weeklong summer camp for employee kids—all for a nominal fee.

Dad brought his Christian values to his workplace. What that meant in practice was that he brought the same values to his work that he upheld at home: the importance of family, the dignity of the individual, and the joy of giving.

When Prince Corporation hit its stride it became what was called a Tier One supplier to the auto industry. We worked directly with the car companies with no middleman in between. As a consequence, Prince employees had to be in Detroit all the time. Another business leader might have opened up an office in Detroit and required employees to either move from Holland or lose their jobs. Dad didn't do that. He became one of the leading Big Three auto parts suppliers and never opened an office in Detroit. Instead he bought a twin-propeller airplane to shuttle employees back and forth from Holland to Detroit. He wanted his employees to be able to live in Holland and be home with their families in time for dinner at night, just as my mother wished for our family. The plane allowed Prince employees to do that. It often made multiple trips back and forth to Detroit in a day.

Giving back was important to both my parents. Dad told us all the time that he had his business to make money so we could do good things. In the mid-eighties, he started a Christmas tradition at Prince. Each year, a rotating group of employees identified a group of local nonprofits that were doing good work. All the employees were then encouraged to give to one or more of them. Prince matched their gifts dollar for dollar.

They called it the Care and Share program. Some Prince employees had their first experiences in charitable giving through the program. Over the years Care and Share has raised more than $24 million for Holland nonprofits and continues today in the companies that now operate out of the Prince factories. Dad's absolute favorite moments were when representatives of the charities came to the factory and talked about who and what their giving had impacted. He loved seeing the joy of both the charities that had benefited and of all the employees who had given.

In the late 1970s and early 1980s, shopping malls cropped up on the outskirts of Holland, just as they did in towns across America. As the number of malls grew, businesses in Holland's historic downtown began to fail. My mom and dad were horrified. They knew that a healthy, thriving community needed a healthy, thriving downtown. They decided they weren't going to sit back and watch downtown Holland die like so many other towns. They started buying vacant stores and historic buildings, renovating them, and leasing them to merchants at well below cost. Dad and Mom knew that they would probably never see any financial benefit from what they were doing, but they thought it was the right thing to do.

Once again, Dad envisioned a future that no one else could see. When he proposed to use waste heat from the power plant to heat the streets and sidewalks of Holland's main street to keep them clear of snow, the city powers-that-be thought he was crazy. They refused. So my parents donated half the funds needed to accomplish the project and the city officials came around to the idea. Thanks to their vision and the hard work of many other Holland residents, the downtown is thriving today. The heated sidewalks keep the downtown businesses and offices pleasantly accessible all year round—even in the heart of the snowiest Michigan winters. And what was once dismissed as crazy is now a main marketing feature for the town.

It was years later, on March 2, 1995. I had married Dick and had given birth to my kids. We were skiing in Colorado when we saw our name on the emergency message board by the chairlift, telling us to contact the ski patrol. Something was wrong. Our minds immediately went to Dick's father, who had had two bypass surgeries and was continuing to fight heart failure.

But it was my father. Earlier that day, Dad had finished lunch at Prince headquarters with some members of his leadership team. It was a daily ritual. On any other day, Dad would bound up the steps to his third-floor office two at a time. On March 2, he took the elevator. About ten minutes later, an employee wheeling a large cart called the elevator. When the door opened, he found my father inside, dead. He was sixty-three.

To this day, I can't get off a chairlift at the top of a ski run without thinking of that day.

I try not to think about all the "what ifs." What if Dad hadn't taken the elevator—would he have been discovered sooner and survived? What if he had had the follow-up care he should have had after his first heart attack? What if he hadn't been under such stress from pressure to expand the company? What if he had exercised more?

We were a family in shock. Somehow, we had a visitation for Dad in the Prince athletic facility. Mom was strong but very broken. My sister Emilie was eight days away from giving birth to her fourth child. Erik gave the eulogy.

In theory, Dad would have loved it if one of his children had wanted to take over his business. Prince had allowed him to do good things—for his family, for his employees, and for his community. But he never wanted any of us to feel pressure to live a continuation of his life. He always urged us to pursue things we had an interest in doing. After his death, we made the decision to sell Prince Corporation to Johnson Controls Inc. of Milwaukee. Mom took $80 million of the proceeds and gave bonuses to the Prince employees who were responsible for so much of my father's success.

In keeping with their faith, my parents have never spoken much about their contributions to their community. They didn't make them for the accolades or attention. In a particularly fitting way, there isn't a towering statue of my dad on a pedestal looking down over downtown Holland. Instead, his footprints are embedded in the brick at the corner of Eighth Street and Central Avenue. The simple plaque reads, "We will always hear your footsteps."

I hear my dad's footsteps often, even more loudly in the years since his death. I wouldn't say I try to emulate him—there's only one Ed Prince. But I do try to live out the lessons he taught me, including being deliberate and generous about caring for others and always trying to figure out how to make things work better. If there's a Prince family tradition, that's it.

After I graduated from high school, I went "away" to college— thirty miles away, that is, to Calvin College in Grand Rapids. It was there I would discover my love of politics, my passion for public policy, and the man with whom I get to spend the rest of my life.

CHAPTER TWO

THE UN-AMERICAN EDUCATION SYSTEM

Few people give much thought to the quality of their schools until their first child is born. Even then, most don't get serious about it until a few years later, when it's nearing time for their preschooler or kindergartner to attend.

It wasn't until it was time for our first child, Rick, to go to school that I had my epiphany about education in America. In this country we believe that it doesn't matter who your parents are; we *all* have inalienable rights to life, liberty, and the pursuit of happiness. But when it comes to education in America, it *very much* matters who your parents are. Parents who can afford to find the right schools for their children do so, either by moving to a suburb with "good" public schools or paying for private education. Parents who can't afford to send their kids anywhere other than where their local school district assigns them—well, they have to do what they're told and hope for the best.

It's very un-American.

Rick came into the world a healthy eight pounds, two and a half ounces. A few hours later, the neonatologist told us he had only a fifty-fifty chance of living until morning. Rick had somehow acquired bacterial pneumonia. Words can't begin to describe our emotions. We were first-time parents with a seemingly perfect child. How could this be? Dick shared my hospital bed, and we spent a fitful night with lots of prayer. Thank God, Rick awakened the next morning. But he spent the first week of his life in the Butterworth Hospital neonatal intensive care unit, or NICU. There he was, my big eight-pound boy, in an incubator, surrounded by tiny preemies.

While we weren't prepared for that introduction to parenthood, once that scare was over and we settled in, Rick was just like any other kid. All I saw when I looked into his eyes was unlimited potential. Every new mother—and father—sees this. Every new mother and father wants the best for their child—for them to become everything they are capable of. And that begins with education.

My K–12 years were all spent in Christian schools. The reason was no more complicated than the fact that my parents wanted it that way. My mother had gone to Christian schools in Holland. My father probably would have done the same, but as a young widow, his mother could never afford it. My parents wanted the Prince kids to grow up with the same values they had. They had to stretch to afford it while we were young, but you stretch for the things that matter— and a Christian education definitely mattered to my mom.

Dick, on the other hand, had always gone to public schools. Both Dick and I received perfectly fine educations. But, if we're honest, both of us were also bored in school. The traditional American model—of twenty or twenty-five kids seated in row upon row of desks, with one teacher up front, all reading and working through the same textbook— didn't do much to spark our imaginations or creativity.

We knew we wanted something better for our children, and we were open to a variety of options. What I wanted most for Rick was to find the right fit for our curious, creative little boy who was thriving at a Montessori preschool.

One of the first schools we visited was a small, K–12 school in Grand Rapids called The Potter's House. I knew a little bit about it because it was founded by four remarkable fellow Calvin College alumni.

After graduation, the four classmates had each taken a look at their lives and concluded they weren't living out their faith. Their faith taught them to be concerned about the poor, but they didn't really know anyone who was poor. Their faith taught them to respect and value all people, but they didn't know many who were different from themselves. Their faith taught them to serve others, but they didn't believe they were being good stewards. So they decided to do something about it. They sold most of their possessions and moved into a house together in Roosevelt Park, a poor neighborhood in the heart of Grand Rapids.

One of these remarkable people, John Booy, taught fifth and sixth graders at a Grand Rapids public school. At night he and his housemates from Calvin began hosting dinners and sing-alongs for the adults in the neighborhood. When the local kids heard the music, they started to show up at John's house, peering in the windows from the front porch. It was only a matter of time until the Calvin College crew felt compelled to let the kids in. Tuesday nights were set aside for kids to eat and play foosball and air hockey at the house. They shared about what was going on in their lives. Some of what they shared was good, but a lot was about drugs, violence at home, and worse. Much worse. Before long, 150 kids were coming every Tuesday night. Even so, John and his friends didn't feel like they were doing enough. The public school the kids were assigned to in Roosevelt Park was ranked the third lowest in the entire state of Michigan. John knew they couldn't make up for that experience in just two hours every Tuesday night. So he and his friends started The Potter's House school.

Discovering The Potter's House was like finding a treasure. I saw firsthand what every school can and should be. The Potter's House school showed me that even in the poorest neighborhoods— *especially* in the poorest neighborhoods—there can be safe, enriching places for children to learn. It showed me how loved every child can and should be.

The Potter's House school showed me a place where children, not adults, were at the center of the school's mission.

The story of The Potter's House is one of faith and determination overcoming tremendous odds. It started with twelve kids in a church basement. Thanks to the unwavering commitment of John and his friends, it has grown into a K–12 school with more than six hundred students today. Parents pay what they can. No child is turned away because of their family income. The Potter's House takes in children who are very poor. It takes in children who speak no English. It takes in kids who have been falling through the cracks in the public education system. Kids who have been bullied in the system. Kids who have been suicidal in the system. Every child is welcomed. Every child is valued.

John and his friends' commitment humbled me. What they had built inspired me. So I began visiting The Potter's House school to read to students. I talked to parents. I heard how the school had changed their children's lives for the better.

Not long after I started volunteering, I met a shy, quiet five-year-old named Steve. One day, Steve's mother dropped him off at the house of a woman known in the neighborhood as Aunt May. I'm uncertain whether Aunt May was Steve's actual aunt or not. All I know for sure is that his mother never came back for him.

Aunt May was in her eighties, with a big heart but not much else she could offer Steve. So she brought him to The Potter's House. I met him when he was in kindergarten. We were an unlikely couple. I was a woman who had been blessed beyond measure; someone who had never known a day of true want. Steve was a young boy who had been abandoned by his mother, father, and, seemingly, by the world. What he needed was an adult he could rely on. Someone invested in his success. So we read together and I tried to be his friend.

Steve was the first of a number of children I mentored and Dick and I supported at The Potter's House school. We took on a child from The Potter's House for sponsorship—that is, we paid their tuition—as each of our four children came of school age. As our children grew and our opportunity to give grew, we supported the tuition of many others. The school didn't extend to high school when Steve was a student, so his time at The Potter's House was more limited than it would be today.

John Booy still hears from Steve. John says he still has troubles, but he's surviving.

"He's a rough-around-the-collar kid," says John. "But he's still alive. He's not in jail."

It's not a storybook ending, but it's a better ending than so many kids from the "wrong side of the tracks" have. More kids like Steve deserve that chance.

In the end, the right fit for Rick was a school closer to our home and work—a small, faith-based school called Ada Christian. Dick and I made that choice because we could afford that choice.

Although Rick didn't attend, it was at The Potter's House that I began to think more deeply about children who weren't as fortunate. Who a child's parents are should *not* determine whether they get an education or not. It shouldn't determine whether they stay out of jail or not—or whether they live to adulthood or not. Not in America.

Before there were my children, before there was a Potter's House school, there was Dick DeVos. I met him during my sophomore year at Calvin College. After graduating from high school two years before me, Dick had tried a semester at Calvin but he was bored sitting in his classes. His major goal at the time was to see how few days he actually had to attend a class and still pass it. Not surprisingly, as the end of the semester neared, Dean Stob called him into his office.

"Dick, your GPA is really bad," he said. "You just need to know, if you're still enrolled at the end of next week, your grades will become a part of your permanent record. But if you're not enrolled they will disappear like vapor."

Dick is a quick study; he never went back. He later pursued higher education through independent study at Northwood University in Midland, Michigan. Northwood was founded with a heavy focus on business and entrepreneurship. Dick could attend class on his own time and go as quickly or as slowly as he wanted, which suited him. He earned his bachelor's degree just after we were married, graduating with highest honors. It was another early lesson in education freedom for me: Different students learn in different ways.

Like Dick, I was impatient with school and I was geared toward action from an early age. I was not shy. My recitation of the Pledge of Allegiance when I was two, a skill my mom recalls I picked up from *Romper Room*, included a very hearty emphasis on "'liverty' and justice for all!" I enrolled at Calvin College at seventeen after graduating from Holland Christian High School. At the time, I aspired to be an interior designer. I still love design, but my wise advisor at Calvin suggested I might be too strong-willed to work for other people. So I majored in my own unique combination of subjects: business and political science. Somehow I became increasingly drawn to politics and public policy while managing to avoid being influenced by the Marxist who taught in the economics department. One likely reason for that was Paul Henry, one of my professors who was also the Kent County Republican chairman at the time. Soon he would be the congressman from our district.

Paul was a compelling teacher, encouraging his students to test the teachings of our church and to join God's work in redeeming the world. At that point, my political experience consisted of little more than shaking President Richard Nixon's hand at the Battle Creek airport when I was in fifth grade, and acing my favorite class, U.S.

Government, in high school. But Professor Henry inspired me to run for the student senate at Calvin. I won. (My winning slogan: "Put a Prince in your future and vote for Betsy.") Next, I did what most college students do to get involved in politics: I volunteered on a campaign.

They called us "Scatterblitzers." We were energetic, optimistic college kids in matching T-shirts who both "scattered" and "blitzed" for our hometown candidate, Gerald R. Ford. Ford had become president when Richard Nixon resigned after Watergate. In 1976 Ford was running for his first full term as president. We Scatterblitzers were bused into neighborhoods throughout the Midwest—in Michigan, Ohio, Indiana, and Wisconsin—to campaign door-to-door.

Being a Scatterblitzer got me a ticket to my first national political convention, the 1976 Republican National Convention in Kansas City, Missouri. We had to pay our own way, but our campaigning efforts were rewarded with tickets to events. It was a blast. Kansas City was the last national party convention that featured anything close to real drama. Ford narrowly survived a challenge for the Republican presidential nomination from a former California governor named Ronald Reagan. There was tension in the air. We didn't sleep. We ate plenty of junk food. We had fun doing what we viewed as important work.

At the time, politics was something fun and interesting, not something I saw myself spending much of the rest of my life around. But things happened during that election year that would very much influence my life trajectory. I didn't know it at the time, but that campaign would eventually cause me to double down on my desire to engage in the world and try to make it better.

The unlikely agent of my fate in 1976 was the governor of Georgia, Jimmy Carter. Education wasn't much of a national issue in 1976. Schools were still the domain of states and localities. When Carter became the Democratic nominee for president, he made a deal that changed that. For the first time, education became part of the national political conversation.

At the time, to the degree the federal government was involved in education, it acted through the old Department of Health, Education, and Welfare (HEW). The teacher union bosses had been agitating for years to create a new federal department dedicated exclusively to education. In 1976, Carter cut a deal with them. Out of view of most Americans, he made a promise to the leaders of the nation's largest teacher union, the National Education Association (NEA), to create the U.S. Department of Education in exchange for the union's support in the election. [1]

The move was controversial—even among some Democrats. So Carter and his running mate, Minnesota senator Walter Mondale, mentioned their promise to create the Education Department frequently in front of union audiences, but rarely in front of general audiences. The result was that the political press virtually ignored the issue.

In his memoir, Carter's secretary of HEW, Joseph Califano, talked openly about Carter's political motivation for creating the new department.[2] Califano himself was opposed to a Department of Education because he believed it would take state and local control of education and turn it over to the unions. The *Washington Post*, believe it or not, agreed with Califano. Here's what the *Post* editors had to say about the legislation to create the department:

"The bill is the inspiration of the NEA, an organization that has much the same relation to the public schools as the plumbers union has to the plumbing business."[3]

Even the mainstream media saw it coming: Placating the school union bosses was the first step in making children second-class citizens in their own schools.

After some arm-twisting by the Carter administration, the legislation passed. In exchange for the NEA's first ever presidential endorsement and the active support of thousands of union members, the U.S. Education Department was created in 1979. The NEA quickly became the single most powerful special interest in the Democratic Party, if not the entire country.

Of course, none of this was on my radar screen when I returned to Calvin after campaigning for Ford. Classes kept me busy and college social life beckoned. That fall I dated a fellow Scatterblitzer named Bill Swets a couple of times. It was very casual. I knew early on that it wasn't going to be a serious relationship.

One night, Bill asked my cousin Heidi and me to dinner at the old farmhouse he and his roommate were renovating in Ada. They had done a lot of work putting in counters and laying carpet (with staples by the thousands). It was not bad for a bachelor pad. When we sat down to dinner, there were four of us: Heidi, Bill, me, and Bill's roommate. He was a slightly intense, fit guy with intelligent brown eyes named Dick DeVos.

There are unusual similarities in Dick's and my childhoods. We are both the oldest children of medium-sized families. Our families worshipped at churches within the same denomination. We both had innovative, entrepreneurial parents who came from nothing. We were both middle-class kids who grew up to be a part of the so-called one percent. We were born and raised less than forty-five miles from each other.

Dick is the oldest child of Rich and Helen DeVos. Rich cofounded Amway, which would become a global, direct sales company, with his partner Jay Van Andel in 1959. Dick was four. The DeVos and the Van Andel families grew up next door to one another, in houses both sets of parents lived in until they died.

Rich and Jay were high school friends and, later, serial entrepreneurs. When they came back from World War II, they started a flying school in Grand Rapids. They weren't pilots. They recruited students for the school and hired pilots to teach them. Then Rich heard about something out in California called a "drive-in," so they started one in Michigan. Eventually they sold the restaurant and the flight school and bought a boat to sail around South America. Off the coast of Cuba, the boat sank. Rich's and Jay's parents experienced several frantic days after the boat failed to arrive in Cuba. The boys had to be rescued by a freighter on the high seas.

Next, Rich and Jay sold imports they found in South America. They sold wooden toys. They sold bomb shelters during the early days of the Cold War.

Then they tried something different. They heard about a unique, person-to-person sales model selling natural vitamins and food supplements. The product was called Nutrilite. Rich and Jay gave the Nutrilite business a try and did well, building an enthusiastic organization. Soon they expanded their product offering to an organic all-purpose cleaner. They operated their young company out of the basements of their houses and named it Amway. Rich and Jay eventually built a headquarters in Ada that remains the company headquarters to this day. Dick's first job was watering trees and pulling weeds at the first small Amway building. In high school, he gave tours of the growing facilities to Amway distributers under the name of Dick Marvin, his first and middle names. Going by DeVos, he said, prompted too many extraneous questions.

Much has been written and said about Rich DeVos and Jay Van Andel since they built Amway into the leading direct-selling company in the world, but I was blessed to actually know Rich DeVos. He was an unabashed, unapologetic optimist—not just about life but about other people's potential.

Rich was known for always encouraging people with "You can do it." It was more than a catchphrase for my father-in-law. Jay's and his model of capitalism didn't depend on crushing the competition.

It didn't depend on anyone else failing. It depended on bringing out the best in ordinary people—unlocking their potential—and creating shared success. Rich had an extraordinary gift for that. The result was that his success has been shared by millions of people throughout the world.

When I met Dick that night at the farmhouse, he was working with the Amway travel team, organizing distributors conferences. I was drawn to his maturity, among many other things. Dick would later say that meeting me was easily the best thing he gained from attending Calvin College. When he found out that his roommate and I weren't serious, Dick asked Bill if he could ask me out. We were married in February 1979 at the LaGrave Avenue Christian Reformed Church in Grand Rapids. The press later called it a "merger," not a marriage. But they were wrong. Forty-three years and four children later, we are more devoted to each other than ever.

The 1980s and early '90s were a period of change and growth for my family and me. Elissa, Andrea, and Ryan joined Rick to make us a family of six. As our family grew, education became something we thought about more and more.

Our experience with The Potter's House had shown us what was possible when it came to giving all kids a chance to have a great school. I knew that for every family who had their children at The Potter's House, there were many more families that wanted the same opportunity for their children. Dick and I were in the position to help build and support a new vision of education opportunity. We knew from the start that it would be focused on one thing: giving those parents who wanted to send their children to a school like The Potter's House the opportunity to do so, regardless of their income.

We didn't want to limit ourselves to writing checks to distant organizations. We wanted to help *kids*. In our view, it was immoral to force kids and parents to wait out the five- and ten-year timelines the education establishment said they needed to fix schools. We wanted parents to have opportunities *now*. After all, children only grow up one time. They can't afford to wait years for their school to improve.

We founded the Dick and Betsy DeVos Family Foundation in our early thirties, about the same time we founded The Windquest Group, our family business. This was the beginning of a new and tremendously fulfilling chapter in our lives.

In our business dealings, Dick and I are naturally driven, type-A personalities. Our philanthropy, however, comes from a different place. We could be on an island somewhere, just enjoying ourselves. But, honestly, that would be boring. And, more important, it wouldn't be a responsible use of our God-given gifts. Chalk it up to the influence of our faith or good old-fashioned "Dutch guilt"—probably both. Either way, we place a high value on giving and on the stewardship of all the resources that have been entrusted to us.

Our focus from day one was to support students, not systems or buildings. When the school my children attended, Grand Rapids Christian High School, asked us to contribute to their capital campaign, we said we'd prefer to fund a scholarship program to ensure more families could choose the school for their children even if they couldn't afford the tuition. We have been able to help hundreds of local kids who wouldn't otherwise have had the opportunity to attend a school that better matches their needs, desires, and values.

In 1993, we founded the Education Freedom Fund, which gave scholarships to lower-income Michigan families to help them attend the school of their choice anywhere in the state. A few years later, businessmen John Walton and Ted Forstmann established similar scholarships through the Children's Scholarship Fund, enabling students in New York and other cities throughout the country to attend schools their families choose. The Education Freedom Fund has given thousands of Michigan students the opportunity to improve their education. Nationally, the Children's Scholarship Fund has done the same for nearly 200,000 American families.[4]

At the same time, I began to join with other education choice advocates and school reform experts to give parents choices nationwide. I joined the boards of two nonprofit education groups that were lobbying for school choice in states across America: Children First America and the American Education Reform Council. Later I also served on the board of the Alliance for School Choice, which was formed in 2004 on the fiftieth anniversary of the landmark *Brown v. Board of Education* decision and eventually became one of the largest school choice organizations in the country.

Through these groups, I met and worked with the giants of the education reform world, people like civil rights leader Howard Fuller, education reformer John Kirtley, banker Peter Flanigan, investor Bill Oberndorf, Washington, DC, school choice activist Virginia Walden Ford, Milwaukee school choice activist, and Susan Mitchell, as well as Walton and Forstmann.

These were some of the people present at the infancy of the movement. They represented a different kind of political activist. Most people who donate to causes or become involved in organizations move on to something else after their ballot measure loses or their legislation fails. The founders of the education freedom movement refuse to do that. They keep fighting, through obstruction, corruption, and, yes, the occasional loss in the statehouse or at the ballot box. They inspired me with their vision and determination.

We made progress in a handful of states initially, but I also wanted to do something more personal for kids who were being overlooked by the system. The young man I had worked with at The Potter's House, Steve, had reminded me of the innate value of every human being, regardless of where they came from or what they looked like. Like my friends who founded The Potter's House, I wanted to do something that really honored the unique potential of every child. Like them, I felt called to get out of my comfort zone and really give of myself.

That opportunity came through another organization I was involved with, Kids Hope USA. This West Michigan–based organization was founded on a simple premise: A local church of any denomination partners with a local public elementary school to provide adult mentors for at-risk kids. Mentors commit to meet with their student at school for one hour once a week, for at least one school year. The idea was to give kids a reliable adult who would show up consistently to love and encourage them. For many of them, this was something new. More than once, students would ask their mentors, "Who are you going to meet with next week?" When we answered, "I'm here for you and only you!" they would look at us with disbelief. It was heartbreaking—and heartwarming—to help give them the love, consistency, and encouragement they craved.

With my advocacy, our church started a Kids Hope program at one of the most challenged elementary schools in Grand Rapids. The percentage of kids who were at grade level in reading and math at the school was in the low double digits. The *lowest* double digits.

I began mentoring a young girl named Sasha (I've changed her name to protect her privacy). My time with Sasha is a story that doesn't necessarily have a happy ending. But it was a learning experience and an important one for me, I think. It opened my eyes and it humbled me at the same time. Despite many ups and downs, I took away and learned far more from the kids I mentored than they ever took from me.

When I met Sasha she was seven years old. She came from a chaotic background. Her dad was seldom in the picture and her mom had trouble with relationships in general. At first, Sasha and I met at school. We talked and read and worked spelling words and crafts. Slowly, I got to know her and then her family. There was just Sasha, her older sister, and her mom. They were struggling, like so many families. Her mom was only sporadically employed. The older sister was reaching an age where she could make mistakes that would impact the rest of her life. I became close with all of them.

Sasha and her family lived in an apartment when I met them. When they couldn't pay their rent and were evicted, they went to live in a pay-by-the-day motel. One night, just a few rooms down from theirs, someone was murdered. This was now a family that I knew and cared about. I had brought Christmas dinner and presents to Sasha and her family by that time. So I insisted that Sasha and her mom and sister move out of the motel. We rented another apartment for them and later Dick and I helped them find a house in a safe neighborhood.

Meanwhile, Sasha languished at her school. My relationship with her and her family had grown well beyond the one hour, one day a week. I wanted Sasha to become equipped with the learning necessary to break the cycle of poverty her family knew. I couldn't see things improving much for her at her assigned school, so Dick and I told Sasha's mom we wanted to give Sasha the chance to attend a different school. She jumped at the opportunity. We paid Sasha's tuition through the end of high school. I continued to meet with her regularly. Our whole family took presents and Christmas dinner to her house each year. I was convinced we could help put her life on a different and better trajectory if I just tried hard enough.

But in the end, I couldn't. While Sasha was in high school, her older sister got pregnant. Then Sasha got pregnant. We arranged for her mother to work at a hotel but she lost the job. The family continued to spiral down. Dick and I came to the heartbreaking conclusion that we couldn't change Sasha's life. In the end, *she* had to decide her future.

After she had her baby, Sasha graduated from high school with an alternative degree. We continued to support her and her family as we encouraged them to get back on their feet. Eventually they left Grand Rapids and we lost contact with them.

It was tempting to walk away from our experience with Sasha believing it is impossible to change people's lives, so why try? Some would argue that families like hers are incapable of making good choices for themselves. They don't know what's good for them, they say, so government must decide where they go to school and even where they live. I couldn't disagree with this more. We tried to give Sasha and her family the ability to make their own choices. The fact that they didn't make good ones doesn't mean other families shouldn't have the power to choose. It's like a sinking ship that has lifeboats for all the passengers. If some passengers choose not to take a lifeboat, that doesn't mean *no one* should get a lifeboat.

This argument—that simply being less advantaged suggests you aren't capable of making decisions in your best interest—infuriates me. It pretends to be compassionate when in fact it's elitist. I refused to let their false argument stop me from helping other families build better lives for their children.

I began to mentor another child from Sasha's old school. She was a first grader named Elena (I've also changed her name to protect her privacy). Both her parents were from the Dominican Republic and her father was still there when I met Elena. Once again, I found myself becoming more and more involved with her family. Dick and I spent time with them at Christmas and Elena's birthdays. When she was in elementary school, we gave her the chance to go to The Potter's House. She thrived there ("It's a private school but there are lots of people like me," she once told me).

I did a lot of the same things with Elena that I did with Sasha but the results have been dramatically different.

We found the family a house near The Potter's House. We helped Elena's mom secure a good job. She went on to become more than a diligent, capable employee—she has become part of our family. Meanwhile, Elena is at Grand Valley State University, majoring in nonprofit administration with an emphasis on community development planning.

She is minoring in Latin American studies. She may add an international business minor as well. I am so proud of her, as is her family.

———————————

B efore I started mentoring students personally, I had yet another education revelation. It was true that our support for students in Michigan through the Education Freedom Fund, The Potter's House, and Kids Hope USA was making a difference in kids' lives. But there wasn't enough philanthropy in the world to fix American education. Taxpayers spent more than $750 billion on K–12 education last year alone. That's quite a bit more than the total net worth of Bill Gates, Warren Buffett, Elon Musk, and Jeff Bezos—combined. Still, our education system is failing the kids who need it most.

Dick and I had started out with the belief that if we contributed enough, we could spur change in the system. If we showed enough people the unmistakable benefits of giving students the chance to go to the school of their choice, we thought, the practical and emotional appeal of this cause would spread to others. And some of that definitely happened. Philanthropists and advocates have given well over a million kids a shot at a good education through charitable giving. But eventually I realized that the system was too broken to be fixed through private philanthropy alone. Laws had to change. Governments had to change. That required political muscle.

We continued to give scholarships and to mentor students, but slowly we focused less on appealing to philanthropists to mitigate the worst effects of the system. We turned our efforts to building the political culture to *change* the system. In Michigan, we were fortunate to have a powerful ally.

John Engler was elected governor of Michigan in 1990, at the outset of a decade in which governors of states—not politicians in Washington—were the policy innovators who challenged the status quo in American politics. Among the education reform governors—people like Wisconsin's Tommy Thompson and Flori-da's Jeb Bush—Governor Engler was a pioneer.

In his first term, John challenged the Michigan legislature to allow students to attend a new kind of public school that had been pioneered in Minnesota just two years before. They were called char-ter academies or charter schools—public schools that were freed from teacher union rules and regulations and given the freedom to experi-ment with new ways of teaching kids.

Even though the unions were not as hyperpartisan back then as they are today, the Michigan Education Association (MEA) recog-nized charter schools for what they were: a threat to their educa-tion monopoly. They fought Governor Engler's proposal hard. Also, despite the fact that there were Republican majorities in both houses of the legislature, John's bill to authorize charter schools in Michigan was far from a sure thing. Dick and I worked hard to build support among state legislators.

The chief roadblock to passage of the charter school law was one we have encountered again and again in the fight for education free-dom: risk-averse politicians from both parties who fail to see how more education freedom can benefit their districts and, therefore, them. In Michigan, it was particularly members from rural areas, like the Upper Peninsula, who were convinced that the education status quo was just fine. After all, they already had a "good" school in their district—why pick a fight with the unions and the educa-tion establishment? In the end, a huge compromise was made to the bill to win over these hesitant members: a cap on the total number of charter schools. Even then, the bill passed by a razor-thin margin.

Governor Engler signed the law to create 150 charter schools in Michigan on January 14, 1994.

We had won the battle, but the war was far from over. That fall, the MEA filed a lawsuit challenging the constitutionality of the schools. They argued that charter schools didn't deserve public funding because they were not controlled by local school boards. It was a red herring dressed up as educational accountability. But the unions' cries of alarm were falling on increasingly deaf ears. That October, the cover of *Time* magazine featured a Michigan charter school student named Zach Leipham under the headline "New Hope for Public Schools." The spark had been lit.

Well before the time we worked to pass the charter school law in Michigan, I had become active in the Michigan Republican Party. I started as a volunteer for the local Kent County GOP and worked my way up through every single party office to become Republican National Committeewoman for Michigan. In 1992 I challenged incumbent Ronna Romney—daughter-in-law of former Michigan governor George Romney, and sister-in-law of Senator Mitt Romney—for the job of Republican National Committeewoman. I won.

Then, in 1996, Michigan GOP state chair Susy Heintz resigned her position to run for Congress, and I was elected state party chairman for the balance of the term. I was then elected and reelected to full terms in 1997 and 1999. I came into the chairmanship of the party full of energy, confidence, and a touch of naïveté—a potentially dangerous combination. I knew what I wanted for my party and my state and I wasn't intimidated by the opposition. I was ready to play hardball.

A key weapon of choice for opponents of education freedom, in Michigan and just about everywhere else, is a provision written into most state constitutions called a Blaine Amendment.

The amendments got their name from the late-nineteenth-century congressman James Blaine of Maine. He first proposed an amendment to the U.S. Constitution in 1875 to prohibit public funding of "sectarian" schools. "Sectarian" was code for Catholic. At the time, Irish, German, and Italian immigrants were pouring into U.S. public schools. The new students were mostly Catholic, but the men who controlled the schools were almost exclusively Protestant. They saw public education as a way to spread their doctrine. Horace Mann, the creator of the industrial model of public education, openly embraced this nativist, religious bias in public schools. The American "common" school, Mann said, was designed to "Americanize" Catholic immigrants into "least common denominator Protestantism."[5]

When American Catholics protested and called for public funding for Catholic schools, Representative Blaine introduced his amendment. It narrowly failed to pass in Congress, but many American states began passing bigoted amendments of their own.

Blaine Amendments are ugly, unconstitutional statutes that should have been consigned to the ash heap of history long ago, but they're still with us. Today thirty-seven states have Blaine Amendments on the books. They're certainly no longer used to promote Protestantism, but they are handy tools for school union bosses and others who oppose public funding being used for anything other than traditional public schools. Michigan has one of the worst, and most proscriptive, Blaine Amendments.

Michigan's was one of the last Blaine Amendments passed after the unholy ménage-à-trois of nativists, religious bigots, and union bosses had been consummated. This twisted threesome has only worsened in the years since the Blaine Amendments went on the books. Today's defenders claim that "public" education will be destroyed if the government allows parents to spend "public" dollars on a private or religious school for their child. The real reason the education establishment hides behind measures as ugly as the Blaine Amendments is not that they fear government support of religion. It's because they fear competition to their monopoly control of education.

We had a chance to help put an end to bigoted Blaines while I was secretary. A courageous mother named Kendra Espinoza had sued her home state of Montana after it refused to implement a modest school choice program because of Blaine. When the case made its way to the U.S. Supreme Court, we worked with Attorney General Bill Barr to ensure that the Department of Justice stood against bigotry and for parents. Barr was a willing and able partner, who shares many of my views on both education and religious liberty. We argued strongly that Montana's refusal to let kids use the school choice scholarships violated their constitutional rights. The Court agreed with our view and overturned Montana's ruling, dealing what should ultimately prove to be a fatal blow to Blaine. As of this writing, the Court is considering another case about religious liberty in education in which we had intervened, fittingly originating from Maine.

Unlike many of the outside activists and union lobbyists who shamelessly use Blaine Amendments to prevent education freedom, Dick and I have seen firsthand how denying choice to students in failing public schools has damaged children.

Dick spent two frustrating years on the Michigan state board of education in the early 1990s. They seemed like two decades. The board was stubbornly bureaucratic and deeply dedicated to defending the education status quo.

Now, Dick is the kind of guy who would rather act than talk, so the snail's pace of the education board deeply frustrated him. His service was not an experience he looks back on fondly. But it did give him an up-close and personal look at the Michigan education system and the cabal that controlled it. Dick became convinced that, as long as power resided with the bureaucrats and insiders on the board and not with parents and students, schools were not going to change.

The last straw came in 1999, when the Education Freedom Fund, the donor-funded school choice program we had started, received 64,000 applications from desperate Michigan parents for just 4,000 scholarships. The need and the desire for more than a few thousand scholarships created with private dollars was clear. The system had to change.

"When I sat with Betsy and read the letters of parents and grand-parents, they would make you weep," Dick told a group of reporters at the time.[6]

We brought together a coalition of inner-city black leaders who wanted better schools, religious leaders who wanted the ability to run better schools, and business leaders who knew their future depended on better schools. We started a group called Kids First! Yes! with the goal of amending our constitution to get rid of the Michigan Blaine Amendment and allow public funds to follow students to private schools. Our early meetings featured a cross section of Michigan-ders hoping to change our education system that, when described, sounded like the beginning of an old joke. There were typically a few inner-city ministers, a rabbi, a couple of priests, an Episcopal school superintendent, and a businessman from the Chamber of Commerce, in addition to others.

As state Republican Party chair, I had to be careful not to use any party resources in the Kids First! effort, but I helped Dick in any way I could. By early 1999, we had succeeded in getting a measure on the 2000 ballot in Michigan. A "yes" vote was a vote to amend the constitution—eliminating the "Blaine" language—and to create a $3,300 voucher for any student who wanted one in a failing school district. A "failing" district was defined as one that graduated fewer than 66 percent of its students. Parents in school districts that grad-uated a higher percentage of students could decide by a vote of their school board or a group of citizen electors whether—or not—to allow students to use vouchers.

We went into the ballot measure with our eyes wide open. We had at least two significant strikes against us. First, in any question on the ballot, it's always far easier to get voters to vote "no." A "yes" vote is a vote for changing the status quo, after all. If opponents can raise doubts in voters' minds about that change, it is much more likely voters will oppose it.

Second, we were going up against the most powerful special interest in the Democratic Party, possibly even the state: the Michigan Education Association. Not only would they have loads of cash (taken from teachers' paychecks) to throw into opposing the measure; they would also have thousands of teachers and other allies to enlist in the effort.

But there was an additional obstacle to passing the measure that we didn't anticipate going into the fight. At a biennial Republican Party conference on Michigan's historic Mackinac Island in September 1999, Governor Engler announced that he would not support the school choice measure. My friend and education reform ally was careful to say that he agreed with the change we were seeking; he just didn't agree with the timing.

Michigan voters would be voting for president at the same time they voted on the education measure in 2000. Former Texas governor George W. Bush was campaigning to be the Republican nominee and Governor Engler was chairman of the Bush campaign in Michigan. Senator Spencer Abraham, whose first campaign for the U.S. Senate I had chaired, was also on the ballot that year. He was facing a tough reelection fight. Governor Engler feared that the education measure would bring out voters who would oppose Governor Bush and Senator Abraham—voters who might not bother to vote in the absence of the school choice question.

Dick and I were always skeptical of Engler's reasoning. In presidential races, it is the *presidential candidates* that drive people to the polls, not ancillary ballot questions. Plus, well before the voters had the chance to decide, Engler was open about the fact that he believed the ballot measure couldn't win against the union political machine. Before a single vote was cast, the governor called the measure a "stone cold loser."[7] He argued that we should put off the fight for another election cycle. As the Republican Party chairman, it gave me no joy being at odds with my governor. I liked and respected John, but

Dick and I felt strongly that we needed to pass the measure in 2000. Low-income Michigan students couldn't wait four years or more for the opportunity to choose decent schools.

John was right about one thing: The union bosses fought hard against the measure, and they fought dirty. We used the Freedom of Information Act (FOIA) to uncover documents showing school districts using public dollars to campaign against the measure. Anti-choice propaganda was sent home with kids from their public schools. The Oakland County public school district used taxpayer funds to create email campaigns, videos, and PowerPoint presentations to lobby against the proposal.

Most egregiously, the MEA conducted dual, racist whisper campaigns to encourage Michiganders to vote against the measure. In the suburbs, they sent out coded messages to convince voters that their schools would be overrun by poor, black kids if the measure passed. And in inner-city Detroit they circulated fliers claiming that poor, black kids would never be allowed to attend good schools, voucher or not.

Former Michigan governor James Blanchard, a leader of the opposition, managed to make both racist insinuations in a single op-ed. In the *Detroit News* a month before the vote, Blanchard darkly warned that vouchers would "discriminate against children with our tax dollars." Private schools, he wrote, would "have the power to pick and choose the students they want based on race, religion, a student's grades or athletic ability or even parents' income." The message to poor African-Americans was unmistakable: School choice will give private schools the ability to discriminate against your kids with public dollars.

At the same time, the op-ed made a thinly veiled racist appeal to white suburban voters. Blanchard warned that the "hidden agenda" of the proposal was to damage all public schools, even safe, white, suburban schools. "In fact, every school district, *even highly acclaimed* *districts*, could be affected by this voucher proposal," he wrote (emphasis mine). The message to white suburban voters was unmistakable: School choice will ruin your good schools by allowing inner-city kids to attend them.*

We began the campaign with polls showing the measure attracting around two-thirds of Michigan voters, in some places an even higher percentage, particularly in African-American communities. Dick set a goal to raise $5 million and succeeded in raising more than $12 million. He brought in the leaders of the national school choice movement to support the effort. People like John Walton, Bill Oberndorf, Howard Fuller, and Susan Mitchell actively supported the campaign. So did Cory Booker, who at this time was a city councilor in Newark, New Jersey, but was a rising star in the school choice movement. We had a who's who of education freedom warriors on our side.

As the campaign gained momentum, Governor Engler's dissatisfaction with the measure—and with me—grew louder. By December 1999, the governor's discontent was impossible to ignore. He was giving me a choice: Get Dick to pull down the ballot campaign or lose my position as state GOP chair. I didn't doubt that John would follow through on his threat.

I thought hard about how to respond. John was an ally in the fight for education freedom. I didn't like being at odds with him. But he was forcing me to pick sides. And if he thought I was going to throw Dick and the Kids First! Yes! effort under the bus in favor of my party chairmanship, he thought wrong. As far as I was concerned, the governor's political considerations did not outweigh the education

---

* Blanchard failed to mention an important detail in his own history. While serving as governor, he had chosen to send his son to a suburban school district that was predominately white and upper income, as opposed to the urban high school his son was residentially assigned to in Lansing. Blanchard's reasoning was that the Lansing high school was not safe enough for his son. Such hypocrisy is all too common among union-backed politicians: "Choice for me, but not for thee."[8]

crisis in Michigan. Our constitution had to change before our schools could change. And Michigan wasn't alone in being hamstrung by the Blaine Amendment. This was our opportunity to lead the country—possibly ignite a movement—in creating better futures for kids.

On February 2, 2000, I called a press conference at the state capitol. The tension between the governor and me was the talk of Lansing and the room was packed. It seemed like every reporter in the capital was there.

"It is no secret to any of you that Governor Engler has been unhappy with my refusal to go along with all of his requests," is how I began my remarks.

"It is obvious that the governor prefers a follower in the job of party chair, not a leader," I continued. "I have never been a rubber stamp. I have been a fighter for the grassroots, and following is admittedly not my strong suit."

With that, I announced that I was resigning as Michigan Republican Party chairman effective immediately. To say the announcement was unexpected would be an understatement. There were audible gasps in the room. A reporter from the Associated Press asked me if Governor Engler knew I was resigning.

"I assume he's finding out about this right now," I replied.

In fact, as I spoke, Engler was in Washington, DC. He cut his trip short and came back to Michigan that evening to announce a committee to find my replacement.

My feelings are mixed when I look back on this unpleasant episode. I didn't want to resign as party chair, especially in an election year. But the friction between the governor and me was hurting both the party and the constitutional amendment campaign. There was no other choice. I wasn't going to stop the campaign. And if it continued, the governor would make it impossible for me to continue as party chairman. So I made the hard call. The measure went on, and I resigned. In the end, Engler's pick to be my replacement was proof

I had made the right call. His search committee miraculously landed on his own communications director, Rusty Hills, as my replacement.

———————————

I was now free to get more actively involved in the campaign. Many of my key state party staff joined the campaign along with me, including my state party executive director, Greg Brock, and communications director, Greg McNeilly. From the beginning we were fighting the opposition's strategy of creating doubt in the voters' minds about whether they personally would benefit from school choice. Part of that strategy was to create doubt about the motives of the ballot measure's supporters. The unions brought out the kind of personal attacks that would become very familiar in the following years. Dick and Betsy DeVos, they said, were rich Republican capitalists out to destroy public education and the people who rely on it most. Of course, precisely the opposite was true. Our proposal was aimed directly at lifting up poor kids.

In any school choice plan, it's always a tough decision whether to allow all students to use public funds for the schools of their choice, or to limit choice to poor kids in failing schools. We made the conscious decision to focus the Michigan vouchers on poor kids in bad schools who had no other options. We had two reasons. First, it meant the program would be smaller and less expensive, so it would theoretically be an easier sell to the voters. Second, and most important, we felt it was the right thing to do.

Throughout the spring, summer, and fall of 2000, we made our case to Michigan voters that education freedom was a question of justice and equality. On the surface, our argument sounded a lot like the argument some Americans would make decades later that the United States is systemically racist against minorities. This argument is wrong. America is *not* a racist nation. But in one important area—education—we *do* have a system that is institutionally racist against blacks and other minorities; a system that traps them in failing schools and with no possibility of escape.

"In America and here in Michigan we do not have equality in education and we should not kid ourselves into thinking we do," Dick told audiences on the campaign trail. "We like to perpetuate the myth that all kids, regardless of their race, religion, creed, or income, are guaranteed an equal opportunity to a quality education. It may have been this way once—I don't know. It is not this way today."

The argument we made then, like the argument we make now, goes to the heart of what woke warriors claim is wrong with America: We are systematically failing poor, minority kids. On this, Dick and I agree with the left. The question is, what are we going to do about it? The education establishment's solution has been to spend more and more money funding the same failing system. At the same time they have fought, tooth and nail, against every attempt to give poor, minority kids a way out of schools that are failing them.

Our solution was to do something different, to stop perpetuating a systemically racist system by giving black and brown parents the opportunity to escape it. But when forced to choose, the education establishment chose politics over justice. It chose adults over children. In 2000, when the teacher unions and their allies were given the chance to end this education system in Michigan, they refused. They attacked supporters of choice as racists even as the union bosses defended a racist system. And their strategy worked. On November 7, 2000, the school choice referendum failed, 31%–69%.

It makes me wonder how all the voices calling America "systemically racist" would react when confronted with the same choice today. Would social justice—or politics—win?

———

Defeat is painful, of course, but it can be clarifying. California also had a school choice referendum in 2000 and it, too, failed.

After their loss, the supporters of that referendum largely moved on to other issues. Our loss in Michigan was bruising and disappointing, but I had no intention of abandoning the field of education reform. If anything, I was more determined than ever to fight. There was still a lot of energy in Michigan around school choice. I wanted to harness that energy to continue to fight for kids.

Dick and I came out of the voucher campaign smarter and more experienced than we were before. We had tried philanthropy. We had tried working to change the law. We had tried giving the voters a chance to amend the state constitution. In the end, we had learned from the opposition. We had to beat them at their own game.

Democrats in the state legislature—and many Republicans—lived in fear of losing the financial support of the powerful Michigan teacher union. Many more lived in fear of provoking the union's wrath by opposing their agenda. We decided we needed the same combination of respect and fear if we were going to be successful in Lansing. Legislators needed to understand there would be political peril in opposing education reform legislation. Instead of trying to get all the same players to do the right thing, we needed to change the players. We needed to build a political majority for school choice in the state legislature.

Together with Greg Brock, I created a political action committee called the Great Lakes Education Project (GLEP) in 2001. The idea was to support Michigan candidates who favored giving more families education choices by raising the cap on charter schools in the state. The original limit of 150 charters had quickly been met after the charter law was passed. Tens of thousands of Michigan kids were left on waiting lists.

For the first time, GLEP provided a counterweight to the teacher unions in Michigan elections. We were bipartisan. We sent every person who filed to run for the legislature—Republican or Democrat—a questionnaire. Our only criterion for supporting a candidate was that he or she supported lifting the cap on charter schools.

The Michigan teacher union was shrewd in those days. Outside of Detroit, the MEA liked to back Republican candidates who opposed school choice but were still conservative enough to win in largely conservative districts. Maybe the candidate was pro-life and pro-gun—the MEA didn't care—as long as he or she supported their education monopoly. This tactic gave the unions a surprising amount of clout in some GOP races. The result, particularly in the statehouse, was that there were a number of members we called "MEA Republicans." They were self-identified Republicans who opposed lifting the charter cap and didn't dare cross the unions. For years they had told their constituents they were conservatives while they voted like liberals on education. We concluded that this had to change if we were going to build a pro-school-choice majority.

Initially, GLEP focused its efforts on the August 2002 Republican primary. We concentrated on open seats where we had a better chance of winning. Our endgame was expanding charter schools, but there was a challenge. Education wasn't widely talked about in the election. Plus, explaining an issue as complex as lifting the limit on charter schools in a fifteen-second radio ad or a campaign flyer was virtually impossible. So we made the strategic decision that our communications with voters—mostly direct mail and radio in these rural districts—wouldn't be limited to education. We would highlight any relevant issue to help our friends and hurt our opponents.

More than once we got creative with our message. A case in point was a primary challenge to one of our candidates, an underdog who believed in education freedom. Barb Vander Veen was a West Michigan freshman representative who was challenged for the Republican nomination by three-term state senator Leon Stille. Stille was losing his Senate seat to term limits so he was trying to continue his political career in the House. A month before the primary, Stille looked like a shoo-in. He had high name identification, lots of friends in Lansing, and the backing of the MEA.

Then, about a month before the primary, Stille was caught dumping trash from his daughter's wedding into a dumpster of an elementary school in his district. An eagle-eyed constituent had seen a man matching Stille's description throwing tires, cans of paint, and other trash into the dumpster. That fact, and the fact that the car the man was driving had a Michigan State Senate license plate, pointed directly at Stille. He was busted.

We knew West Michigan voters wouldn't take well to a politician using taxpayer property for his own benefit. So GLEP mailed a flyer to voters in the district with a certain dyspeptic green monster who lives in a trash can on the cover. We called him "Oswald the Grouch." Inside the flyer we reprinted the *Grand Rapids Press* article about Stille's dumping incident.[9] "Oswald" just wanted to remind voters that Stille had been caught using public property to get rid of his trash.

The piece of mail was silly, but it got people's attention. Barb Vander Veen came from behind to win the primary and she kept her state House seat. Stille, on the other hand, used the remainder of his Senate term to vote against education reform. In December 2002, he was a key Senate vote in defeating the creation of fifteen additional charter schools in Detroit—charter schools with buildings that would be paid for by a private donation. Sadly, it was kids who lost.

GLEP didn't always win, but we always made our point as we held politicians accountable for their votes on education, something only the unions were doing at the time. In one race, we recruited a primary challenger against a state representative named Mike Pumford, who was a strong and vocal opponent of lifting the charter school cap. We didn't succeed in unseating Representative Pumford—not in 2002 anyway. But we did succeed in educating Michigan voters about his record. We sent a piece of mail to voters in his district that noted, correctly, that Pumford was supported by the same groups that had supported Al Gore for president. Pumford was outraged. In the media, he asked indignantly if we were "impugning" his Republican credentials. Our answer was an emphatic, yes, we are.

I'll be the first to admit we played hardball politics—but that is exactly what the unions had been doing for decades. We wanted candidates and politicians to understand that things were different now. Education freedom supporters would no longer look the other way when politicians opposed education choice. There would be consequences at the ballot box. Word started going around Lansing that we were making a difference in state elections.

GLEP came out of that first election cycle with some high-profile wins on the board. Soon after the primary, we met with school choice supporters who included board members I worked with on the various national school choice organizations. John Walton, Bill Oberndorf, and John Kirtley were there. Greg Brock and Curt and Wes Anderson, two campaign operatives with whom I had worked for several years, were also involved.

I made a presentation about GLEP's first election cycle track record. We had managed a half-dozen high profile victories in 2002 and were on track to building a majority in the legislature. More than that, GLEP was gaining a reputation as a serious and effective player in Lansing. We had sent the unmistakable message that candidates in both parties would be held accountable for their votes on charters and choice—especially candidates who were trying to sell themselves to the voters as conservatives.

The group was impressed with our results. John Walton immediately picked up on the idea and suggested we take the GLEP model—supporting candidates who supported education freedom and challenging those who don't—and deploy it in other states. If it worked in Michigan, it could work elsewhere.

From that pivotal meeting came the mandate to create a national PAC that would target states that were ripe for creating education choices. We called it All Children Matter. After a few successful years, All Children Matter and the Alliance for School Choice gave way to the newly created American Federation for Children (AFC), a full-spectrum education, advocacy, and political organization. We chose the name very deliberately to contrast with one of the main national teacher unions, the American Federation of Teachers (AFT). They were "of teachers" (or so they claimed), but we were "for children."

The American Federation for Children represented the amalgamation of the considerable wisdom and experience our group had gained from fighting the school choice fight. We had learned that successful advocacy of education freedom required coordinating a lot of moving parts. We had to focus on helping to get the right people elected, crafting good school choice legislation, getting that legislation implemented when it became law, and then helping students and their families exercise their choice to find the right schools. That meant hiring teams and opening offices in multiple states across the nation.

It wasn't long before our comprehensive approach started showing results. We had already helped Pennsylvania create a tax credit for corporations who contributed to school choice scholarship organizations. In 2004, Ohio enacted a voucher program for students with autism. That same year, the U.S. Congress created the DC Opportunity Scholarship Program for low-income students in the nation's capital. In 2006, Ohio, Iowa, Rhode Island, and Arizona created choice programs.

We worked with then-governor Bobby Jindal to give Louisiana kids in low-performing schools the opportunity to go to another school. In 2011, we worked with then-governor Mitch Daniels to create in Indiana one of the largest education freedom programs in the country. John Kirtley, who worked closely with Governor Jeb Bush on Florida's education reform, later credited our approach as the turning point in transforming Florida's schools.

By 2013, more than 250,000 students were benefiting from thirty-three publicly funded, private school choice programs in seventeen states and the District of Columbia. And we were just getting started.

With the exception of another term as Michigan Republican Party chair, I invested the sixteen years after Michigan's voucher campaign advising governors, designing legislation, raising money, and supporting campaigns for AFC and its forerunners. By the time I was nominated to be education secretary, the American Federation for Children was the largest and most effective school choice organization in the country, with chapters in multiple states. Through helping create new choice programs and expanding existing ones, we helped provide education opportunity to hundreds of thousands of children and families.

After years of fighting in the education reform trenches, we had hit on something that worked. It wasn't enough to donate money to education reform causes. It wasn't even enough to advocate for them. The public had to be educated. Supporters had to be elected. Consequences had to be paid.

We were fighting for nothing less than a revolution in America's K–12 education system. Parent by parent, legislator by legislator, and state by state, we were breaking down the barriers to education freedom for America's children. Little did I know that this battle would soon bring me to challenge the greatest obstacle of them all: Washington, DC.

CHAPTER THREE

"THE REAL DEBATE ISN'T BETSY DEVOS"

t was later in the day—the day after election day in 2016—by the time I got back to Jeb. He had emailed me that morning to ask if I would ever consider being U.S. secretary of education. I responded that evening the only way I knew how: with candor and curiosity. I told him the thought of being a cabinet secretary had truly never crossed my mind. But if he was serious and the opportunity actually presented itself, of course I would consider it. He swiftly emailed me back.

"I don't have a lot of influence with the campaign," he wrote (emails don't convey sarcasm very well, but no one could miss the sarcasm in this). "But I do have some friends who might."

Jeb Bush was probably the last person you would expect to be recruiting for the Trump cabinet. As one of candidates running for the Republican nomination in 2016, he had been the constant target of attacks and school-yard taunts from Donald Trump. It had been ugly and personal. But I wasn't at all surprised Jeb still cared about who would be Trump's secretary of education. No governor in America had spent more time and done more to give all kids the chance to attend a great school. And no governor had been more successful. Under Jeb's leadership, Florida students moved from near the bottom in reading and math achievement to scoring among the best in the nation.

I had known and worked with Jeb on education reform for twenty years. The secret of his success was the same passion that drove me. As governor, Jeb gave Florida students more options for where and how they could get an education than students in any other state. Jeb tripled the number of Florida charter schools. He instituted virtual learning, supported homeschooling, and gave students public school choice. He instituted standards and accountability. He helped foster better options for children with disabilities. He preached high expectations for every student.

Critically, Jeb also created the first statewide private school choice program in the country. By the time we connected after election day, the Florida Tax Credit Scholarship Program had grown to be the largest education freedom experiment in American history. More than 100,000 Florida students annually were benefiting from using public dollars to attend the school of their choice.

Jeb got beat up for challenging the education status quo— something I've become familiar with. Opponents accused him of trying to "privatize" public schools. Union mouthpieces charged him with practicing "corporate education reform" and somehow "profiting" by destroying schools for poor, minority students.

But something remarkable happened as Jeb's reforms took hold and grew in Florida. The arguments his opponents used against him were proved wrong. Dead wrong.

Opponents had said vouchers would destroy traditional public schools. But study after study showed that the competition produced by school choice *improved* traditional public schools results in Florida.[1] As a matter of fact, the improvements in public school student achievement were greatest where there was the most competition. Opponents also said poor, minority kids would be hurt most by school choice. In fact, it was these public school students whose reading and math ability improved the most. They even improved in school attendance and graduation rates.[2]

Jeb was a living, breathing refutation of the deceitful arguments of the education establishment. He had compassion, vision, and guts. I was humbled that he would recommend me to be education secretary.

Later, Jeb shared that he reached out to me after raising the idea with Mike Pence, President-elect Trump's running mate and vice president. After checking in with me, he had relayed to the vice president–elect that I was open to the idea. Not long after, I saw Mike at an event. He caught my eye from across the room and asked to talk after dinner. I had worked with Mike when he was a member of Congress and when he was governor of Indiana. I knew he was a brother-in-arms on the issue of school choice. Jeb's recommendation certainly carried weight with Mike as well. He called me the next day to ask if I would meet with the president-elect and him at Trump's golf club in Bedminster, New Jersey, that Saturday, November 19. I said, "Absolutely."

Dick and I flew from Michigan to a small airport near Bedminster Saturday morning. More precisely, *Dick flew* us out to New Jersey. For as long as I've known him, Dick has had a passion for aviation. He's been a pilot for more than twenty years. He likes to joke that he's "just Betsy's pilot" on trips like this. Dick is many things—father, husband, businessman. The aviator part is just a bonus for me! Still, true to form, as I went off to Bedminster, he stayed at the airport, watching the action on the television in the air service lounge.

Trump had commandeered the clubhouse at Bedminster to have his meetings with potential cabinet secretaries. The dining room was set up as a "greenroom" with food and beverages while the interviews were conducted in what appeared to be a boardroom or private dining room on the other side of the clubhouse. Mitt Romney was in an interview when I arrived. James Mattis, Trump's future secretary of defense, was in the greenroom. I had never met General Mattis before and I found him to be interesting and easy to talk with. Not surprisingly, we got on the subject of education. He told me how moving it had been for him when he was a commander in Afghanistan to have his Marines protect Afghan children as they went to school. He would later tell me—on more than one occasion—that no one in the cabinet had a harder job and was doing more important work for the future of America than I was.

Former DC public schools chancellor Michelle Rhee was also there with her husband, former Phoenix Suns point guard and Sacramento mayor Kevin Johnson. When it came time for Michelle to meet with Trump, Kevin joined her and together they were ushered outside and around to the front door of the clubhouse rather than going directly through the interior door to the meeting room. General Mattis took the same route, as did I when it was my time to meet.

The press was lining the stone driveway in front of the Georgian Revival mansion, and apparently the president-elect had decided it made for better theater for his visitors to greet him on the front steps.

The president- and vice president–elect came out on the landing as I walked up. I have known Mike and Karen Pence for years so I instinctually extended my hand to Mike first. But as I approached him, Mike tipped his head toward Trump as if to say, "Say hi to the big man first!" I quickly corrected, shook hands with Donald J. Trump for the first time ever, and we went into the meeting.

In addition to the president–and vice president–elect, Ivanka Trump, Jared Kushner, Steve Bannon, Reince Preibus, and Stephen Miller were in the room when I walked in. Everyone asked me questions about my background or an education policy. Trump homed in on career and technical education—"vocational school," as he called it. His background in construction made him familiar with graduates of these programs.

"How come these kids are being told to go to college?" he said. "There are all these great jobs and they would make a lot more money. We need to be focusing on that." I told him I completely agreed. Then we talked about school choice and accountability for a while. The meeting ended without a job offer. It was hard for me to tell how it had gone because I had never met with Donald Trump before. I left Bedminster unsure what, if anything, would happen next. Dick flew us back to Michigan.

It was clear Trump was looking to shake up the education status quo, and we couldn't have agreed more on the need for that. The press quickly declared that the choice for education secretary was between Michelle Rhee and me. *BuzzFeed* said I was the "conventional" choice, while Rhee, a Democrat and a veteran of fierce battles to reform Washington, DC, schools, was the "f--k you" choice for the teacher unions. I wasn't so sure about that. The teacher unions and I had been going round and round for decades. I wasn't their candidate, and I didn't want to be.

Dick said that the idea of me being education secretary became real to him when the news showed me walking up to Trump and Pence at Bedminster. But even after the interview, it was still very theoretical to me. When I got home, I resumed normal life. I had already talked to Dick about going to Washington. We talked again, more seriously and practically this time. I had also talked to my kids and taken the temperature of close friends about the possibility. Most were enthusiastic—to varying degrees—but some were skeptical. Some of my kids were concerned about the target that would be painted on my back and the beating I would most likely take getting confirmed by the Senate. I wasn't worried about me, though I was worried about the impact it could have on them and my grandkids. I had withstood attacks before—or so I thought. Looking back, I underestimated how vicious the process would become.

On November 22 I was meeting with the CEO of one of our businesses in Holland when my cell phone rang. It was a 212 number—a New York City area code. I told my colleagues, "I think I'd better take this one." I went into another room and said hello.

It was the president-elect. "BETSY!" he boomed into the phone. "YOU'RE GOING TO MAKE A GREAT SECRETARY OF EDUCATION!"

That was it. There was no small talk, no questions, just an enthusiastic declarative statement. And I was going to Washington.

Almost immediately, my life was no longer my own.

Being nominated to a cabinet position sets off three necessary but—I'll just be honest—*unpleasant* processes for the nominee. First you have to get your security clearance.

Because the secretary of education is in the line of succession for the presidency (it's sixteenth, but it's there!), the position requires a high security clearance. That begins with a 136-page form on which you have to list descriptions of every job you've had, everywhere you went to school, everywhere you've lived, everywhere you've served, and everywhere you've traveled in the last seven years. Among other things. You also have to include dates and names, and if you get them wrong, the maximum penalty is jail time. Then you have to allow a small army of federal agents and investigators to cull through the details of your life.

I'm not complaining. The reason made it an honor to be vetted. As complicated as it was, the security clearance process is necessary and useful. What was significantly more time consuming and invasive— and in desperate need of significant modernizing, in my opinion— was the financial disclosure process.

Federal law rightly requires nominees to list all their sources of income in order to make sure they have no conflicts of interest with their future position. A person can't be the secretary of energy, for instance, and own stock in an electric vehicle company (or at least that was true until Joe Biden became president, but that's a different story[3]). The problem is, the financial disclosure law was passed in the 1970s, and the world of finance has changed dramatically since then. Add to that the fact that our family finances are admittedly complicated. The result was our financial disclosure process was long, confusing, and expensive. Dick called it "financial proctology." In the end, we divested from companies and funds that we knew weren't conflicted. We just wanted to get the process over with.

But even after going above and beyond the letter of the law in our financial disclosure, a favorite tactic of the opposition was to accuse us of trying to profit somehow from the world of education. And if not from that, then from some other governmental activity. Every one of the accusations was baseless, some of them absurdly so. For example, my family had long supported a wonderful nonprofit named Bethany Christian Services and its mission to provide adoption, foster care, and refugee services to needy kids. When Bethany got a contract to provide temporary housing to undocumented kids separated from their parents at the border, stories started to appear in the press darkly questioning my "financial ties" to Bethany and the Trump policy of family separation. What the reporters didn't seem to understand was that my "ties" to Bethany were charitable *contributions*. Contributions to charities don't pay you anything. They can't make you rich—only *less* rich.

Finally, in addition to getting my security clearance, finishing the grueling financial disclosure process, and finding a place to live, I had to get ready for my confirmation hearing before the United States Senate.

The notion that the Senate is responsible for confirming the secretary of education is really only true on paper. In reality—as we would see later during the COVID crisis—it's the teacher unions that control the process, at least for Democrats.

Since the unions are so central to this tale, I want to say a few clarifying words about teachers. Most American parents love their children's teachers, and for good reason. Most of us have known teachers who made a real difference in our lives (for me, Mrs. Walcott, my second-grade teacher, comes to mind). We all know teachers who are conscientious and inspire our children and grandchildren. A great teacher can impact a child's life forever. Most teachers work hard and care about their students.

When I talk about "teacher unions," I'm not talking about the men and women who are in the classroom teaching our children. The unions don't do a very good job representing those people. It's one reason I call them "school unions," not "teacher unions." If they really cared about teachers, then teachers would be paid better, among other things. Instead, the school union bosses care about one thing: their power. They maintain that through their political advocacy, which they fund by constantly seeking new dues-paying members.

The National Education Association (NEA) and the American Federation of Teachers (AFT) contributed more than $66 million to candidates in 2020, and virtually all of it—98 percent—went to Democrats, from President Biden to local school board members. During COVID, when schools were closed and the bosses were demanding ransom before they would allow them to open, their political giving spiked. Their contributions more than doubled between 2018 and 2020. And, like Pavlovian dogs, congressional Democrats rewarded their giving with $280 billion in emergency relief in 2020.[4]

Now, I support political giving. Dick and I have done our share of giving to impact our community and our country in positive ways, and we will continue to do so. We give because we believe deeply in ideas and causes, and we support candidates who share those views. We've never given for access, power, or personal gain, like all too many others seem to do.

But political contributions from public employee unions are different—very different. In most parts of the country today, there are no alternatives to public schools for parents and children, and these schools are staffed by dues-paying union members. When a public sector union uses Americans' tax dollars to support just one party—when their members make up more than 10 percent of the delegates at that party's convention—the leaders of these unions are effectively buying protection for their monopoly. The people who fund the system—the people the system is supposed to serve—don't have a voice. And the party in question—the Democratic Party—enacts legislation that is good for its union benefactors, not necessarily good for students.

So it didn't surprise me at all that the school union bosses started attacking me the day the Trump transition team announced my nomination. AFT president Randi Weingarten said my selection by Trump "makes it loud and clear that his education policy will focus on privatizing, defunding and destroying public education in America."[5] She went on CNN and said I was "the most anti-education nominee who's ever been nominated."

Lily Eskelsen García, president of the NEA, took longer to say it but she was just about as welcoming. "Betsy DeVos . . . has done more to undermine public education than support students. . . . She has consistently pushed a corporate agenda to privatize . . . public education," Eskelsen García wrote. "By nominating Betsy DeVos, the Trump administration has demonstrated just how out of touch it is with what works best for students, parents, educators and communities."

Look at their words closely. Here the union bosses argued that I am an enemy of public education. But later they would focus on another insult—that I was unqualified to be the secretary of education. The fact that they pivoted is revealing. Polls showed majorities of Americans favored what I had long championed: more school choice. And that support would climb even higher when schools remained closed during the COVID-19 pandemic. The unions and the education establishment knew education freedom was supported by Americans. So they had to make their defamation campaign not about the need to change the system, but about *me*.

As if on cue, Massachusetts senator Elizabeth Warren wrote me a rambling, *sixteen-page* letter charging that "[t]here is no precedent for an Education Department Secretary nominee with your lack of experience in public education." Her statement was brash. Definitive. And wrong.

America's first secretary of education, nominated by Jimmy Carter, was a federal appeals court judge whose work in education amounted to writing a few op-eds. Fourteen years later, President Bill Clinton nominated Richard Riley, a partner in a South Carolina law firm with no background in public education. In fact, only three out of the ten education secretaries who preceded me ever taught in a K–12 classroom.[6]

I had thirty years of background in education reform. I had met with thousands of kids and hundreds of teachers. I helped my husband create a charter school. I guided governors in building school choice programs. I had convinced uncertain state legislators to fund school choice. I had mentored students.

In other words, I had lots of experience in education—just not the kind of education Elizabeth Warren agreed with, or would ever support for any kids but her own. The sad part was, a decade earlier, in a book written with her daughter, Warren had agreed with me. She correctly diagnosed that the problem in American education was that parents with money already had school choice—by moving to a good school district. Meanwhile, middle- and lower-class families were stuck in bad schools. She wrote:

> It's time to sound the alarm that the crisis in education is not only a crisis in reading and arithmetic; it is also a crisis in middle class family economics. . . . At the core of the problem is the time-honored rule that where you live dictates where you go to school. Any policy that loosens the ironclad

relationship between location-location-location and school-school-school would eliminate the need for parents to pay an inflated price for a home. . . . A well-designed voucher program would fit the bill neatly.[7]

In a complete about-face, when she needed to curry favor with the school union bosses, Warren forgot about the middle- and lower-class families stuck in failing schools. She lobbied hard against any kind of school choice—even charter schools. Warren had sent her child to a private school. She had exercised her choice. But she fought my nomination because I believed all parents should have that same choice.

But Senator Warren got one thing right: I *was* an unprecedented choice for education secretary. Not because of my resume but because I wanted to fundamentally disrupt the education status quo. Most education secretaries—Democrat and Republican—had only tinkered around the edges of the American model of public education. I wanted to see that model—created more than 150 years ago to prepare children to work in factories and be good Protestants—fundamentally changed. Some kids learn just fine sitting in rows in a classroom all day. But many others need something different. Central planning in Washington doesn't work to meet those needs.

Only the creativity and competition fostered by education choice can finally fix American schools.

The one-size-fits-all model of government dictating where children go to school and how they learn works fine for the adults who profit from the system, but not for kids who depend on it. I went to Washington thinking I could change that, and it won me few friends, on either side of the aisle. Even Jeb Bush, who was largely responsible for me being nominated and who had led bold reforms in Florida, said later that if he were president, he didn't know if he would have had the guts to appoint someone like me education secretary.

The school union bosses' problem with me wasn't that they thought I was unqualified. It was that they knew I was dangerous to their agenda.

———————

The path to my confirmation hearing was a fifty-day sprint. That's what separated the day I got the job offer from the president-elect and the day the Senate Health, Education, Labor and Pensions (HELP) Committee would hold my confirmation hearing. Mine was one of the first confirmation hearings of the new cabinet—scheduled for January 11, 2017.

One of the first things you do as a cabinet nominee is "make the rounds." You stop in and visit with the senators on the committee who will determine your fate. In my case, that meant meeting with twelve Republicans, including friends like Senators Orrin Hatch and Tim Scott.

Tim has a way with words that I, admittedly, sometimes do not. I thought he summed up the coming confrontation well: "The real debate isn't Betsy DeVos," he said. "It's a generation of kids who are caught in underperforming schools."[8]

As for the Democrats on the HELP Committee, they clearly didn't agree with that assessment. Their membership included a cast of the party's most high-profile and ambitious politicians. An idealist might say they were there as a testament to the importance of education to the party. A pragmatist, on the other hand, might say they were there as proof of how eager Democrats are to keep the union bosses happy. Whichever you believe, the HELP Committee was home to Democratic power players like Bernie Sanders, Tim Kaine, and Al Franken (before he resigned in disgrace amid sexual harassment revelations).

Throughout the first part of January, I met with all of the members of the committee. I met with the chairman, Tennessee senator Lamar

Alexander. Lamar is a friend and former education secretary. You might argue that that makes him uniquely able to assess who is, or is not, qualified for the role, as opposed to, say, Senator Warren. Lamar worked hard to see me through the confirmation process, and I am grateful to him.

My meetings with senators revealed some surprising—and some not so surprising—things about them. In all my visits, I was accompanied only by the staffer assigned to me by the presidential transition. These aides are affectionately known as "sherpas" and mine was there mostly to take note of requests—and promises!—members made. These were supposed to be "one-on-one" meetings, and I didn't need or want a lot of staff in the room.

One of my first meetings was with Washington senator Patty Murray, the highest-ranking Democrat on the committee. We walked into her office and were seated in chairs directly across from the senator. She had an array of staffers around her, some sitting and some standing. They would occasionally whisper in her ear. They also asked most of the questions. A typical exchange involved an aide asking me a question and Senator Murray following up with, "Yeah, what about that?"

Most senators, even ones I knew disagreed vehemently with me, were cordial. Al Franken was one. Susan Collins of Maine was up-front with her misgivings about my nomination, but she invited me to come up to her state to see Maine's limited system of school choice. I also met with Vermont senator Bernie Sanders. His office was decorated in lots of plaid and smelled like a lot of mothballs. Still, he was mostly pleasant. Elizabeth Warren, on the other hand, was one of the coldest people I have ever met. That meeting was one of my shortest.

In most changes of administrations, incoming presidents have transition teams in place long before election day. These are usually made up of people experienced in policy and the ways of the

Washington bureaucracy. They provide options to the president for filling top-level posts, as well as names of qualified candidates for lesser offices. They guide the new team through the process of forming a government.

The problem—or the blessing, depending on how you looked at it—was that Donald Trump was not a creature of Washington. He had never worked in government. He didn't have networks of experts to help him build his administration, and he didn't care to. Trump's willingness to disrupt the establishment and play by his own rules was one of the best things about him. It led him to nominate me for education secretary. But his tendency to shun the establishment also had downsides. Turns out, some norms exist for a reason.

Self-created chaos dogged the Trump transition from the start. Two days after he won the election, President-elect Trump fired the man who had been preparing his presidential transition, former New Jersey governor Chris Christie. Trump then put Mike Pence in charge of the transition. He couldn't have made a better choice, but with the change, the effort lost valuable time. Reportedly, some thirty notebooks full of information on potential hires compiled by the Christie team went out the door when Christie was let go.

One of the main responsibilities of the presidential transition team is to guide candidates like me through the details of confirmation by the Senate. The most significant part of that process is to prepare for the confirmation hearing. Teams conduct "murder boards," or mock trials in advance of the real thing. Transition staff play the roles of opposition senators peppering the nominee with questions. The idea isn't necessarily to master the policies—although becoming familiar with them was part of it. Mostly, murder boards are a tool to give the nominee experience under fire.

The Trump transition team was put together on the fly—while everything else moved forward. That meant that even as I was busy navigating the endless security and disclosure processes, my team was also dealing with a changing cast of transition staff. Many came from backgrounds other than education—some were just individuals who had been on the campaign. The result was that, when we did our mock hearings, many of the transition staff asked me questions *they* didn't know the answer to. Out of necessity, they coached me repeatedly to stick to generalities and not commit to any specific policies in any of my answers. I had never gone through a confirmation and transition before, so I had to trust the advice I was given. Their risk aversion rubbed off on me, and I became uncharacteristically cautious.

Looking back, the biggest mistake made during my confirmation process was allowing the opponents of my nomination eight weeks of unanswered attacks. There is an unwritten rule that nominees don't talk to the press before they are confirmed. All communications must go through "official" channels, in this case the transition team. The Trump transition enforced this rule relentlessly. The problem was, they also didn't communicate much of anything in response to the attacks.

On January 9, two days before the hearing was scheduled to occur, the HELP Committee suddenly announced that it would be delayed for a week, until January 17. The only explanation the committee offered was that the delay was at the request of the Senate leadership.

I had already been badly battered in the press, with little pushback from the transition team. The hearing delay left me exposed for an additional six days, effectively gagged from speaking publicly.

The unions took advantage of this extra time to step up their campaign to portray me as somehow both unqualified and dangerous. The media proclaimed me Trump's "most controversial" nominee. Late-night comedians weighed in. Each day that ticked past, the stakes for the hearing grew higher. Even before the delay, my nomination had attracted unprecedented attacks from Democrats and their allies. Over the course of those additional six days, the tension built, and the hearing became political "must-see TV."

And I had to stay silent.

I t is a sad fact that congressional hearings in the age of social media have become more political theater than public service. They are opportunities for members of Congress to perform for the cameras. Hearings are used less to ask substantive questions of the witness and more to obtain thirty-second snippets of dramatic outrage to post on Facebook alongside fundraising pitches.

Expecting the worst, when the day of my hearing arrived, I wanted my friends and family close. A large Michigan contingent joined me in Washington. John Booy came from The Potter's House. Denisha Merriweather was there, a friend who had beaten the odds to become the first in her family to graduate from high school and go on to college, thanks to Jeb Bush's school choice program. Of course Dick was there, along with most of my kids and some of my grandchildren. We opted not to subject the grandkids to the hearing and kept them at the hotel. But my kids sat right behind me in the hearing room. Dick claims he was seated out of camera range so no scowls or visibly mouthed insults at members of the committee would be caught on tape. He may have been on to something.

From the moment Chairman Alexander gaveled in the hearing, the Democrats on the committee engaged in what can only be called theatrical antagonism. Their objective was to catch me in a "gotcha" moment.

With the cameras on him, the jovial Al Franken I had met in his office two weeks earlier became a hard-bitten prosecutor. He asked me questions and then cut me off, not allowing me to answer. You may have watched a clip of him asking me if I thought "growth"—how much a student has learned since they were last measured—or "proficiency"—if a student is performing at the expected level—was the best way to measure student progress. My answer was, neither. I believe in mastery. Only when a student truly commands a topic or concept can we say they've succeeded in learning it. But Franken had no interest in giving me airtime to explain that.*

Other senators did the same regarding funding children with disabilities under school choice. The truth is there are many great school choice programs across the country that are targeted specifically at aiding students with disabilities. But protecting children with disabilities is not a question that can be answered in a ten-second sound bite—or at least I hadn't yet mastered that ability. Again and again, committee Democrats asked big, political hot-button questions, few of which had anything to do with education. They allowed little time for me to answer. Topics like gay conversion therapy and climate change came at me rapid-fire.

When they weren't firing "gotcha" questions at me, they were asking me to commit to policies that were, in my view, responsible for keeping our schools under the thumb of an education monopoly and a nineteenth-century model of education. I didn't agree with most of these policies and was not going to pledge to continue them with the hope of winning over Democratic senators.

Chairman Alexander and the committee Republicans were more substantive. But even some of these exchanges were used out of context against me.

In my office visit with Senator Mike Enzi of Wyoming, he had told me about a small elementary school in Wapiti, Wyoming, that has a ten-foot fence around its playground to keep grizzly bears out. We revisited that school's unique problem—and how it needed the

---

* I would have enjoyed asking Franken about his own K–12 education at an elite private school, or about his children's experience at the *very* elite private school he chose for them. He probably didn't want to try to explain that.

latitude to address that problem—early in the hearing. Later, Democrat Chris Murphy of Connecticut asked me what I thought about guns in schools for safety. Being a federalist and a supporter of the Second Amendment, I said that was a question best left to the states and districts. Recalling my conversation with Senator Enzi, I said the administrators at the Wapiti school could probably use a gun as additional protection for their students against grizzlies.

Granted, it was an unusual answer—perhaps a little more of a contrast than the question called for—but when considered in context it made an important point. Different communities have to be free to create schools that address their unique needs. No school in Murphy's hometown of Hartford, Connecticut, was going to need to protect its students from bears (or would they?*) but the folks in Wapati did. They should be able to do so in the way they see fit. Without fail, the press repeated my answer to Senator Murphy without mentioning my earlier exchange with Senator Enzi.

That answer is one of the things I might do differently if I had to do it all over again. But it's also a telling example of the state of policy debates in our country and the gulf that exists between Americans who live in their own, unrelated bubbles. My critics were far more interested in having a raucous laugh at my expense than in talking about the real questions impacting teachers, families, and kids.

The hearing didn't begin until 5 p.m. and continued over three long hours.

Finally, nearing 9 p.m., it was over. I was exhausted but thankful I had survived. While everyone was milling about the hearing room I approached Elizabeth Warren to shake her hand. She was gathering her papers up from the dais and we made eye contact. Instead of taking my outstretched hand, she whirled away and exited

---

* Interestingly enough, a year and a half later, when I was education secretary, a school in Connecticut had to go on lockdown because there was a bear on the playground. We sent the clip to Senator Murphy. He was uncharacteristically silent in response.

the hearing room. I was left standing with my arm outstretched. Al Franken noticed what happened and stepped in. I shook his hand as I shrugged my shoulders over what I had just witnessed.

Everyone was hungry. So, together with a few members of my staff who had helped me through the confirmation process, we met my family and friends for dinner at a restaurant near Capitol Hill. We walked into the dining room thinking the hearing had gone fairly well. I knew I had had a couple of slip-ups, but nothing too damaging. Or so we thought.

But when we talked to people who had watched the hearing on television, we got a very different perspective. My performance was being portrayed in the media as a disaster. As if in one voice, the pundits declared that the hearing had left me "unqualified" to be the secretary of education. I was surprised. I knew that I had made a few mistakes and I owned them. But the magnitude of the negative reaction was puzzling. It didn't take long for the reason to become clear. Democrats would later say that it was *the hearing* that led them to oppose my nomination. The not-so-hidden message was that they had been fair and open before the hearing but afterward, everything changed. In their rewriting of history, it was my performance, not the political pressures on them from the education establishment, that disqualified me.

On January 31, the HELP Committee approved my nomination on a party-line vote. The next step was a vote by the whole Senate. Anyone who thought the opposition would back off after having failed in the committee was dead wrong. The closer the Senate got to voting on my nomination, the louder the volume of the establishment's animosity became. Using social media and texting campaigns, the teacher unions and their allies created an Astroturf campaign of opposition directed at Capitol Hill. The phone lines and inboxes of Senate offices were deluged with strangely similarly worded messages.

Democratic activist groups organized "protests" outside wavering senators' offices and even outside of our home in Michigan.

In previous transitions, education secretary nominations have been so uncontroversial that they've often been approved by a voice vote of the Senate. Members don't even bother with going on the record with individual votes. In the cases in which there have been recorded votes for education secretary nominees, the margins have been lopsided. Even Bill Bennett, Ronald Reagan's outspoken secretary of education, was confirmed by a vote of 93–0 in 1985.

In my case, Democrats in the Senate first attempted to filibuster the vote on my nomination. On February 3, the Senate voted along party lines to end the filibuster and allow the vote to occur. Then, two Republicans senators, Lisa Murkowski of Alaska and Susan Collins from Maine, announced that, even though they voted for me in the HELP Committee and supported ending the filibuster, they would oppose my confirmation in the final vote. That meant that in a Senate with 52 Republicans and 48 Democrats, my nomination was deadlocked at 50–50. Democrats tried desperately to recruit one more Republican senator to vote against me. They even held a twenty-four-hour talkathon the night before the vote, each of them dutifully addressing a chamber that was empty except for the C-SPAN cameras.

But in the end, it didn't matter. Our Constitution articulates only two roles for the vice president: becoming president in case of the president's death, and presiding over the Senate. In practice, the vice president's job in the Senate is pretty limited. But they do have one important power: They are allowed to vote when there is a tie. On February 7, the Senate finally voted on my nomination. When the vote tied at 50–50, Vice President Mike Pence walked into the chamber and took the gavel. For the first time in United States history, the vice president voted in the Senate to break a tie for a cabinet nominee. My nomination was confirmed. I was the eleventh U.S. secretary of education.

They consumed all that time "debating," I thought, and they would have gotten the same result with a voice vote.

───────────

At around the six-minute mark, C-SPAN viewers watching the vote closely in the Senate could see Senator Cory Booker of New Jersey enter the chamber, walk directly up to the dais, give a quick thumbs-down to the clerk, and silently leave the chamber.

For me watching, it was deeply disappointing. Cory's "no" vote wasn't just another senator registering his choice. For me it was the personification of what happens when a party is controlled by a special interest group—a special interest group that is holding American children as hostages to their cause. No member can cross the group, not for any reason. To his credit, Booker was amazingly open about how the unions responded to his attempts at reform.

"I was literally brought into a broom closet by a union and told I would never win office if I kept talking about charters," he once said.[9]

Cory and I had a long history. He first rose to political fame as a young, Democrat, African-American city councilman in Newark in the early 2000s. The Newark school system was a corrupt patronage machine that was taken over by the state of New Jersey in 1995. The Democratic state government's approach to fixing the system was to pour more money into it. Ten years later, Newark was spending twice the national average and yet one of every two Newark students failed to graduate from high school and students in every grade tested dead last among their peers in the state.[10]

Cory had another idea to fix Newark's schools: give parents and students publicly funded vouchers to take to the school of their choice. It was a bold move for a young Democrat. When Dick and I heard about it, we reached out to Cory, offering support and solidarity.

Cory and I went on to serve together on pro-school-choice organization boards throughout the 2000s. He had campaigned for the 2000 state constitution amendment in Michigan. He keynoted two American Federation for Children (AFC) meetings when I was chairman—once as mayor of Newark and again as a U.S. senator. He drew standing ovations from the crowd. Cory's was a valuable voice for the school choice movement. He spoke on behalf of the Americans who were being hurt the most by the current system. He was aggressive and direct about all the failed promises poor families had been given.

At the time of my nomination, I hadn't seen Cory since the May 2016 AFC event when he told the audience that "the mission of this organization is aligned with the mission of our nation." Later, when he was asked by the press if he supported me as education secretary, Cory refused to comment at first.[11] But eventually he began to express "serious concerns" about my nomination.[12] I reached out to him to meet, both before and after my confirmation hearing, but he was never available. In mid-January he announced he would vote against me on the floor of the Senate.

I've been involved with politics a long time. I know politicians can be . . . let's just say, *morally malleable*. But Cory's betrayal hit deep. He not only turned his back on me, he turned his back on millions of children counting on someone like him to do what's right.

What's more, he offered a completely contradictory rationale for opposing me. At the AFC meeting in May, he spoke movingly about what defines us as a country—our commitment to freedom and equality. The battle for education freedom, he said, was critical to "who we say we are as a country." The fight being waged by the people at the AFC meeting was part of realizing the promise of America that every human being has innate value. We were fighting, he said, the "last battle of the civil rights movement."

Eight months later, when he stood up to speak in the Senate, the Cory Booker I thought I knew was unrecognizable. He directly negated the view of freedom—and the role of education within it— that he had expressed just eight months earlier.

He would vote against the "nominee," Cory said, because she is "someone who has been silent on the issues that are so critical to this country *being who we say we are*."

The federal government, not citizens exercising their freedom, he said, was the key to realizing the promise of America. He never said my name. He just said that "the nominee" had no commitment to defend the rights of minority children, gay children, and children with disabilities—literally all the same virtues he had ascribed to the school choice movement at the meeting in May.

Even for Washington, it was a breathtaking reversal. Cory had been right the first time. It's not the federal government that determines our rights. Our Constitution rightly declares that our rights come from our Creator—they cannot legitimately be tampered with or taken away by any government. He said it himself: The current government-imposed system has "imprisoned" inner-city kids in "institutions of failure." It will be a free people, exercising their choice to educate their children in the way they see fit, that will give all American children the right to safe and functioning schools.

I was disappointed and hurt by Cory's actions, but I wasn't surprised. He was running for the nomination of the Democratic Party for president in 2020. He couldn't betray the well-funded, well-organized interest groups that held his political future in the palms of their hands—and held our children as hostages to their self-interested cause.

"Grandma, why does it say 'DeVos' on there?" my six-year-old granddaughter asked, looking at a C-SPAN feed on my phone, cuddled up to me in the Suburban's third row.

While the Senate was voting on my nomination, we took a family tour of the Smithsonian's National Air and Space Museum, just a few blocks down the National Mall from the U.S. Capitol. It's an oddly powerless position to watch a hundred people, most of whom barely know you, debate in public whether or not to hire you. My nervous energy pushed me out of the museum and into the backseat of that SUV. I wasn't planning for Clara—my first grandchild—to come along, but looking back, I'm glad she did.

There's a certain calm you get from having a small child by your side; a reminder about what's most important in life. It also helps you bite your tongue when you see people you do know—people who should know better—turn their backs on you.

In many ways, those fleeting moments were a beautiful microcosm of what would come next. I was thinking about the child next to me, and millions more like her. The people on the screen were thinking about their adult issues.

I hugged Clara and thought, Welcome to the politics of education.

CHAPTER FOUR

THE SWAMP

I t was a crisp, clear day in Washington, DC, and I was on my way to a middle school in the capital's inner city. It was my second day as the U.S. secretary of education, and I wanted to show my support for public education. So we worked with the District of Columbia government to use that sunny, February day to visit Jefferson Middle School, a public school in one of the more disadvantaged neighborhoods of the city.

We intentionally decided not to announce the visit to the media. I wanted to talk with students, parents, and teachers without the lights of TV cameras intruding. The visit wasn't about good press or public relations. I was new on the job. It was about building a relationship with local school leaders, students, and their parents. But when we pulled up to the school it was clear that DC officials had leaked word of my visit to the unions and their allied groups. Dozens of protestors were gathered in front of the building, carrying signs and chanting "Dump DeVos!" "Go back!" and other insults that don't bear repeating. They chanted "shame" at me. But it seemed to me the only "shame" of the scene was what the innocent kids inside the school were forced to witness.

I was traveling with two security officers assigned to me by the Education Department. I would go on to receive so many credible threats against my life that I became the first education secretary in history to be assigned security provided by the U.S. Marshals Service. But that came later. That day, even with the department officers in tow, getting out and navigating the crowd was a risky move. But being intimidated—staying in the car and driving away—felt even worse. So one of the security officers and I got out of the SUV.

Immediately the crowd closed around us. The officer was clearly rattled as we pushed through the throng, but we kept going. When we reached the steps leading up to the schoolhouse door, several protestors rushed ahead of us to block our way. The scene was chaotic; people were shouting and shoving. A protestor on the steps above pushed me (and was later charged for assaulting a DC police officer). As I nearly fell backward down the concrete stairs, I made a wry mental note: Next time, wear lower heels.

I was more irritated than afraid when my security officer took my arm and ushered me back into the car. We sped off in the black SUV. A few blocks away, he said, "Ma'am, I don't think we should go back there." I instinctively knew that what I did next would set the tone for my entire time as education secretary. The unions were determined to manufacture a fight. They wanted to keep the cameras on conflict between *adults*, outside the classroom, where they had the advantage. I wanted to turn the nation's eyes on the children they were supposed to be educating.

"We are going back," I told the officer, trying hard to keep a lid on my frustration.

We returned to Jefferson Middle School and managed to enter through a side door. My experience that day confirmed what I already knew. Good teachers want to teach. Children want to learn. And parents want a say in their children's education. The problem is that the education establishment—led by the school union bosses—didn't want to let me in the door. It was going to be a long four years.

———————

The centralization of education policy in Washington had been going on for two decades when I became secretary of education. Administrations of both parties were responsible for consolidating more power at the federal government level. President George W. Bush's No Child Left Behind Act, despite its admirable intentions, resulted in Washington's permanent bureaucrats—not exactly reform-minded folks—being in charge. President Barack Obama initially seemed like he might break from the controlling, systems-first Democratic mold of education. But the Obama administration ended up imposing damaging new federal regulations on schools, from Common Core to race-based discipline quotas to robbing students of due process.

I came to Washington after almost thirty years of working with innovative governors and state legislators. This is where America's real education policies are made. States test different approaches and learn from each other. All my time and effort had been invested *outside* Washington—outside the Department of Education, outside the education establishment. Coming to Washington did nothing to convince me that I had been wrong in focusing on the states. As a matter of fact, it firmly reenforced my belief.

One of the hardest things I did as secretary of education—though it shouldn't have been—was to fight for federalism. That is, defending the principle that most government decisions—but *especially* education—should be made in the states and local communities, closest to the people they will affect. Of course, Democrats had never been fans of federalism in education, not since they ignored Joseph Califano's wise warnings and created a federal Department of Education in 1979.

What was surprising to me, though, was the extent to which federalism needed defending from *Republicans* in Washington. I had to invest a lot of energy, for instance, trying to convince Senator Roy Blunt why we should simplify the federal education funding streams to give states and localities more flexibility to make decisions. Our system gives that power to states and local school boards; our Constitution doesn't say "education" once, making it a power reserved to the states. And that makes sense. What works for families in Miami, Florida, is different than for those in Fairbanks, Alaska, and vice versa.

Sadly, Washington is a lonely place for federalists. As secretary of education, I found myself in the paradoxical position of being in the seat of government power while actively working to send that power back to the states. I aimed to make my job irrelevant. However, creating new federal programs is an activity that is rewarded in the nation's capital, not discouraged. And too many members of Congress, from both parties, are addicted to the federal dollars that come with federal programs.

In short, Washington isn't particularly receptive to the message of federalism—even in the best of times. I had the added weight of having just gone through a confirmation battle that was waged to impair me as secretary. More than at any time before in my career in education, I was fighting headwinds in those first months in Washington.

———————

The Department of Education occupies three separate buildings in downtown Washington, DC, including one unattractive structure the size of seven football fields. On my first day as secretary, I walked every floor of every one of these buildings and introduced myself to every employee. I covered roughly four and a half miles. I was wearing heels—another unfortunate footwear choice. The arthritis in my big toe is a long-term reminder of that epic trek.

I had given thought to how I would spend my first days as the secretary of education. During the confirmation process I was forced to be silent while Democrats, the media, and the education establishment conducted a multimillion-dollar attack campaign. Their goal was to portray me as a kind of rampaging monster—an enemy of public education out to do as much damage as one could conceive. The level of personal vitriol was amazing. It was an ominous example of what our political dialogue would devolve into over the next few years. Both sides increasingly regarded people who didn't share their views as, not simply misinformed, but *bad*. Evil, even.

As unprecedented and unfair as the campaign against me had been, the damage was done. For those in the education establishment it was practically a requirement to oppose me. Activists and the media were dug in. But all the noise and opposition wasn't going to stop me from doing what I had come to Washington to do. If my opponents thought they could convince me otherwise, they were wrong.

On my first day I gathered the department's employees to introduce myself—this time on *my* terms. I wanted to show them that, despite what they might have thought, I did not have horns—and I have a sense of humor.

"I won't pull any punches," I told Education employees gathered in the department's auditorium and watching online. "For me personally, this confirmation process and the drama it engendered has been . . . a bit of a bear."

Laughter rippled through the room as the audience caught on to the joke. But then I turned serious. I noted that the last few weeks had raised more questions than they answered—precisely the opposite of what the confirmation process was supposed to do. I told the department that I was a "door-open type of person" who was ready to work together with anyone who was interested in helping children. I asked that everyone join me in personally committing to being "more open to and patient with views different than our own." I offered an olive branch.

Nearly all of the employees who had gathered to listen were career staff at the department. These are the people who stay in their posts from administration to administration. They have powerful civil service protections that make it almost impossible to hold them accountable for their work or fire them. Their salaries and positions are tied to the length of time they spend in government, not the quality of work they do. They are the "bureaucrats."

There are many fine professionals that serve in the federal government. But there is also a lot of deadweight and inefficiency.

For example, not long after I became secretary we were made aware that there was a treasure trove of books sitting in the basement of the building gathering dust. I thought we should distribute these books to students and schools that could actually use them. Easy, right? Wrong. It turned out that thanks to the byzantine rules of the federal bureaucracy, there was only one guy who had the key to the storeroom, and he was only there Tuesdays and Thursdays. On top of that, he was on leave. So we found someone who could unlock the basement, but it turned out the books could only be moved by designated union employees, who weren't there that day. It literally took weeks to schedule a time when the guy with the keys and the guys who could move the books would be at the department on the same day.

One root of the problem was the extremely expansive telework policy that had been put in place during the Obama administration. Many Department of Education employees teleworked 100 percent of their time—they literally never came into the office. Some had even moved out of state. Remember, this was well before COVID-19 forced many Americans to work from home. The absurdity of the telework policy really came home to me on the first Friday I was secretary. My deputy chief of staff for operations, Dougie Simmons, went to ask the two employees who staffed the reception desk a question. They weren't there. The reception desk sat empty. Dougie called the office manager and was informed that the two career employees "teleworked" on Fridays. My jaw dropped. Only in the federal government could employees whose job it is to receive people be allowed to "telework." I changed the policy and limited teleworking to one day per week, and only for those who could actually do their work from home.

I came into office with every intention of minimizing the Washington education bureaucracy. All federal employees—whether they were at work or not—cost taxpayers money. When I became secretary, the Education Department had more than four thousand full-time employees and thousands more contractors. The average salary was more than $100,000. All these people were putting a federal imprint on schools. We eventually scaled the number of employees back by nearly 20 percent. It was not nearly enough, but it was a start.

I meant it when I told the department staff that first day that I wouldn't pull any punches. I acknowledged that I had a lot to learn about the work they did and wanted to earn their trust. I asked that we set aside our disagreements and find common ground for the sake of students. I was sincere.

That same day, I also reached out to the school union bosses. I called Randi Weingarten of the AFT and Lily Eskelsen García of the NEA with the same message I had given the Education Department staff: I hoped we could find common ground on behalf of students.

Admittedly, I didn't hold my breath. The union bosses rightly recognized me as a threat to their education policy monopoly. For decades, they justified their monopoly with the promise of giving every American child—regardless of race or income—a safe, quality education. For decades they failed to deliver on that promise. They *had* to make it personal between them and me. Otherwise they would have to talk about how and why they were failing.

I wish I could say we all locked arms and went on to work for the good of America's children. To be fair, there were individual leaders within the Education Department who were committed to working hard for students, despite their political leanings. But these bright lights were inevitably clouded by the recalcitrance of so many of their colleagues and by the whole ossified system. Former education secretary Bill Bennett called the enormous, congealed mass of federal and state bureaucrats, unions, and other outside groups dedicated to the education status quo the "Blob." Like in the movies, the Blob exists to survive and to grow by devouring everything in its path. That's its reason for being. Get out of its way and give it what it wants or it will chew you up and spit you out.

The education establishment would not accept a truce with me. We never even accomplished a cease-fire. The first bad sign was my first official school visit, which I described earlier. The one where union-organized thugs and protestors literally blocked me from entering the school.

Then came another—one that was so absurd it would have been laughable if it hadn't signaled something much more serious. My first week in office, I was accused of "disappearing" the landmark Individuals with Disabilities Education Act (IDEA). Yes, "disappearing"—the kind of thing mob bosses and drug cartel leaders are accused of doing.

From its digital age infancy, the Education Department's website had grown like kudzu, with no rhyme, reason, or pretense of thoughtful planning. Different offices added webpages whenever they chose to and however they liked. The resulting product was a sprawling, disconnected menu of individual websites, most of which hadn't been updated in years. When I became secretary, the department boasted something like 97 Twitter handles and 60 "official" Facebook pages. All told, the Department of Education's "website" was actually a labyrinth of hundreds of independent websites hosted by 107 different servers.

One of these websites had been created under the George W. Bush administration to inform parents of their rights under IDEA. It was unclear whether anyone at the department remembered the website existed, much less how to access and update it. Yet someone, identifying themselves only as "anonymous," reported that the website had gone down on my first day on the job. Within hours, rumors were hurtling across the internet that I had purposefully removed the site as the first step in a wicked plot to take away the parental rights of children with disabilities.

It was absurd, but that didn't stop Senator Patty Murray, the ranking Democrat on the HELP Committee, from performing a classic Washington Democrat publicity stunt. She authored a letter addressed to me expressing her "concern" that the website had "disappeared"—and simultaneously leaked the letter to the compliant press. Murray's home state newspaper, the *Seattle Post-Intelligencer*, played right along. It published an article with the headline "Website for disabled kids disappears as DeVos takes office."

All of this was a little too convenient for the establishment groups that opposed me. How did someone even notice that this obscure website had gone down? And how had that managed to happen on my first day in office? "Anonymous," who started the rumor, was never identified, if that person ever existed. Patty Murray's "concerns" were not realized and IDEA remained unchanged. But something good did come out of the debacle. We created a new, interactive website for parents of children with disabilities—and we updated it regularly.

Coming into the job of secretary, I knew that the federal bureaucracy was big and cumbersome. I didn't expect that it would take three weeks to get books out of the basement or that receptionists can "telework"—but I had a general idea about bureaucratic bloat and inefficiency. What I didn't fully understand was how willful and underhanded the permanent Washington bureaucracy could be. Politicians come and go in Washington, but bureaucrats are there to stay. They have the power to obstruct and even destroy policies that threaten them. And their civil service protections make them brazen.

While I had learned some valuable information, the website debacle was just the tip of the iceberg. I soon learned more about just how low the Washington bureaucracy will go to resist change.

The budget process in Washington is a convoluted mess. Spending is out of control. And when government spends money to create programs, something pernicious happens: It creates people and groups that benefit from the program—people and groups that fight hard to preserve the program. Thus, cutting spending is one of the hardest things to do in Washington. It takes guts, careful political navigation, and thoughtful discretion. When a budget cutter shows her hand too early, advocates for the status quo gear up and go into battle. The result is rarely a victory for the forces of reform. The permanent bureaucracy knows this and they play the long game.

To the extent that the budget process has any rhyme or reason at all, it begins with the White House putting out its yearly proposed budget. Congress, of course, has the last word on spending, but the White House budget guidance comes first. Then the details of the proposed budget are hammered out in negotiations with the various cabinet departments before the document is unveiled and sent to Congress.

The Trump White House's first budget contained deep cuts for education programs. This set off a back-and-forth with the White House over where to prioritize the cuts versus where further investments might be warranted. As anyone who's ever developed a budget knows, this is a deeply sensitive process. It cannot be conducted in the open and certainly not in the press.

We were deep into negotiations on the morning of May 17 when I opened the *Washington Post*. Inside, our entire budget proposal was laid out, cuts and all. Someone had leaked the whole thing. Small leaks here and there are unfortunate but routine in Washington. But never before had the entire education budget been leaked. It was more than a breach of trust by an employee; it was an act of political sabotage. Someone was trying to stop the budget cuts before they could be debated and acted on by Congress. I was furious.

We quickly identified the leaker—a career employee in the Budget Service Office. She admitted to leaking the budget to the *Post* and would later go on to declare herself a "whistle-blower." Whistle-blower protections were created to give people who witness corruption or wrongdoing in government protection from retaliation. But there was absolutely nothing improper or corrupt about the budget. It just proposed to scale back the federal role in education and give parents more power to control their children's schooling. The leaker's motives were political; she openly and proudly acknowledged that fact. But we were essentially powerless to hold her accountable. The strongest disciplinary action we could take against her was a five-day suspension *with pay*. She appealed the case and, as of the time I left the department, she still had not served her suspension.

The bureaucracy was not the only obstacle to commonsense budgeting in Washington. In each of its yearly budgets, over my objections, the White House proposed zeroing out federal spending for Special Olympics. The proposed cut was actually pragmatic. Federal funding for the program is quite limited, with most support coming from the private sector. I have donated to Special Olympics myself. It was pragmatic policy, but it was *very* bad politics. I was one of the most budget-minded members of the cabinet, but even I thought the move was counterproductive. Congress was *never* going to agree to it. Period. All that would be accomplished in calling for the elimination of Special Olympics funding would be to give the media and activists "proof" to portray us as coldhearted and hostile to education. I had my eye on major changes to our education system. Spending precious time and political capital defending a cut that was never going to be approved by Congress made little sense to me.

After the White House's third budget proposing to defund the Special Olympics came out in 2019, something happened that I was surprised hadn't happened before: a tweet went viral asserting that I had "cut all funding" to the program. It wasn't true. It was only a proposed budget—no cuts had been made. That same day, I had to appear before the House Budget Committee to defend the administration's budget. Always on the lookout for good YouTube and fundraising fodder, the members of the committee raked me over the coals for the nonexistent funding cut.

The next day, when I appeared before the Senate Budget Committee, Democratic senator Dick Durbin of Illinois upped the competition for media clicks by saying I deserved a "Special Olympic gold medal for insensitivity."[1]

I did my job defending the budget, making the perfectly valid point that taxpayers can't fund every worthy program. The more dramatic scenes from the hearings went viral, just as the members of Congress designed. When the president saw the coverage, he was incensed. The next day, on his way out to Marine One, Trump announced, "I have overridden my people. We're funding the Special Olympics."

I promptly called the president to thank him for doing what I said we should have done all along.[2]

It's true what they say: If you want a friend in Washington, DC, get a dog.

While I worked hard to forge relationships with the permanent career staff, I was also hard at work hiring my own senior staff. In contrast to the career employees, these were the "political" employees who serve, ultimately, at the pleasure of the president. In other words, they can be fired. They are there to implement the administration's agenda.

The Department of Education has fifteen senior appointments that require confirmation by the Senate. Typically, in a change of administration, these are uncontroversial votes. But again, it should be said, I was not part of a typical administration, and I was not a

typical cabinet member. When Trump education nominees came
before the HELP Committee, it seemed the Democratic members
were still angry that they hadn't succeeded in killing my nomination. They did everything they could to argue, delay, and draw out
the process of confirming my appointees. The disorganization and
paranoia in the new White House staff didn't help.

While lacking attention to detail elsewhere, the Trump White
House personnel people were scrupulous about vetting potential hires
for past criticisms of the president. They combed through every aspect
of a nominee's public life: speeches, articles, and years-old social
media. Nate Bailey, who became my communications chief and later
my chief of staff, raised red flags in the personnel office because of an
op-ed he had written in 2015. In it, he had lamented what he called
our "reality show" electorate. His point was to criticize our political
process as more concerned with performance than results. The White
House took the op ed as a criticism of the president. In the end, Nate
was hired, but it took a conversation with Reince Preibus, the White
House chief of staff, to keep him on my team.

It wasn't the last time I'd have a run-in with the White House's
personnel office. Later in the term, the president put his twenty-nine-
year-old former travel aide, Johnny McEntee, in charge of the hiring
and firing the more than four thousand political appointees in the
White House and cabinet agencies.

Multiple times, McEntee or his deputy tried to force us to hire
political loyalists with no qualifications to work at the Department
of Education in roles that we did not want or need to fill. One was
a woman who had been fired from the Department of the Interior
earlier in the term for spreading conspiracy theories and making
bigoted comments on social media. Others had no relevant experience whatsoever (for example, a commercial real estate lawyer, or a
retail clerk from New York). More significantly, in the last months
of the administration, he and his sidekicks attempted what can only

be described as a purge of employees they deemed to be insufficiently loyal to the president. At one particularly low point, McEntee's deputy handed me three prewritten resignation letters for three of my most senior and trusted staff. They have to go, he said. I disagreed, quite vehemently. They stayed.

But the far more serious obstruction to building my team came from Senate Democrats. They seemed determined to replay my confirmation process with every senior education nominee that came before the Senate.

One of my first choices for senior staff was a longtime education reformer named Jim Blew. Jim had decades of experience with innovation in education. He should have been a shoo-in for quick confirmation. He had been a Democrat most of his life and had worked with Democratic senators Cory Booker of New Jersey and Michael Bennet of Colorado. But in the eyes of committee Democrats, Jim had a fatal flaw: He was an advocate of school choice. They bitterly opposed his nomination and then slow-walked his confirmation. Republicans on the committee weren't much help. It took more than ten months for Jim to receive a vote in the full Senate. In July 2018 his nomination was approved without the support of a single Democrat—including Senators Booker and Bennet.

Congressional Democrats worked to obstruct even employees that didn't require Senate confirmation. In February I chose as my special assistant a veteran of the George W. Bush Education Department named Bob Eitel. Bob had an encyclopedic knowledge of education law—particularly higher education legal issues—and he was willing to take on the establishment when necessary. He was the lawyer I wanted by my side as we did legal battle with the forces of the status quo.

When I hired him, Bob was working for a company that owned and operated several for-profit colleges (a position he'd held for only a few years and that was his first work in the for-profit education sector during his thirty-year legal career). That put him in the crosshairs of HELP Committee Democrats who were waging a long-term battle against for-profit schools as part of their ultimate goal of "free" higher education. They have great disdain for for-profit institutions as exploitative and untrustworthy. And it was true that some for-profit institutions, just like some nonprofit schools, have made promises to students they couldn't deliver on after graduation. Bob's former employer had agreed to repay students who were allegedly misled by the terms of their loans.

I did not have a dog in this fight. I was neither "pro" nor "anti" for-profit education. My feeling was that transparency and honesty across the board were needed most to solve the student debt crisis. First, there needed to be more transparency about what a particular degree from a particular college will provide a student. Before students enroll in a school and decide on a major field of study, they should have full knowledge of how similar graduates are employed and what they make. If schools fail to provide this information or if they lie about it, then they should be penalized. But being organized as a for-profit institution is not a crime and the government shouldn't treat it as such.

Second, I argued, along with President Trump, that students needed to be more clear-eyed about exactly why they should go to college. For many young people, a four-year degree is not a wise investment. They may be better suited for, and may earn more by pursuing, vocational, shorter-term, or other education pathways.

Liberal senators felt otherwise. They wrote me a letter about their "concerns" over Bob's hire and leaked it simultaneously to the media. The same day the letter arrived, the *New York Times* had a front-page, above-the-fold story about Bob—right next to one about how North Korea had fired another ballistic missile at the West. They seemed to think the two articles had similar import.

Bob had jumped through all the hoops. He had consulted with Education ethics advisors before taking the job. He had committed to recusing himself from working on anything that impacted his former employer. But the senators who wrote the letter regarded the fact that Bob had worked in the for-profit sector as disqualifying. Their philosophical jihad led to an investigation of Bob's hiring by the Department of Education inspector general. Bob was cleared of any wrongdoing, but not until April 2020. It was an attempt at political assassination. Thank God it failed.

Thanks in part to baseless allegations and political machinations like those employed against Bob, I didn't have a senior staff in place until over a year after I became secretary. The Department of Education was dead last among the federal agencies in the number of senior staff who had been confirmed by the Senate in the spring of 2018.

We ultimately did put together an outstanding team. In addition to Nate, Dougie, Jim, and Bob, we were able to bring on an unprecedented staff of education reformers. Mick Zais, the former South Carolina schools chief and a retired Army brigadier general, became deputy education secretary. Ebony Lee was my deputy chief of staff for policy, overseeing our K–12 agenda. Washington veteran Jim Manning oversaw higher ed, and then Federal Student Aid. Bush alumna Diane Jones led our successful effort to overhaul the higher education accrediting process, having worked previously in every sector of higher education. Bob King, who had run higher ed systems in New York and Kentucky, joined to push forward the rest of our higher ed agenda, especially improving our grant making. Two men who had been instrumental in helping Jeb Bush transform Florida K–12 schools, Frank Brogan and Carlos Muñiz, came on board. Candice Jackson acted as our assistant secretary for civil rights until Ken Marcus, who had held the job previously from 2003 to 2004, was again confirmed. Kim Richey and Johnny Collett served students with disabilities. Steven Menashi ran the general counsel's office, until he was appointed to the U.S. Court of Appeals; Reed Rubinstein took over, spearheading a critical effort to expose the influence of foreign donations to educational institutions. Career and technical education veteran Scott Stump brought his expertise to our efforts to diversify higher education options for Americans. Longtime Hill aide Peter Oppenheim was our liaison to Congress. Educator José Viana oversaw our Office of English Language Acquisition. Capitol Hill and TV news veteran Liz Hill ran our communications office.

There were also tremendous members of the career staff who were true public servants and worked hand in hand with our political team. Phil Rosenfelt—who has been working on federal education policy since before Jimmy Carter created the Department of Education—was one of the best lawyers we had. I also chose to elevate Denise Carter and Jason Gray to assistant secretary roles, rather than adding political leads in their respective departments. There was no reason to bring in additional staff, at additional taxpayer cost, when the staff already in place were more than capable of doing the job.

Together, they all ably led teams who went to battle every day to improve options and outcomes for America's students.

———

The first major policy issue I was forced to deal with as education secretary was—to my regret—at the heart of the culture wars. I am a conservative. But when it comes to issues of race and gender, I am a reluctant culture warrior. My passionate advocacy of school choice has always been driven, in very large part, by our education system's systemic failure of poor, mostly minority students. In practice, this has meant holding together an uneasy coalition of advocates for the urban poor, religious educators, and white suburbanites who are generally happy with their public schools. Upsetting this careful balance is something I've always tried to avoid.

After the nightmare of my confirmation, the last thing I wanted was another national controversy. I had my eyes on the prize—the transformation of our education system. I was intent on educating Congress and the American public about what education freedom really means—that it means more than a choice of different buildings. That it's really a virtually endless menu of choices of different ways and places to learn. I wanted to spend my time reaching out to potential allies in Congress and the states. I was not naïve. I knew I would have to deal with plenty of opponents of education freedom. There was a lot of work to do. So I didn't want my first major action as secretary to be on an issue as sensitive and divisive as gender politics. But Attorney General Jeff Sessions had other plans.

First, some context. My faith teaches me that every man and woman is uniquely created and worthy of love and respect. I've always believed that in a free, multicultural, multi-religious, and multi-ethnic country like the United States, the best way to live together is to deal with each other as fellow human beings with inherent worth. If we respect and honor each other, we can live together without one-size-fits-all requirements from Washington. Family by family, community by community, and school by school, we can find the right solutions for the people involved.

An example: In the mid-1990s, when I was chairman of the Michigan Republican Party, we had a group of employees who were paid to work the phones to raise money. They were "dialing for dollars." There was one employee who was in the process of transitioning from male to female. Some of the largely female staff objected to this person using the women's bathroom. I knew we could find a solution. What guided me was my belief that, however we resolved the situation, we would respect the dignity of *all* persons involved. We did just that. Everyone was allowed to use the bathroom, but we made a sign that indicated it was in use, effectively making it a single-occupancy restroom. Anybody could post it while they were inside. Everyone was accommodated. Everyone was respected. No lawyers were needed.

In the last months of the Obama administration, the Department of Education directed all American schools to handle the issue of transgender students and bathrooms in a very different way. The Obama Education Department sent a letter to schools across the country notifying them that from now on, transgender students would have to be allowed to use the bathrooms that comported with their stated gender identity, not their biological sex. Mind you: The administration just sent a *letter*—a threatening letter that meaningfully altered the behavior of every school in America. Nothing that remotely resembled a new regulation, let alone law. The letter was written by Catherine Lhamon, who was then the head of the Office for Civil Rights (OCR) for the Obama Education Department. Lhamon would later be President Biden's choice to lead OCR and her confirmation had to be won by not one but two tie-breaking votes cast by Vice President Kamala Harris.

The Obama letter referenced Title IX, the law that prohibits discrimination on the basis of sex in any federally funded education activity. That's the standard written in Title IX—"discrimination *on the basis of sex*." When the law was passed in 1972, "sex" unquestionably meant biological sex. I'm not sure it is any less definitive nearly fifty years later. Regardless, if the Obama administration intended for Title IX to encompass gender identity, they should have lobbied Congress to change the law. But they didn't do that. Instead they sent a letter that effectively rewrote Title IX to define "sex" as "gender identity." It was not the first time that unelected and unaccountable bureaucrats in the Office for Civil Rights took it upon themselves to change the meaning of Title IX, and it wouldn't be the last.

As soon as I became secretary, there was a lot of pressure—rightly—to undo what Obama had done. The Obama/Lhamon letter had been issued jointly by the Department of Education and the Department of Justice in 2016. For it to be withdrawn by the Trump administration, both departments would have to act together.

Attorney General Jeff Sessions was, from the beginning, eager to immediately withdraw the Obama directive. I fully agreed with him that the letter needed to be rescinded. In May 2018, the parents of a five-year-old girl in Georgia filed a complaint with OCR alleging that the girl had been assaulted in her school bathroom by a boy who identified as "gender fluid." The complaint alleged that the school district's policy of allowing transgender students to use the bathroom of their choice made the assault possible. This was a very real, legitimate concern for parents. A federal dictate that all school bathrooms be open to both sexes threatened the privacy and safety of all children.

I believed that individual schools and districts were best positioned to manage their bathrooms in a way that ensured all students were safe. There were examples of that approach working all across the country. But I disagreed with Attorney General Sessions on the best path to success. I felt we needed to take the time to educate the public about what we were doing and why. I'm not a lawyer, but I know it's hard to win a case you haven't prosecuted. I had seen it time and again. When no groundwork is laid for a controversial move like this, the media steps in with their own rationale. For the Trump administration, that meant the reversal of the Obama transgender bathroom policy would be attributed to the worst possible motives. It would be defined as an act of bigotry rather than an attempt to empower schools to manage any situations that arose.

The attorney general and I went back and forth about when to rescind the letter. We had some pretty intense arguments. The attitude of the AG and his staff was that we should just make the change—rip off the Band-Aid. Sure, we would have a few days of bad media coverage. But after that, they argued, people would just forget about the issue.

But I was all too familiar with education establishment battles. I knew transgender activists would not just "forget" about abruptly changing the federal guidance they prized. They would make it an issue—a big issue—and we needed to prepare the American people for that.

Sessions and I eventually ended up in the Oval Office, arguing the decision in front of the president. The attorney general made the legal case for reversing the Obama guidance. I didn't disagree. My objection was practical.

I told the president we needed to take the time to explain to the public something very few people understood about Title IX: that the Obama administration had overstepped its authority in replacing "sex" (by which the law clearly meant biological sex) with the ever-evolving concept of gender identity. We needed to frame the issue in terms of what was best for all kids, I argued. These were personal and sensitive matters. They shouldn't be decided by bureaucrats in Washington. If a president wanted to change the law, he or she had to ask Congress to change it. I made that point very clearly at the time.[3] Directives from Washington can come and go. Actually shaping public opinion, though it takes more time and effort, has a more lasting impact.

When I left the meeting, I believed we had won some more time. A few days later, on February 22, I was in a senior staff meeting when my assistant said the White House was calling. I left the meeting to take the call and learned that the decision had been made to rescind the Obama guidance. President Trump had sided with Attorney General Sessions. Despite the accusations of the groups that had attacked me, this was not how I wanted to begin my time in Washington.

The next day, at the annual Conservative Political Action Conference, I took the opportunity to explain myself to a like-minded audience.

"The media has had its fun with me, and that's okay," I said. "My job isn't to win a popularity contest with the media or the education establishment here in Washington. My job as secretary of education is to make education work for students."

It was a bit of an understatement, but I meant what I said. I was a member of the president's cabinet. I was prepared to carry out his policies. I was prepared to take my hits in the media. I was even prepared to be fodder for late-night comedians in order to do my job.

Less well known are the overreach and bad ideas we *stopped* from occurring. Stephen Miller, President Trump's policy guru, summoned Nate and Ebony from my team to the White House for a discussion. After failing to properly clear them through White House security, Miller's aides took them to a nearby restaurant (Cosi, for those who know the area) to have their meeting.

Over the din of patrons slurping lattes and crunching salads, Miller's men described a plan to put U.S. Immigration and Customs Enforcement (ICE) agents into schools under the pretext of identifying MS-13 gang members. The plan was, when agents checked students' citizenship status for the alleged purpose of identifying gang ties, they could identify undocumented students and deport them. Not only was the prospect of this chilling, but it was also patently illegal. Nate and Ebony turned them down cold. But that didn't stop Miller from subsequently calling me to get my thoughts on the idea. They were the same as Nate and Ebony's: no. *Just no.*

To his credit, President Trump saw the value in supporting historically black colleges and universities (HBCUs) almost immediately in his presidency. President Obama had all but ignored them. For President Trump, showing the administration's support for HBCUs was a way to appeal to African-Americans. It was both good policy and good politics.

In late February, the evening before President Trump issued an executive order giving more federal priority to HBCUs, I released a statement expressing my admiration for the schools, noting that historically black colleges originated from an absence of higher educational opportunity and access for black Americans. So African-Americans "took it upon themselves to provide the solution." In that way, I said, "HBCUs are real pioneers when it comes to school choice."

My opponents "pounced." They accused me of ignoring the shameful history of racial segregation that made HBCUs necessary. The way the statement was drafted admittedly gave them this opening. I should have explained the sentiment differently. The next day at a session with HBCU presidents at the White House, I offered needed clarification.

"Your history was born, not out of mere choice, but out of necessity, in the face of racism, and in the aftermath of the Civil War," I told the presidents. African-Americans had been denied the opportunity for higher education so they made their own opportunity. The reason why these schools needed to be created was unforgiveable. But the black community's grit and determination to educate their children in the face of this segregation was admirable.

Two months later, when we announced that Bethune-Cookman University, a historically black university in Daytona Beach, Florida, had invited me to give their commencement address that May, the same critics were outraged yet again. By inviting me, they said, Bethune-Cookman University had "sold their soul for a check."[4]

It was a shame that they saw fit to run down Bethune-Cookman for the sake of taking a shot at me. The university was founded by Dr. Mary McLeod Bethune, a fearless advocate of education for African-American children. It remained a leading light among HBCUs. I had close friends in Orlando who were in a Bible study group with people from Bethune-Cookman for years. They knew that I had been working for more than three decades to give poor, African-American kids access to schools that work for them. They knew what was in my heart, so they communicated the university's invitation to give the commencement address.

By the time I gave my speech on May 10, the Bethune-Cookman students had been primed by weeks of media and activist agitation about my presence at Bethune. Sitting on the dais, before the ceremony began, I saw people run up and down the aisles among the graduates, waving and gesticulating, as if choreographing their actions. I wasn't surprised about what happened next, but I was deeply disheartened. The boos began as soon as I opened my mouth to speak. More than half the graduates stood up and turned their backs to me. I had to shout to make myself heard above the din.

"Anytime we meet someone new, we have two options," I called out. "We can focus on differences that might divide us or we can choose to listen, to be receptive and to learn from others' experiences and perspectives. In my life, I have endeavored to do the latter."

The faculty and administration at Bethune-Cookman had been warm and welcoming to me. I could see the embarrassment on their faces as the crowd continued to heckle. At one point, Dr. Edison O. Jackson, the university president, took the mic and warned he would be forced to mail the degrees to graduates if the behavior continued. The crowd didn't let up, but I persevered with my speech. I had a message for these students, one that I had been struggling to articulate since I had clumsily called HBCUs "pioneers" of school choice. These students were graduating from a unique institution, whose creation defied all the odds, but whose purpose was to give the gift of education to everyone who sought it. We had a lot of work to do before the American K–12 education system lived up to the promise of opportunity and excellence inherent in Bethune-Cookman University. But it had been my life's work to try.

"America is too great a country to deny any child this equal opportunity," I said, as the jeers continued.

It was a difficult experience, to say the least. But I'm still glad I went there, and I'm thankful I had the opportunity to deliver my message. Someone said that if they had mailed a copy of my commencement speech without revealing who wrote it, everyone behind the melee would have hailed it as a fitting tribute to the Bethune-Cookman University graduates. That would have been an interesting experiment.*

In spite of frequent chaos created within the Trump White House by individuals like Omarosa Manigault Newman, the reality-show television celebrity turned presidential advisor on issues including HBCUs, President Trump was in fact a champion of historically black colleges.† He restored more than $250 million in funding and reconstituted the President's Board of Advisors on Historically Black Colleges and Universities. We eliminated regulations and policies that illegally restricted the schools' First Amendment right to live out their religious mission. I met quarterly with the leadership of the HBCU network. I even intervened to provide debt relief to four HBCUs that were still trying to recover a dozen years later from damage inflicted by Hurricane Katrina in 2005.

Regrettably, this record—like other things we accomplished—was overshadowed by missteps and impulsive rhetoric from the White House. For example, every year, the Department of Education hosts a weeklong conference for historically black colleges and universities in Washington. It is the president's and the administration's most significant opportunity to showcase their support for HBCUs.

---

* Should you want to try the experiment, the speech's text is available here: https://time.com/4774574/betsy-devos-bethune-cookman-university-commencement-2017-speech-read/.

† When she served in the White House, Omarosa consistently made everything more difficult. Inexplicably, she viewed herself as an expert on education. On more than one occasion, Omarosa inserted herself into policy or events. In this case, she invited herself on the trip to Bethune-Cookman in spite of the fact that she didn't have a role there. She even crashed the receiving line, positioning herself on the stage to shake the hands of the students as they received their diplomas. Bethune-Cookman administrators finally ushered her off.

In 2017, the conference was scheduled to occur just over a month after a woman was killed during white supremacist rioting in Charlottesville, Virginia. Following the riot, two Virginia state troopers were killed when the helicopter they were using to monitor the crowds crashed. President Trump infamously said that there were "good people on both sides" of the riot. In the fallout, we canceled the conference and so missed an important opportunity to showcase the president's and the administration's support for HBCUs.

It was the first time that I seriously considered whether I could continue serving in the Trump administration. I wrote to the Education Department's staff, sharing my feelings:

Team,

I write today with a heavy heart for our country. While we should be anticipating and celebrating students' returns to campuses across the country, we are engaged in a national discussion that has stirred ugly, hate-filled conversations and reopened hurtful wounds from shameful portions of our nation's past.

There is fear, pain, anger, disappointment, discouragement and embarrassment across America, and I know, too, here within the Department.

Last weekend's tragic and unthinkable events in Charlottesville, which stole three innocent lives and injured many more, were wholly unacceptable. The views of white nationalists, neo-Nazis and other racist bigots are totally abhorrent to the American ideal. We all have a role to play in rejecting views that pit one group of people against another. Such views are cowardly, hateful and just plain wrong.

This is what makes our work so important. Our Department, and particularly the Office for Civil Rights, exists to ensure all students have equal access to a safe, nurturing, quality learning environment free from discrimination or intimidation.

Our own difficult history reminds us that we must confront, head-on, problems when and where they exist with moral clarity and conviction. Our nation is greater than what it has shown in recent days.

Violence and hate will never be the answer. We must engage, debate and educate. We must remind all what it means to be an American, and while far from perfect, we must never lose sight that America still stands as the brightest beacon for freedom in the world.

My hope is that we will use this as an opportunity to show that what unites and holds America together is far stronger than what seeks to divide and draw us apart. We can all play a role. Mentor a student. Volunteer at a school. Lend a helping hand and offer a listening ear.

Our work is truly the bridge to a stronger future. Let's recommit ourselves to ensuring the future is brighter for all.

After navigating the first few months of my time in Washington—the hostile press, the mammoth bureaucracy, the dysfunctional Congress, and an undisciplined White House—I was eager to get out of Washington and show my fellow Americans the world of options they have when teachers are free to teach and families are free to choose.

CHAPTER FIVE

THE SCHOOLS OF THE FUTURE ARE HERE TODAY

The local media was full of headlines speculating about why the U.S. secretary of education was visiting a small, private high school in Kansas City, Missouri. The local NPR station warned, "A Tiny Kansas City Private School Wonders if Betsy DeVos Knows What She's Getting Herself Into."

"Who Is Betsy DeVos and Why Is She Visiting a Liberal School Like Kansas City Academy?" wondered a local weekly.

The *Kansas City Star* simply quoted a student in its headline: "'Why Us?'"

So it was no surprise that there was palpable tension in the air when we drove up to the Kansas City Academy (KCA) in September 2017. The protestors outside easily outnumbered the students within. People lined the last two blocks before the school holding accusatory signs of all sorts. One woman, without appearing to understand the irony of her statement as she stood outside a private school, held up a hand-scrawled sign that said, "School Choice is Discrimination."

Education secretaries typically do a "back to school" tour in the fall when classes start. They get a bus, decorate the outside with the theme of whatever policy they're promoting, and go around the country doing press conferences. During the Bush administration, the policy

Margaret Spellings promoted was the No Child Left Behind law. For Arne Duncan in the Obama administration, initially it was Race to the Top, a competitive grant program meant to incentivize school districts to innovate. When that program proved unacceptable to the education establishment, Duncan was reduced to traveling the country promoting the education status quo, with a tiny tweak here or there.*

When I traveled the country as secretary, I always did so as a representative of kids and their futures. So in my first fall as secretary, we decided to do things differently. We didn't do a "back to school" tour; we did a "Rethink School" tour.

Doing innovative things that centered on improving student success was the primary criterion for the schools I visited. I went to institutions, public and private, that were thinking and acting outside the box, engaging kids who wanted or needed something other than the typical school. I wanted to showcase these schools for American families, to show them that the benefits of education freedom are not theoretical; they're tangible. When rigorous academics are combined with more choice for parents, more focus on students, and more freedom for teachers, education is transformed. Students are transformed. It's happening right now. It's just not happening in enough places for enough students.

KCA was one of the most unique schools I visited, the kind of school environment I loved to experience. All forms of art—visual, applied, performing, culinary—were integral to KCA, with hands-on learning that encourages innate creativity and curiosity. Students learn to think critically and to take risks within the bonds of a tight-knit community. The KCA school building was an old red-brick structure with creaky wooden stairs; it reminded me of where I went to junior high school.

---

* There was good reason to believe Duncan was earnest in understanding what it took to improve schools. He had co-founded a charter school earlier in his career (as had John King, Duncan's successor and my predecessor). It was a shame the unions' bare-knuckled demands, including calling for Duncan to resign, forced them both to abandon their reformer roots.

There were a number of gay and transgender students at KCA. There were lots of expressive clothing choices, hair, tattoos, and piercings. But contrary to what the media was saying, none of this surprised me, nor did I find it off-putting. That was the whole point of the school. Families at the academy sought out the school because their kids were bored at assigned public schools or they didn't fit in or they were looking for a different experience. Parents chose KCA because their son or daughter was a budding artist or a chef. Or because they were looking for a learning environment that inspired their child's imagination and creativity instead of stifling it into submission.

They were there because they *chose* to be there. That was why I came to this small, private, liberal school in the middle of America.

———

After the debacle at Jefferson Academy in Washington on my first school visit, the unions and the usual suspects feigned that things would be different in the future. Obama education secretary Arne Duncan tweeted, "Agree or disagree w @BetsyDeVos on any issue, but let's all agree she really needs to be in public schools. Please let her in."

When I returned to the Education Department after the Jefferson visit, I had a flurry of phone calls and texts from my brother, Erik. He was furious. He knows more than a little bit about security and he thought the security I had at Jefferson was completely inadequate. He's a very protective brother, but I tended to agree, as did others. The department security officers who were traveling with me were well-intentioned but naïve. They had made crucial mistakes. They failed to secure a route into the school ahead of time. They allowed the mob to surround me and physically keep me from entering the school, pushing me and assaulting a DC cop. Everyone seemed to agree that I needed better protection. The question was: Where would that come from?

Despite the close call at Jefferson, I was very reluctant to have a wall of security between me and the students, parents, and teachers with whom I visited. Over the weekend following the school visit, my chief of staff, Josh Venable, talked to White House chief of staff Reince Priebus about what to do. At the White House's request, the Secret Service did what they call a threat assessment. They reviewed the numbers, content, and the seriousness of the people who were threatening me through phone calls, letters, and social media. They made the determination that I was one of the most threatened members of the administration. The risks to my safety were quite real, and would-be attackers probably only felt more emboldened watching that regrettable scene in the school parking lot at Jefferson.

With the Secret Service stretching resources to protect the large Trump family, the decision was made that the U.S. Marshals were best situated to provide me with the needed, round-the-clock security. When I returned to work on Monday, I had a much different security detail at my side.

From that point on, the Marshals did a quarterly threat assessment and briefed me on it. In between, they notified us about specific threats that arose. It was deeply unsettling to hear what they found in these assessments. People threatened me with murder. Kidnapping. Rape. Torture. At times there were thousands of threats—they escalated after I received heavy media coverage. Much of these were just talk, of course. But at any given time there were a dozen or so threats the Marshals took seriously enough to investigate, talk to the people, meet with them, and even make arrests. They also tracked stalkers—people who consistently showed up at my events. They gave my team and me pictures of them so we would recognize them in the crowd.

I wouldn't have chosen to travel with an entourage of U.S. Marshals, but I was grateful for them. I became close to many of these amazing men and women, and they literally made it possible for my staff and me to do our jobs. They allowed me to venture out beyond "safe" communities and to showcase schools in neighborhoods that might not have been as congenial if I had visited under other circumstances. Every once in a while, a bomb-sniffing dog sent in advance reminded me of that fact.

Despite the unions' and Arne Duncan's appeals to take things down a notch, protestors were a frequent part of my school visits. I generally ignored them and kept my mind focused on visiting with students, teachers, and parents. My staff, however, could see the hostility that had been ginned up in the crowd of protestors when we visited the Kansas City Academy. There were more than three times as many protestors as there were students at KCA. I avoided making eye contact as we went into the school through the throngs of people, some holding young children and yelling obscenities at me.

Inside the school, it was quieter but there was a kind of manufactured tension in the air. Students had been told that they could take a "mental health day" and not come to school on the day of my visit. Those who were there seemed scared and nervous at first, as if they had been told that my presence was a threat and not an opportunity to show off their school.

When I entered the school, students were in their various classes. They were working on pottery, fashion design, and other self-directed art projects. I love the arts, and I love to see students engaged and learning. As a result, I tend to lose track of time when visiting with kids. The same was true at KCA, despite the chill in the air. I talked with the students about what they were making and tried my hand at the pottery wheel. I was enjoying myself. My staff, on the other hand, was worried that the situation could explode at any moment.

The head of school showed me around and introduced me to various students. As he was doing that, my staff noticed two girls who were whispering to each other conspiratorially and trying to get close to me. The Marshals noticed them, too. When I saw them I could tell they wanted to say something to me. So I approached them and spoke first.

One girl was wearing a particularly creative outfit. I have sewn a lot over the years and I love clothing design, so I asked her, "Did you design your outfit? I love it!" We got into a fun conversation about sewing and fashion. She told me about other work she had done and I told her about the people I knew in the business. Before long, whatever the girls had planned to confront me with was forgotten. They thanked me for talking with them. My staff was visibly relieved.

Later I talked with a civics class at KCA and took questions from the students. Some of them were pointed. But I listened, took them seriously, and answered them fully. The students appreciated that. I think they were expecting to disagree with me but found out that they really couldn't. I talked with them about an education model that allows every student to find the best fit for their learning style—precisely what they were doing inside KCA. I'm sure I didn't convert all of them to my way of thinking, but we had what ended up being a great visit.

A few weeks later I got a letter from the head of school who had shown me around KCA. He was very candid. He admitted that he had had a negative view of me and was hostile to my ideas. Prior to my visit, he wrote, he had never really contemplated the fact that he ran a private school that families chose because they could afford it. My visit had made him confront the fact that there were families who wanted the same kind of choice but couldn't afford it. He said he was a liberal, and as a result, felt obliged to be reflexively pro "public" education. But our time together had forced him to realize his work was actually much more aligned with my worldview. It was a courageous and respectful letter to write. I appreciated it very much.

My first "Rethink School" tour also took me to Wyoming, Colorado, Nebraska, and Indiana. In Colorado Springs, in a first for an education secretary on a back-to-school tour, we went to a barbecue for parents and students who homeschooled. Our memorable "school visit" was to the backyard of a suburban house. Dozens of homeschooling families joined us and shared their perspectives on how and why that form of schooling was a fit for them.

I visited a public school district in Casper, Wyoming, that is among the most unique in the nation. It is a 100 percent choice district—basically an open system of what are often called magnet schools. Every school is different. Parents choose the school that meets their children's individual needs.

The concept is simple but revolutionary. The parents have choice, the money follows the child, and the local community figures out what educational options to provide. I went to an elementary school that was entirely teacher-led. There was no principal. The school was run by a board that includes parents and teachers. The lines between grades were blurred and students moved freely between them according to their different learning levels.

This system of customized learning for Casper's kids wasn't directed by government from the top down. It evolved organically to meet the unique needs of that particular community. They had a classical, Latin-based school. There was a dual-language immersion school where students learned half the day in English and the other half in Mandarin Chinese. There was a school that was student-led and focused on individualized learning. Yet another offered preschool–12 with a shorter school week to accommodate children from distant ranches or farms.

By giving parents the opportunity to choose, Casper turned the traditional model of public education on its head. There was a different school for virtually every different kind of child—and they were *public* schools. But the sad fact is that this kind of public school choice is something that can only be achieved in a community where the teacher unions lack controlling power. When I was in Casper, I kept contrasting what I saw with the experience Dick had serving on the Michigan State Board of Education. There every request for a child to go to a school other than their assigned school had to be approved by the state board. It was a night-and-day contrast. Dick told me he never thought twice and voted yes on each and every request. The others from the education establishment who sat around the table with him simply could not understand his automatic vote for the families who made the requests.

In Colorado I visited Firefly Autism, a school for students on the autism spectrum. There were protestors outside that school as well. A very common attack on education freedom is that special needs students have to "sign away" their rights under the Individuals with Disabilities Education Act (IDEA) in a system of school choice. But the Firefly school is a brilliant example of how school choice actually expands the options available to parents of students with disabilities, students who are often failed by the one-size-fits-all traditional system.

In 2010, the parents of a student with autism named Endrew F. took him out of his assigned public school and sent him to Firefly because Endrew wasn't getting the specialized help he needed to progress. Then his parents sued, arguing that the law required the school district to pay Endrew's tuition at the Firefly school. The case, which went all the way to the U.S. Supreme Court, became about whether public schools should be required to provide the minimum standard of progress for a child with disabilities or whether they should be expected to do more. That's not much of a quandary for me. Fortunately, the High Court sided with Endrew. Unfortunately, other children with disabilities continue to be routinely shortchanged by the system. Endrew's parents saw something better for him at the Firefly school and they pursued it. Our education system should facilitate this, not prohibit it.

In Indiana we visited another unique school. Hope Academy in Indianapolis is a charter school created for recovering addicts. Hope calls itself a "safe, sober, and challenging academic experience." I met with high school age kids who had struggled with substance abuse and were, against the odds, getting their high school degrees. I talked to parents who were tearfully grateful that their children had found a safe place to learn. All the students at Hope were there by their own choice, and that was a key contributor to the fact that 94 percent of Hope graduates go on to higher education.

One of the last stops on our "Rethink School" tour was in Lincoln, Nebraska, to showcase yet another interesting school. I had heard about Lincoln Public Schools' Science Focus Program, more commonly known as the Zoo School. The school was created in partnership with and on the grounds of the Lincoln Children's Zoo. In the mid-1990s, Lincoln parents wanted more schooling options and the Zoo School was the result. The students were engaged in hands-on, real-life science learning. I watched as students cared for different animals, including feeding an iguana sweet potatoes. The students shared how bored they had been at their previous schools, and how Zoo School had rekindled their love of learning, while also giving them a running start toward a future career.

One peculiar thing struck me about my visit to the Zoo School. It was common to other innovative public schools I visited at other times: the protestors. Outside the Zoo School there were 75–100 people holding anti-school-choice signs. They didn't seem to understand, nor did they care, that I was showcasing a *public* school of choice. So what exactly was the problem?

I thought about something similar in Omaha when I visited Nelson Mandela Elementary School, which is a wonderful private school that is tuition-free to its students, thanks to generous backers. As I visited this private school, all the innocent young children had been plastered with stickers saying, "I [heart] public schools" . . . while the adults eagerly showed me around their *private* school. Regrettably, the kids were being used as props in an adult political statement. The school was privately funded but they were trying to pass it off as a public school. It didn't matter. I was there because of the kids.

––––––––––––––––––

On the grounds of Gerald R. Ford International Airport in Grand Rapids is a most unique school. When you walk into the airy, window-lined common room, two airplanes hang suspended from the ceiling: a 1947 Piper Cub and a 1961 open-cockpit Corben Ace. Flags of dozens of countries circle the room, representing the home countries of students who attend the school.

This is the West Michigan Aviation Academy, a one-of-a-kind charter school. The Aviation Academy is the only high school in America that offers flight training as an integral part of its curriculum. Students can learn to pilot airplanes there before they are old enough to buy a beer. The Aviation Academy is the creation of my husband, Dick DeVos. It combines two of his passions—education and aviation. I suggested he start a school following his valiant but unsuccessful bid to become Michigan's governor in 2006. The Aviation Academy is his labor of love.

First, a word on exactly what a charter school is. Critics like to use terms like "private charter schools" to imply that these schools are not public schools. This is totally false. Charter schools are public schools funded with public dollars. They can't discriminate or "cherry-pick" which students to enroll. All are welcome. If there are more applicants than there are spaces at a charter school—which is often the case—the schools have a lottery to see who gets in. These lotteries, which parents and their children attend in person, are known as "cheers and tears night." In a country where every child is supposed to have an equal chance at the American dream, some kids win and some kids lose on cheers-and-tears night. It's completely random, operated in exactly the same way a casino worker calls bingo numbers. It is heart-wrenching watching young lives consigned to that kind of chance.

Many people first came to understand a charter school lottery from the documentary *Waiting for Superman* (2010). It follows five low-income students from Harlem and the Bronx as they submit to the lottery process. The students are trying to escape their failing schools for coveted New York City charter schools. The film made a dent in the public consciousness—the families met with President Obama in the Oval Office. But, sadly, it didn't do much to change things for most students.

There's an easy explanation for why: The fact that charter schools exist at all is a direct refutation of the education establishment. These schools are different from traditional public schools only in that they are free of the restrictive union rules and unnecessary bureaucratic entanglements that undermine parents and tie the hands of principals and teachers. Charter schools have the freedom to recruit and retain staff that work hard and are committed to their mission. Importantly, they have the freedom to fire those who aren't. They can set their own hours, curricula, and method of teaching. In short, they are built to ensure that students learn, not to protect the interests of the adults in the school system.

As a result, it's little wonder that when parents are given the chance to send their children to charter schools, they grab it. It's estimated that one million kids are on waiting lists for charter schools across the country. Those numbers grew significantly during the coronavirus pandemic, as charters often found ways to offer better options and experiences than traditional public schools did. That's the story of the charter movement.

The founding history of public charter schools might surprise you. The first charter in America opened its doors in 1992 in Minnesota, thanks to the leadership of a Democrat state senator named Ember Reichgott Junge. She had support for the concept from the then-head of the American Federation of Teachers, Albert Shanker. They knew that disadvantaged students needed better options if they were to overcome their life circumstances, and they knew that teachers needed more opportunities to improve what was happening in the classroom. But the system stood in the way. Shanker summed it up well: "One of the things that discourages people from bringing about change in schools is the experience of having that effort stopped for no good reason."[1]

Shanker turned his back on charters not long after, as the pressures of being a union boss overtook his education reformer heart. But it hardly stopped the movement. New York City had one charter school in 1999. Today it has over 270 charter schools, serving 145,000 students. There are nearly 50,000 more on wait lists in New York City alone, each wishing they had won the lottery.[2] Nationwide, charter schools serve 3.3 million students today, double the number served in 2010.[3]

Nearly half of public school students in cities including Detroit and Washington, DC, attend a charter school.[4] One-third do in Philadelphia and Newark. About a quarter of students in Los Angeles, Boston, Memphis, Columbus, and Wilmington, Delaware—President Biden's hometown—are learning in public charter schools.[5]

The fact is, charter schools work. Parents are flocking to them because the success is evident. Consider the aptly named Success Academy network in New York, founded by the matchless Eva Moskowitz. She set out to redefine what was possible in public education by refusing to accept anything that has traditionally limited learning. As a result, Success is now the number one performing school district in the state of New York. Studies have found that students attending a Success Academy received, on average, the equivalent of 137 extra days of learning in reading and 239 days of math versus those in New York's traditional assigned public schools between 2011 and 2016.[6]

Something similar is true in Detroit. Many attempted to malign Detroit's charter schools while I was secretary, but the simple facts speak for themselves. Students attending a charter school in Detroit gain, on average, three months of added learning each year versus staying at their assigned public school.[7]

Remember, these are public schools operating in the same neigh-borhoods and serving the same students. The difference is in approach.

There's also a difference in how charter schools are funded, but not the way the media might have you believe. New York's charters receive, on average, 16 percent *less* funding than traditional public schools do.[8] Charter schools in major cities across American receive, on average, 33 percent less funding than traditional public schools do.[9]

Charter schools do more with less. A landmark study in New York found the city's charter schools were nearly 25 percent more cost-effective at increasing achievement in reading and math. In Indianapolis, the charters there were a whopping 59 percent more cost effective. They were 43 percent better in DC, 30 percent in San Antonio, and the list goes on.[10]

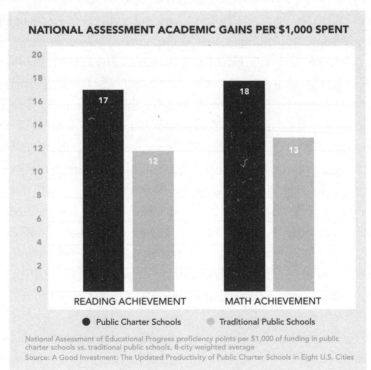

NATIONAL ASSESSMENT ACADEMIC GAINS PER $1,000 SPENT

● Public Charter Schools   ● Traditional Public Schools

National Assessment of Educational Progress proficiency points per $1,000 of funding in public charter schools vs. traditional public schools, 8-city weighted average
Source: A Good Investment: The Updated Productivity of Public Charter Schools in Eight U.S. Cities   11

It's hard to look at these results and argue against making every public school a charter school.

Right from the start, there were two things Dick knew he wanted the West Michigan Aviation Academy to embody. First, he wanted an inclusive school that reflected the whole community. It would have been easy to recruit white kids from the suburbs to go to an aviation school. But he didn't do the easy thing. By starting a charter school instead of a private school, the doors of the Aviation Academy would be open to all students. Dick worked hard to recruit students from poor, inner-city neighborhoods. Also, he wanted the diversity of the school to be more than just skin tone. Students come from farms and cities, towns and suburbs. Some kids have experienced homelessness.

Second, Dick wanted the school to have a culture of high expectations and good citizenship.

The Aviation Academy is committed to academics, but it also teaches students to be young gentlemen and young ladies—a fact that makes them highly sought after in the job market. Students are taught to shake hands and look a stranger in the eye when they meet. Teachers wear business attire to model a seriousness they hope the students will emulate. More important, the teachers are highly collaborative. They work together, share ideas, and clearly care about their students.

On top of that, of course, there is the flying. Every year, a couple dozen students graduate from the Aviation Academy with their private pilot's license. Students learn to fly on small, single-engine aircraft donated by Delta Air Lines and other generous supporters of the school. There is a group of students engaged in a multiyear project to build an entire airplane by the time they graduate. Many students concentrate in the STEM disciplines: science, technology, engineering, and mathematics. All students study robotics and engineering.

But about a third of the kids want to pursue something else entirely. To be accountants. Soldiers. Dancers.

While I was education secretary, I wasn't permitted to even mention the Aviation Academy because the government lawyers had deemed it a conflict of interest—another alleged scheme by which Dick and I would somehow profit by canvassing the inner city for would-be pilots for a nonprofit school. That was unfortunate because there is no bully pulpit for education like being education secretary, and American parents deserve to know about creative, inclusive alternatives like the West Michigan Aviation Academy. The school expects a lot of its students. They have a longer school day and a longer school year. A "D" is a failing grade and students have to complete more credits to graduate than most traditional public schools. Many incoming ninth graders have to come to school early in the year to do remedial work. Some come from their middle schools several grade levels behind, another expense the school has to absorb.

When the day came for parents to sign up their kids for the academy in its first year, Dick was nervous and apprehensive. The physical space was underwhelming at the time. It was a renovated but unimpressive old office building. Tiles were literally falling out of the ceiling. The school was at the airport, a place many of its potential students had never been. Dick feared no one would sign up for school. That evening when he drove up, his eyes filled with tears as he saw a line of families stretching out the door, waiting to get in. The Aviation Academy started in 2010 with 80 ninth-grade students. Today more than 600 attend grades 9–12, from all across Michigan. Some kids commute almost two hours to get to the school. Some live in Grand Rapids during the week with friends or relatives and return to their homes on the weekends. Some take three city buses to get to school every day.

Dick has a saying: "The higher your altitude, the broader your horizons." It's true in aviation, but it's also true in education. When you raise expectations, it's incredible what can result.

When Randi Weingarten of the American Federation of Teachers and I talked briefly on my first day in office, she urged me to tour a school with her. I told her I would welcome that, but she had to also tour a school of my choosing with me. She agreed.

The Department of Education had a permanent apparatus devoted to coordination with the unions. I shut it down as best I could, since our mission was about student opportunities, not labor union desires. Still, it was not surprising that the career staff at the department knew all the details of my school visit with Weingarten before my staff and I did. She chose that we would visit Van Wert, a small, remote town in northwest Ohio. I wasn't overly eager to spend a day with Randi. She had most recently called the day I was confirmed a "sad day for children." But I resolved to be kind and put my differences with her aside for the trip.

The national press that traveled to Van Wert seemed puzzled—and more than a little annoyed—that Randi had chosen such a remote, difficult-to-access place. It was a small, rural town that had voted overwhelmingly for President Trump. And it also had a strong teacher union.

We visited the public preschool, elementary school, and high school and met with engaged students and wonderful teachers. Randi was transparent, somewhat condescendingly, about her goal of "educating" me about public schools. We observed some high school seniors present their capstone projects. One presentation was by students who were raising money for a charitable program run by a local church to provide food to hungry students and families. Randi, apparently missing the irony of it being a faith-based, private effort, surprised me by unexpectedly standing up and announcing the union would donate $2,500 to the charity. Clearly it had been preplanned. I told Dick the story, and he saw to it that our foundation made a contribution as well.

It was a media circus—there were pushy reporters and photographers everywhere. When we toured the preschool, the children had displayed some of their artwork underneath their desks. A couple of them wanted us to see it. So I kneeled down on the floor, craned my neck about, and checked out several masterpieces. Randi had been standing off to the side, looking a bit uncomfortable. The press was snapping pictures and the next thing I knew, Randi was lying on her back under one of the desks, next to a confused-looking kid. It was cute and awkward at the same time.

Randi had chosen the Van Wert schools to highlight a constituency whose elected officials can be more resistant to school choice: rural voters. Van Wert is a small town full of people of faith who were very invested in their schools. I suspect Randi thought it was clever to go to a town of Trump voters who nonetheless were likely wary of school choice.

In Van Wert and everywhere she goes, Randi fights hard to defend the education status quo. To do that she has to try to make people afraid of change—afraid of what education freedom can bring.

But I viewed the trip as an opportunity to educate more parents on the true scope of school choice. Education freedom doesn't necessarily mean just creating new schools or building more buildings. Interestingly, 20 percent of Van Wert parents chose to send their kids to schools outside the district, indicating there was a market for alternatives. For rural families like the ones in Van Wert, an education savings account—one form of school choice—could be used to pay for a tutor, to create a homeschooling learning pod with other families, to take classes online, or to access a myriad of other interesting options. And the competition created by education freedom or school choice would lead to new kinds of educational opportunities, like apprenticeships, vocational education, student-directed learning, teacher-directed schools, and on and on. Once the cycle of creativity is launched, there is no telling what it can produce. The parents in Van Wert deserved to know this.

Sadly, Randi never honored her commitment to visit a school of my choosing. If she had, I might have taken her to the 21st Century Charter School in Gary, Indiana.

The school, which is known as 21C, is in a tough neighborhood in Gary. Its students are 100 percent minority—precisely the students Randi and her colleagues claim to care about the most. But 21C is succeeding where Gary traditional public schools are failing. Its charter status allows it to provide an innovative learning model: Students earn college credits while earning their high school credits. 21C sends students, many of whom are the first in their families to go to college, to any of Gary's local colleges and universities—all free of charge. Fewer than 15 percent of adults in Gary have bachelor's degrees, so few students there have adult role models or any exposure at all to higher education. By facilitating students' learning on various campuses, 21C demystifies higher education and motivates students.

Students at 21C have accumulated hundreds of college credits. When I was there, I met several seventeen- and eighteen-year-olds who were graduating with a high school diploma and an associate's degree at the same time. One young woman, Raven, had graduated with her high school and bachelor's degrees simultaneously. She had now returned to 21C as a teacher. You could see by watching the student body that the success of the older students motivated younger students. It also motivated some of their parents and grandparents to go back to school and pursue degrees.

21C has been undeniably successful, so you would think that education officials would try to replicate its success. You would be wrong. Instead of trying to improve their schools with new options, the Gary public school system calls students in charter schools "lost." In 2019, the city council, which is filled with allies of the school union bosses, did their bidding and proposed to ban more charter schools—to literally hold the children of Gary hostage in assigned public schools. I would have loved for Randi to see how well these "lost" students are doing at 21C.

I toured hundreds of schools as the secretary of education, the vast majority of them public schools, for the record.[12] I also had many "firsts" for a secretary, including the first visit to a Jewish yeshiva. I visited two in New York City. I even visited a school in Alaska for students who don't—or can't—"go to school."

Mat-Su Central School is located in Wasilla, Alaska, about forty-five miles north along the Knik Arm waterway from Anchorage. It's another interesting, one-of-a-kind, K–12 public school that serves children from all across Alaska.

Alaska is the archetypal rural challenge for school choice—the kind of place where choice isn't supposed to work. It's a massive state, with great cultural diversity. The majority of Alaska's students are in its two biggest towns, Anchorage and Fairbanks. But 30–40 percent are scattered across 586,000 square miles.

Alaska's fantastic education commissioner, Dr. Michael Johnson, first told me about Mat-Su Central. He described its innovative approach to education as "à la carte." Families can pick and choose the resources they want or need at Mat-Su, including some in-person classes. Every student at Mat-Su has a personalized learning plan. Some are homeschooled and use the school as a resource center and a place to meet with their academic advisors. Some students live at great distance and can only be physically present in the school a few times a year to pick up materials and check in with their academic coach. Some are enrolled in other schools and use Mat-Su to supplement their education. The school building, which is located in a light industrial park, even has a student-run coffee shop I visited alongside

Alaska's governor, Mike Dunleavy. I ordered a skim mocha, one of the better ones I've ever enjoyed.

On my visit, I met a young man who had dropped out of more than one traditional public school. But before he became a statistic, his mom convinced him to try Mat-Su Central. There he worked with an academic coach who helped him select classes aligned with his interests. For the first time in his life, he took responsibility for his own learning. He went from being a failing student to an A student at Mat-Su. He and his mom both beamed when telling me the story. My heart sang.

The *Wall Street Journal*'s Kimberley Strassel splits her time between Washington, DC, where she covers politics, and Palmer, Alaska, where her children attend Mat-Su Central. Strassel described how Mat-Su Central switched to remote learning during the pandemic more nimbly and successfully than other public schools. Teachers had the latitude to be creative and parents did their part. Strassel credits the school's successful response to COVID-19 to two things: choice and great teachers and administrators. As the school of choice for homeschoolers and remote students, Mat-Su was already familiar with the technology and practice of effective distance learning. And its unionized employees put students first. Superintendent Monica Goyette told Strassel their approach to the pandemic was "meaningful work" and "respectful of tax dollars."[13]

I went to Alaska at the invitation of the state's two U.S. senators. The senior senator, Lisa Murkowski, opposed my nomination. However, I made a commitment to her during our confirmation meeting that I would visit Alaska and I was determined to honor it. I also still held out hope that she would come around on school choice.

Senator Murkowski is the Alaskan version of the Republicans in the Michigan legislature who blocked charter schools to placate the school union bosses. In her 2010 reelection, Murkowski was challenged in the primary by a Tea Party candidate who was far to her right. The teacher unions backed her in the primary to keep the Tea

Party candidate from winning. He won anyway, so Lisa ran in the general election as a write-in candidate. The unions calculated that Murkowski was still their best bet in a three-way race in a red state, even as a write-in. They backed her and helped her win in 2010 and again in 2016.

I had hoped that a trip to Alaska could create some goodwill with Senator Murkowski. But from the outset, her staff sought to control my itinerary, pushing traditional public schools and union offices. If it weren't for the help of Commissioner Johnson, I would never have been able to spotlight innovative schools like Mat-Su Central. Murkowski didn't want us to visit there. Nor did she want me to highlight a great program at the University of Alaska Anchorage that brings bright Native Alaskan middle schoolers to Anchorage for a residential program with a STEM focus. These schools were educating outside of the box.

In the end, despite her invitation, Senator Murkowski didn't seem to really want me in Alaska. She didn't even show up for a visit she had arranged for both of us at a school on Eielson Air Force Base, in Fairbanks. Her staff said she was still in Anchorage because her flight had been delayed by ash from volcanic activity that limited visibility around Denali. Sorry, they said, she wouldn't be able to join me. But a few hours later, Murkowski was spotted at the airport in Fairbanks getting on a plane to leave the state. She had been in town the whole time.

———————————

One of the main reasons for telling my story is to give American families the information they need to give their children the best education they can. The education establishment doesn't want Americans to know what alternatives are possible for their kids. They don't want them to learn that they don't have to be captive to the establishment's ideology and agenda. Some experts, in fact, have questioned whether government-run public schools are even constitutional because they limit parents' First Amendment right to free speech. In a system of assignment, where parents are denied a choice of where their children are educated, they are compelled to have their kids exposed to indoctrinating speech—views on religion, race, and sexuality with which many disagree.[14]

The good news is that there are real options for parents today—traditional public, charter, and private—that are breaking that mold. There aren't nearly enough of them, but there are schools that are great models for groups of parents and communities to adopt. The more American families know about these options, the more they will demand, and the closer we will be to fundamentally freeing up the education system.

I've seen schools in America that are completely rethinking how children learn. They are tossing out the traditional, industrial model of passive, rote learning and unlocking children's true potential.

Some of my grandchildren attend such a school. From the outside, it doesn't look like much. It's two mobile units near a field on the outskirts of town. But inside, young minds are being opened and expanded.

Their school is one of the Acton Academy schools founded by Jeff and Laura Sandefer. Acton Academies are now located across the country and around the world. They are based on the belief that kids are innately curious and that they are capable of much more than traditional education asks of them. Children are considered "heroes" in Acton Academies and they are on a "hero's journey." Their teachers are not their educators but rather their guides. The children themselves must find their way to the calling that is inside each of them. At Acton, it's okay to fail or lose the trail. The value is getting back up, brushing yourself off, and continuing on.

In practice, education is very student directed at Acton schools. Kids set their own learning goals for the week. They learn through hands-on projects that propel them along their personal hero's journey. They write their own constitution. They have jobs and hold each other accountable to a standard of excellence. They don't have grade levels but progress according to their mastery of subjects. They don't just learn to read, they learn to *love* to read. They learn *how* to learn, so that they never stop learning.

Like Acton schools, Design39Campus in San Diego is a preschool through eighth grade school that is trying to harness the natural creativity of kids to learn in ways that are interesting to them. Design39 is not a charter school; it is a traditional public school that acts like a charter. That is, it does none of the traditional things and plays by none of the traditional rules of public schools. It was created within the San Diego public school system thanks to the vision and persistence of its founding principal, Sonya Wrisley. I learned about Design39 through the cofounder of the school, Megan Power, who later became a resident teacher fellow at the U.S. Department of Education.

Design39 is oriented around student-driven, real-world design projects. Students approach subjects from new and unusual angles. They might read a novel and then, instead of writing a book report, collaborate to create a trailer for the book—a short video describing it to potential readers. Kindergartners might study endangered animals and write public service announcements about them. The students have the freedom to work on their projects for most of the day with periodic check-ins with teachers. Grade levels are blurred and student mastery of subject matter is the measure. Design39 is another wonderful "rethinking" of how children learn.

Another such school—a "traditional" public school that looks, functions, and acts more like a charter, or even private, school— made a media splash while I was secretary. Akron, Ohio's I Promise School was started by NBA superstar LeBron James. While it is a public school funded by the Akron district, most of the things that got the attention—free bikes, food and uniforms, the barbershop, added educational supports for parents, and free college tuition—are paid for *privately* by James. The "extras" aren't the only thing that's different. The school has longer school days and a longer school year. It has a summer camp. It has a different curriculum than the rest of the district. It looks about as much like an average public school in Ohio as LeBron looks like an average thirty-something dad on the basketball court. It's a public school in name only, but that name is what really mattered to the education establishment. The school unions could foresee the PR splash I Promise was going to get, and *miraculously* agreed to everything James's team asked of them.

I hold *nothing* against I Promise or James. We need more schools like it, and more people like James to support them. I just wish the unions would be as willing to do what's best for students at *every* school.

For classically oriented parents, the private Thales Academy schools in North Carolina are a great option. They provide a model of learning that is classical, rigorous, and affordable. The curriculum is built around the great books and the great thinkers of Western civilization. Virtues such as self-discipline, responsibility, respect, and humility are emphasized. Thales Academies offer what few public schools provide anymore: a serious study of the ideas upon which the American republic was founded. Students learn about the rule of law, market economics, and the unalienable rights of every human being. And by working hard to minimize costs, Thales is able to deliver this world-class education at a remarkably affordable rate.

For a *60 Minutes* profile in 2018, I took Lesley Stahl and her CBS News crew to a K–8 public "lab" school in Indianapolis called the Cold Spring School. Cold Spring is a high-performing magnet school for the study of the sciences and the environment. It's not a charter school; it's one of a series of "innovation" schools under the purview of Indianapolis Public Schools. But just like charter schools, innovation schools are freed of union rules and government mandates on what and how to teach. They are managed by outside partners. Students are admitted by a lottery.

Cold Spring sits on thirty-nine acres of land. It has a greenhouse, gardens, and hiking trails. Students do much of their learning outdoors when it's warm. Lesley and I toured the school and witnessed the children learning outside.

Cold Spring teachers are also unique. Many come from Marian University's Klipsch Educators College, located next door. Just as innovative schools across the country are breaking the traditional public education mold, Klipsch is breaking the mold of traditional teachers colleges.

Teachers colleges over the last several decades have tended to become very similar in their approach: left-leaning, not very demanding, and with little connection to what it actually takes to be successful in a classroom. Their graduates then bring these attitudes to public school classrooms. Marian has developed a new way of educating teachers. Academic standards are higher for incoming students and they spend less time on education theory and more time on actually teaching children. Marian teachers learn to work with students as unique individuals with different needs.

Lesley Stahl was enamored of the Cold Spring School. She said she'd never seen anything like it.

Lesley and I also visited the Cristo Rey High School in Indianapolis. There are thirty-eight Cristo Rey schools, in twenty-four states. They are Catholic schools that keep their doors open to poor, minority students through a unique education and business model. Students work five days a month at entry-level jobs in a field in which they have an interest. Their earnings go to the school to help pay for their education. But the program is far more than simply work-study. For some of the high school students, it's the first time they have set foot inside a corporate or professional environment. Cristo Rey schools introduce less advantaged kids to a world they might not have previously known. They introduce new role models and experiences into their lives.

Cristo Rey Indianapolis provides students with transportation from their jobs back to the school at the end of the day. Lesley and her camera crew rode along in one of the buses as I talked with the students during the pickup loop. The stories from the kids were inspiring. We had a good time talking with them. Over the course of the day, Lesley also shared about how thrilled she was to be a grandmother and how she had just authored a book about the joy of grandparenting. In the book she notes that grandparents are paying more than $2 billion every year to send their grandchildren to private schools.

But that's not what you saw in the *60 Minutes* report when it aired. To say it was selectively edited would be generous. It was a shame. Lesley claimed to feel bad about it. She called Nate Bailey, my chief of staff, to apologize after the program aired. However, Stahl, a *60 Minutes* star, almost certainly has editorial control of her pieces.

Visiting hundreds of schools has taught me a few things about what sets innovative schools apart. First, behind almost every excellent school I've visited is a visionary leader. You can feel that leader's presence almost immediately when you walk into a school. Children are more engaged. The hallways and classrooms buzz with energy. There is electricity in the air.

Great schools pay attention to individual children. The current model of American education was created, not just to treat all children the same, but to *make* all children the same. When public schools began, religious, ethnic, and cultural differences were intended to be erased to create a common American identity. Differences in children were overlooked in pursuit of providing a monolithic education to all. The education establishment then took this industrial model and enshrined it. Somewhere along the way, this American education machine became self-aware. Its leaders began to fight, not for the children it is supposed to serve, but to perpetuate the machine itself. They brought the educational fads and "woke" theory they learned in teachers colleges into the classroom, contrary to the values and lived experiences of many American families. To date, they've largely succeeded in this fight because they have the ultimate leverage: our children.

All the schools I have highlighted break with this model. They represent opportunities for parents to break out of the top-down, establishment-controlled model and find the school that fits the needs of their unique child. There should be more of these schools. Many, many more. And many schools not yet imagined or created. Freedom is the defining feature of America, yet freedom is viewed as the enemy by the education establishment. This monopoly control must end. It's long past time that all American parents have the freedom to choose the best possible education for their child.

CHAPTER SIX

THERE'S NOTHING CIVIL
ABOUT CIVIL RIGHTS

The young, African-American man's eyes brimmed with tears as he told us his story. His name was Joseph. He had been a student at Savannah State University (SSU), just three weeks away from becoming the first person in his family to graduate from college. He woke up one morning in 2013 to find an email from the Office of Student Affairs.

Joseph recalled the email in his own words. "'You are hereby summarily suspended and if you step foot on campus, you get the threat of expulsion and arrest.'" The email was followed by a campus-wide alert with Joseph's picture, urging anyone who saw him on campus to report it to campus security. Joseph had no idea what he had been accused of. He had never been contacted by the university about any accusation or any investigation, much less any conviction.

Immediately Joseph was locked out of his dorm, he lost access to his computer, and he was expelled from his classes. Still, he had no idea what he had done wrong. He had to submit a request under the Open Records Act to get an answer. He learned that he had been thrown off campus for somehow violating Title IX. On its face, Title IX prohibits discrimination on the basis of sex at educational institutions that receive any sort of federal funds. Over the years, however, courts—working in tandem with activists and federal bureaucrats—have stretched Title IX to cover things far beyond its original mandate, like the bathroom issue.

Even with the Open Records request, the details of the allegations against Joseph were vague. Two anonymous women had complained to the university about "verbal and online" sexual harassment. These complaints alone were enough for administrators to end Joseph's college career and declare him a threat to all students. SSU had not paused for even a moment to deliberate or investigate. The email he received telling him he had been expelled was sent the same day the first complaint was received.

Joseph was one of more than a dozen men and women who came to the Department of Education in the summer of 2017 to share their stories. They had all been denied due process under Title IX. Joseph's story was echoed in the stories of other men and women who had been falsely accused. The stigma of being accused of sexual misconduct led Joseph to relapse and begin drinking again. He tried to take his own life.

"Whatever your accusers say you are," he told us, "is what people believe you are."

That summer, I also heard from men and women who had been the victims of sexual harassment and assault on university campuses. They had all volunteered to talk to me and their stories were chilling. They talked about classmates they thought were friends taking sexual advantage of them. They talked tearfully about having to endure multiple investigations to resolve their cases.

One young woman's story really cut to the core of the problem for me. She had been raped. Later she was accused of assault by a friend. In both instances, she said, her school didn't get it right.

Listening to the two groups of students left me emotionally drained. Every single one of the stories was hard to hear. Every single person I heard from—both survivors and the accused—had been let down by the way their school handled their case under Title IX. After the meetings, I was scheduled to give a press conference to summarize the discussions, but I had to delay it. My heart ached for those students. I needed time to compose myself.

Also listening in on these sessions was a remarkable woman named Candice Jackson. Candice had agreed to serve as the acting head of the Office for Civil Rights for the department while the official nominee was being held up in Congress. She is controversial and fearless. A Stanford-educated lawyer and activist, she had chronicled the stories of the women who accused Bill Clinton of sexual assault and harassment. She later brought all of them to the second presidential campaign debate between candidate Donald Trump and Hillary Clinton.

But these meetings were also personal for Candice. She is a rape survivor. She bravely shared her story in the session with the others, in details too sensitive and intimate to recount here. What she wanted to make clear, perhaps more than anything else, was that they should discount the media narrative that any changes would be drafted without keen sensitivity to or understanding of what survivors endure. Candice, too, bore those scars (as did others on our team who helped write the rule).

Candice overcame the trauma she endured and became an accomplished lawyer. She married a woman and started a family. Being a mom—to a boy and a girl—was now another lens through which she viewed this issue. She hadn't told me her whole story until just before the meetings with the survivors. She was still struggling with her past. It was all she could do to say the word *rape* out loud. But her experience, she said, motivated her to take on the issue of dealing with sexual harassment and assault in school. She wanted, she said, "to get this right, for everyone."

Candice came to the issue of Title IX sexual harassment from a perspective of personal experience. She understood the need for survivors to have control over what comes next. She described the difficulty she had in understanding that what had happened to her was rape. She described the pain of having to be in the same class and the same dorm as her rapist.

Candice also understood the pain of the falsely accused. We both were particularly moved by a mother who recounted how she came upon her son trying to commit suicide after being falsely accused of rape under Title IX. From that point on, she said, every time she opened the door to her son's room she feared she would find him dead. No mother should have to endure such a thing.

As is too often the case with laws, the original congressional authors of Title IX wouldn't recognize the law as it is today. This well-intentioned, straightforward statute was enacted as part of a larger education bill in 1972. It was passed to give women equal access to education and educational services, particularly at colleges, universities, and graduate schools. Over the years, Title IX has been interpreted to cover much more, from standardized tests, to sexual harassment, to its most famous application—the number of women versus the number of men who play sports.

It's not just the fact that this noble law has been stretched beyond any possible congressional intent that is dangerous. The *way* it has been expanded is equally undemocratic. Education officials of successive Democratic administrations have issued "Dear Colleague" letters— literally just letters written by unelected, unaccountable bureaucrats to the education community—declaring that Title IX now means something new. The Clinton administration pronounced in a "Dear Colleague" that if men and women don't participate in sports at equal rates at a school, men could be denied opportunities until the rates were equal.

It was the Obama administration that twisted the meaning of Title IX when it comes to protecting students from sexual harassment. Then–vice president Joe Biden announced what he hoped would "change the culture" on college campuses on the same day in April 2011 that he and President Obama announced their reelection campaign. The Obama Education Department issued a nineteen-page, single-spaced letter to the education community. It became known as *the* "Dear Colleague" letter.

Every procedural change introduced by the letter was designed to increase the likelihood of those accused of sexual harassment and assault being found guilty. According to the letter, "sexual harassment" from that point on would be defined broadly as "unwelcome conduct of a sexual nature"—omitting the Supreme Court's requirement that such conduct must also be "severe, pervasive, and objectively offensive." The letter decreed that a single college administrator could act as both judge and jury in a Title IX sexual harassment case. It also explicitly mandated that a *single* instance of harassment could cause an entire university to be labeled a "hostile environment," launching an investigation costing millions of dollars and lasting years.

Under the Obama Title IX letter, a school could move forward with the prosecution of a case even if the original complainant refused to participate or recanted the charges. The accused didn't have to be told about the allegations before he or she was declared guilty. The accused couldn't demand legal representation at a hearing. They couldn't demand to see the evidence against them. They couldn't cross-examine the witnesses against them.

To top it all off, the "Dear Colleague" unilaterally lowered the bar to determine the guilt of the accused. Previously, Title IX cases had often required a "clear and convincing" standard of guilt or even guilt "beyond a reasonable doubt" to convict the accused. Now it required only that the prosecution prove that the accused was "more likely than not" guilty. This lower standard of evidence, the letter said, applied to Title IX sexual harassment cases even if the university used the higher standard in non-sexual-misconduct cases—or in how they adjudicated faculty accused of sexual misconduct.

The penalty for failure to comply with the rules was high. Colleges and universities could lose their federal funding, a death sentence for basically any school.

In short, the Obama/Biden Title IX "Dear Colleague" letter imposed a system that denied justice by favoring the complainant and denying due process to the accused. And it's important to point out that the new decree did not land in a vacuum. Administrators, and particularly Title IX officers on campuses, were already inclined to err on the side of the accusers in sexual harassment cases. The "Dear Colleague" reenforced these administrators' anti-due-process bias—indeed, that was exactly what it was intended to do. The processes that resulted were nothing short of "kangaroo courts."

One after another, men (it was mostly, but certainly not exclusively, men) were denied due process under Title IX, convicted of crimes for which they had not even known they were being investigated. They were not allowed to have a lawyer present or face their accusers. It was as if all the results were preordained.

One example of the additional bias that was injected into the system was the way colleges and universities trained staff to handle Title IX cases. Schools typically kept the materials used to train Title IX investigators and adjudicators secret. But one accused student at the University of Pennsylvania obtained the school's training materials and a district court ruled that they "framed virtually any permutation of an accuser's behavior as consistent with the guilt of the accused."[1] In English: Heads, I win. Tails, you lose.

The mainstream media was a steady source of support for the new rules. To ensure they did their part, the Obama Department of Education published the names of all the colleges and universities that were under investigation for failure to implement the new Title IX rules. The list was purposefully media-ready—any reporter who wanted to help bully schools into complying with the new rules could consult it. The list included schools that were merely being investigated of violations; no actual sexual harassment had been found to have occurred.

Not surprisingly, outrageous cases of schools trampling on the rights of the accused exploded on college and university campuses.

Students found themselves dragged in front of college tribunals for absurd claims. The accused were given little or no notice of what they were accused. They were denied the ability have anyone cross-examine their accusers. The same university officials were often both "investigators" of allegations and "judges" of the outcomes. Far too often, university administrators showed demonstrable bias against the accused. Some administrators intervened directly into trials to find for the alleged victim.

One such case involved a couple at the University of Southern California (USC) who had been dating for two years when a neighbor saw them "playfully roughhousing" on the lawn in front of the girl's dorm. The activity was reported to the USC Title IX office. The woman denied that any abuse had taken place. But under the Obama rules, that didn't matter. The school went ahead with the case and expelled the boyfriend. When the girl insisted her boyfriend was innocent, she was told she was suffering from battered woman syndrome and didn't know what she was talking about.

Another case that was almost too absurd to be true involved a student at the University of Tennessee. An exam for his earth sciences class asked him to name his lab instructor. He couldn't remember her name, so he took a wild guess: "Sarah Jackson." Unbeknownst to the student, it turns out that there is an adult model named Sarah Jackson. When he got a zero on his quiz, he asked his professor what he had done wrong. The professor said his random answer was offensive and constituted sexual harassment under Title IX according to the Obama rules. The university opened a Title IX investigation of the incident, even though no one filed a complaint.[2] It was just one of many ways in which even benign speech was attacked by the Title IX bureaucracy.

There was another, twisted kind of injustice created by the Obama "Dear Colleague" letter: It often resulted in re-traumatizing the very victims it was supposed to protect. In the years following the Obama letter, hundreds of lawsuits were filed by students who felt they had been treated unjustly in Title IX sexual harassment cases. This led to reopening the cases, making the survivor relive the experience, and often overturning the decision not because someone was innocent but because the adjudication procedures were so fatally flawed.

A male student with a troubling record of misconduct sued George Mason University (GMU) after he was found guilty of sexual assault under Title IX. The student alleged that GMU had withheld evidence from him, and that the administrator who decided his case had already admitted he was biased toward the alleged victim. The court ruled in the male student's favor and he was allowed back on campus. The decision had turned on whether the school's Title IX procedures were fair. The court decided they were not and a student who may or may not have committed sexual assault was free to return to campus.

In total, as of 2019, 300 courts had ruled and in almost half of these cases, the court found in favor of the plaintiff. In seventy-four additional cases, the university settled with the plaintiff.[3] And each time one of these students sued their school for wrongful expulsion, their alleged victims were forced to relive their experiences. Our team felt very strongly that this was wrong. Sexual assault survivors were regularly retraumatized by a system that served neither the accuser nor the accused.

The 2016 presidential campaign made the issue of sexual harassment and assault an even more difficult political knot to untie than before. Candidate Trump had his *Access Hollywood* tape in which he bragged about sexual misconduct. Hillary Clinton's husband had his own long string of sexual accusations. Nonetheless, I came into the job of education secretary determined to undo the harm the Obama administration had done to Title IX enforcement.

From the outset, I made clear we would not "rule by letter." I would not repeat the shortcut previous administrations had used by issuing "Dear Colleague" letters. Unelected, unaccountable bureaucrats wrote these letters and called them "guidance" on how to enforce the law. But the word *guidance* implied that these new rules were optional. They were not. Any college or university that dared not follow them opened themselves up to lawsuits. Or they became the subjects of federal investigations that forced them to either lose their federal funding or "settle" with the department by incorporating the new rules. Either way, they couldn't win. The "Dear Colleague" was, after all, no "empty threat," in the words of Catherine Lhamon, Obama's OCR chief.[4]

The letters were an egregious example of administrative overreach—of the bureaucracy making new law through how it chose to *enforce* existing laws. With a stroke of their pen, Obama bureaucrats changed the law, plain and simple. As anyone who remembers *Schoolhouse Rock* knows, Congress is the branch responsible for writing the laws. Congress had not acted to change Title IX. We had to correct the law's enforcement and do so properly.

The intricacies of how the federal government develops and issues regulations make most people's eyes glaze over, and for good reason. But the details of this process matter. When they are ignored—as they were repeatedly with Title IX—bureaucrats step into the role of Congress and democracy itself is subverted.

I wanted to reverse the Obama directive as quickly as anyone else, but I knew we had to do it the *right way*. My senior advisor, Bob Eitel, argued that the only way to ensure that our policy fix couldn't be reversed with another letter from a future Democratic administration was to work through the long, complicated process of issuing new federal regulations.

First the Obama letter had to be rescinded. Then the proposed new Title IX rules had to be written and published in the Federal Register for a period of public comment, usually sixty days. During that period, anyone could critique or suggest changes to any part of the regulation. And the relevant department—in this case the Department of Education—has to reply to every single comment it receives. Only after these steps are taken can the final rule be issued and the regulation be created.

It is difficult to overstate how controversial it is to try to change Title IX. Or rather, how controversial it is to *limit excesses* under the law. Generations of Americans associate Title IX with progress for women in education and athletics, and rightly so. For feminists of a certain age, it is the weapon with which they have fought for fifty years, not just to create opportunities for women, but to break down the differences between the sexes. Now, with the advent of the transgender movement, Title IX is being used to abolish the notion of biological sex altogether. Making the law more sweeping than Congress intended was pretty easy—Democratic administrations had been doing it for decades. But reining in excesses under the law—*that* was hard.

There are credible legal scholars who argue that Title IX doesn't apply to sexual harassment cases at all. In fact, the minority opinion in a 5–4 case on the topic before the Supreme Court said Title IX didn't have such a broad reach.[5] But we chose not to make that argument. My goal was to preserve the integrity of the law, and the advancements for girls and women within it, while at the same time restoring due process to sexual harassment cases. Our strategy was simple: to do the opposite of what we had done nine months earlier with the transgender bathroom rule. The first thing we would do is explain what we were doing and why to the public, and provide the rationale for changing a landmark civil rights law.

We planned a speech announcing that I was pulling the Obama rule and writing a new one. It would be a major address, scheduled to be given at the University of Virginia (UVA) in Charlottesville in August 2017. The Jefferson rotunda on the UVA campus was a great place to talk about falling short of our ideals but still honoring and pursuing them. There was another reason UVA was a good place to

Above: My parents with my sisters and me (far left), age five, before our younger brother joined the family. *Below:* The "Little Red House" in Holland, Michigan, the first place I ever lived. It still looks much the same today and brings a smile to my face every time I see it.

Above: With most of my cousins on my mom's side at my aunt and uncle's greenhouse, circa 1965. When we got older, many of us worked there, competing to see who could transplant the most seedling plants each day. *Right:* The original Prince Manufacturing Company building, which I helped paint with my dad. Later I worked the night shift riveting sun visors.

Left: Dad showing my older kids some of the machines on the Prince factory floor. Little did any of us know how precious these moments with him would be. *Opposite:* Celebrating my college graduation in 1979 with my husband, Dick.

Above: Enjoying a family moment shortly after the birth of our youngest, Ryan. *Below:* Taking the stage with Dick and our kids at the state convention after being elected Republican National Committeewoman from Michigan in 1993.

Above: With a very special girl I mentored in the Grand Rapids Public Schools. Mentoring was personally rewarding and also gave me firsthand insight into how schools were—or weren't—meeting each child's unique needs. *Below:* Dick combined his passions for aviation and education to form a wonderful school in our hometown of Grand Rapids, the West Michigan Aviation Academy. Students can graduate with their diploma and a private pilot's license. The innovative school has attracted many visitors, including President George W. Bush (pictured), astronaut (now U.S. senator) Mark Kelly, and General Colin Powell.

Above: Most of our family, minus daughter Elissa who was in the middle of medical school, with Vice President and Mrs. Pence following my swearing-in ceremony as U.S. secretary of education in February 2017.

Above: At Butler Tech High School in Ohio, "signing day" involves students announcing what company they will work with, a new play on signing events for college-bound athletes. We emphasized the significant value of career and technical education in helping students pursue well-paying jobs and meaningful careers. (Photo: U.S. Department of Education) *Below:* In the White House Situation Room, beneath the West Wing, where meetings on sensitive topics are held. Here, Vice President Pence chairs a COVID task force meeting in the spring of 2020. (Official White House Photo by D. Myles Cullen)

Above: Visiting with cadets at the New Orleans Military & Maritime Academy alongside House of Representatives leader Congressman Steve Scalise. (Photo: U.S. Department of Education) *Below:* I was the first U.S. secretary of education to visit an Orthodox Jewish school, Yeshiva Darchei Torah in Queens, New York. It was inspiring to visit another kind of school that was meeting the needs of the students it served. All families need that same opportunity. (Photo courtesy of Agudath Israel)

Above: Discussing educational needs and experiences with parents and tribal elders in Kivalina, Alaska, alongside U.S. senator Dan Sullivan and Alaska's tremendous education commissioner, Michael Johnson. *Below:* A fun visit to SLAM Public Charter School in Miami with its founder, worldwide recording superstar Pitbull. Armando Pérez, his real name, opened the school as a way to give back and improve the opportunities available to students in the area where he grew up. (Photos: U.S. Department of Education)

Above: Raven Osborne, pictured here, graduated from 21st Century Charter School in Gary, Indiana, with her high school diploma and a bachelor's degree, thanks to their unique and high-performing model. She raised the bar for the entire community, and she's now giving back by teaching at 21C. ***Opposite Top:*** The D.C. Opportunity Scholarship Program, the only federal school choice program, has helped change thousands of lives in the District of Columbia. My friend Shirley, who worked in the Education Department's cafeteria, was able to enroll her two children in a school that better met their needs thanks to the program. ***Opposite Bottom:*** Celebrating graduation day with students at Dick Conner Correctional Facility in Oklahoma. We expanded the "Second Chance Pell" program, which allows men and women who are incarcerated to pursue education as part of their rehabilitation program. (Photos: U.S. Department of Education)

Above: Updating the president on our plan to advance the education freedom agenda in Congress and across America. It was always a privilege to be in the Oval Office, an awe-inspiring place where you can truly feel the weight of history. (Official White House Photo by Shealah Craighead) *Below:* It was a special treat to cohost, with First Lady Melania Trump, a screening of the film *Miss Virginia* in the White House theatre. The students who joined us are beneficiaries of the work of Virginia Walden Ford, whose advocacy is the inspiration for the film. Mrs. Trump's "Be Best" campaign was an important effort to increase focus on the well-being of the whole child, including emotional health and bullying prevention. (Official White House Photo by Andrea Hanks)

Above: A powerful moment as the teeming room fell silent to listen to Samuel Myers, whose life was changed by a voucher for students with disabilities, share his story with President Trump. The Ohio special needs voucher was championed by Samuel's mother, Tera, seated to his left. (Official White House Photo by Shealah Craighead)

Below: Trying my hand at pottery with students at the Kansas City Academy, a school that centers on art and design. It was always fun and interesting to jump into a lesson alongside students. (Photo: U.S. Department of Education)

Above: Catching up with Iowa's impactful governor, Kim Reynolds. Education is inherently a state and local issue, and our team did everything we could to return power to those closest to students. The cane was an unpleasant reminder of my broken pelvis from an accident a few weeks earlier. *Below:* Highlighting our work to improve the federal student aid process with Senator Lamar Alexander and his trusty FAFSA form prop. That scroll is now in the ash heap of history after we dramatically simplified the application and moved it to a mobile app. (Photos: U.S. Department of Education)

Above: Cohosting a field trip with Ivanka Trump to the Smithsonian's National Museum of American History for girls interested in STEM programs. Ivanka was a great advocate for efforts to expand STEM and coding education, as well as increased opportunities for young girls. *Below:* A great discussion—and some delicious barbecue!—with families who homeschool around Denver, Colorado. It brought back fond memories of when our two girls homeschooled for several years. It is an increasingly popular educational option, putting parents in the driver's seat of their children's learning. (Photos: U.S. Department of Education)

Above: Highlighting the importance of in-person learning during the pandemic with my friend Governor Doug Ducey of Arizona. (Photo: U.S. Department of Education)
Below: Sharing some of my experiences as secretary during "circle time" at a local school. My favorite question from the students: "Why did they put you in a cabinet?" I love kids' innocence and curiosity.

announce our reform of Title IX: The university had recently been tarred with sexual assault allegations that were ultimately discredited. The accuser turned out to be a fraud. And the accused were pronounced guilty until proven innocent.

In November 2014, *Rolling Stone* magazine published an inflammatory report under the clickbait headline, "A Rape on Campus." The article alleged that an undergraduate identified only as "Jackie" had been gang-raped on campus. Investigators later uncovered that the journalist who wrote the piece had been looking for a sexual assault case to show "that there's this pervasive culture of sexual harassment/rape culture" on campus. She found Jackie, who told a horrifying story of going to a party at the fraternity house, being taken into an upstairs bedroom, and serially raped by seven members of the fraternity. The article immediately went viral, attracting more than 2.7 million views online.[6]

Literally days after the article was published, Jackie's account began to fall apart. It was discovered that she fabricated key parts of her story, including inventing a fictional frat brother who took her to the party. *Rolling Stone* eventually retracted the story and settled defamation lawsuits with both the fraternity and the university. But the damage had been done. The narrative depicted in the article—that university officials are indifferent to widespread rape on campus—had trashed UVA's reputation.

UVA had been a victim of the rush to judgment that surrounded many Title IX sexual assault claims on campus. It was a perfect venue for us to announce our intention to reestablish justice under the law. We were ready to go. Then Charlottesville happened.

My speech was scheduled for a just a week after the white supremacist riots. It was a tough time for the administration. UVA dean of students Allen Groves called to say that I was still welcome, but we might want to reconsider coming to Charlottesville just then. Though it was a noble offer from someone who has a spine of steel when it comes to protecting free speech on campus, we told Dean Groves we weren't going to come. I was a lightning rod, the subject was wildly controversial, and the community was already on edge. Speaking at UVA was simply not a good idea.

So we went back to the drawing board. But school after school turned us down when we contacted them to host the speech. Many of the same schools that had quietly complained to us how bad the Title IX rules were lost the courage of their convictions when it came to hosting the speech. After eleven tries, We were concerned I wouldn't be welcome anywhere. We had begun planning to give the speech at the Department of Education when a group of principled and courageous students from George Mason University (GMU) Federalist Society chapter agreed to host the speech at GMU's Antonin Scalia Law School.

On the day of the speech, I arrived at the venue in Arlington, Virginia, to a large group of protestors screaming "Stop Betsy DeVos!" Another group of protestors lined the hallway leading to the auditorium screaming "Rape apologist!" in my face. Thankfully, the audience for the speech itself was attentive and respectful. The theme woven through my address was "a better way." Sexual harassment and assault on campus was a genuine problem, I said, and Title IX had protected students' right to learn in safety for decades.

But there had to be a better way.

I talked about the many students I had heard from since I became secretary whose lives had been forever changed by sexual assault. I talked about the parents who cried as they recounted stories of receiving the phone call from their daughter who had been a victim or their son who had been accused of sexual assault. I talked about being a mom to daughters and sons, and trying to imagine what it would be like to receive that call. This was not a problem we could ignore. It was a difficult conversation we had to have.

"One rape is one too many," I said. "One assault is one too many. One aggressive act of harassment is one too many."

"One person denied due process is one too many."

The Obama rules had failed too many students. They forced the hand of schools and tilted the scales of justice. The new rules compelled colleges and universities to step into roles and deal with situations that were beyond their capabilities. So many instances of sexual harassment on campus were "he said, she said" cases in which the truth is difficult for even trained lawyers and investigators to determine—and completely beyond the scope of most college administrators. Alcohol too often clouded memories and distorted motives. Even university officials with the best of intentions were stretched beyond their capabilities by the Title IX rules. In that environment, nobody wins.

"Any school that refuses to take seriously a student who reports sexual misconduct is one that discriminates," I told the audience. "And any school that uses a system biased toward finding a student responsible for sexual misconduct also commits discrimination."

There clearly was a better way. We were committed to find it by issuing new regulations. We would welcome the feedback of the public, the advice of experts, and the real-world experiences of students. But some lines we would not cross. We would not pit men against women. We would not ignore survivors. We would not cast aside any American's right to due process. We would not punish speech. And we would seek justice for *all* students.

The response to the speech was . . . split. Lawyers, including legal counsels at schools, welcomed the prospect of change. They knew how broken the situation was. Some civil libertarians also welcomed our pledge to restore due process to the accused. But most of the broad Title IX bureaucracy—in Washington, in regional Education Department offices, and at colleges and universities—were vitriolic in their response—extraordinarily so. Catherine Lhamon tweeted absurdly that the new Title IX regulation would be a return "to the bad old days, that predate my birth, when it was permissible to rape and sexually harass students with impunity."

There were some positive reviews—one particularly so. At a Camp David retreat for cabinet members a few days after the speech, President Trump held up a *Wall Street Journal* editorial during lunch. Under the headline "DeVos Pledges to Restore Due Process" was an approving article. Trump brandished the piece and congratulated me. Then he started talking about the Duke University lacrosse scandal.

In 2006, members of the team hired a woman to dance at a party. The woman subsequently charged three of the players with raping her in the bathroom. Despite the fact that her account of the facts changed multiple times; that she couldn't identify any of the accused in a lineup; that there was photographic evidence that the event could not have occurred; and that none of the players' DNA was present on the accuser, the Durham County, North Carolina, district attorney, who was in a close race for reelection, pursued the case for months, permanently scarring the reputations of three men who were eventually declared innocent.

Trump associated Title IX sexual harassment with the Duke scandal, I think, because he knew the father of one of the lacrosse players. He was a filmmaker. One night Dick and I went to the White House with other cabinet members and spouses for a screening of one of his movies. The president once again mentioned how important it was that I was reforming the Title IX regulation, despite the controversy it caused. As we were leaving, he turned to Dick and said, "She's tough. She's tougher than both of us."

The time and effort it took to change just one regulation for one law is why Americans hate the federal bureaucracy. It took more than a year after we rescinded the Obama letter until we were able to publish our proposed new Title IX sexual harassment regulation. Even then, it was just a proposed regulation, not a final one. If you look at the timeline from when the process began, with my meetings with survivors and wrongly accused students at the department, the rule took two and a half years to complete. Multiple cabinet agencies, outside interest groups, and the White House were all involved. Countless meetings. Countless opinions.

The damage that occurred when our budget was leaked to the *Washington Post* was still fresh in our minds. We were determined not to have that happen with our Title IX rule, so we added layers of security protections to an already complicated process. We issued no electronic copies of the proposed rule to anyone. Everyone involved got numbered paper copies that they could edit only in my conference room. They handwrote their edits and left their devices outside. We referred to the project by a code name. It mostly worked, though some parts of the rule did leak out of the Department of Health and Human Services.

After his enthusiasm and encouragement at Camp David, the president and I didn't discuss the Title IX issue while we were writing the new rule. The president's lack of engagement was both a blessing and a curse. It was a blessing because we had the freedom to develop the policy as we felt it should be. But it was a curse because we still had to negotiate the details with the White House staff and, in the absence of clear presidential direction, that could be difficult. Their opinions on what we should do ran the gamut from doing nothing at all to mandating student-on-student cross-examination. What's more, the Trump White House was heavy on generals and light on soldiers. A high percentage of staffers thought *they* were in charge.

Part of the challenge for me with some of the White House staff might have been attributable to the fact that I had not supported Trump in the primary. Anti-establishment feeling ran deep in parts of the White House. I'm not sure I ever passed the purity test for some Trump staffers. The Trump White House had more than its share of politically inexperienced but ideologically driven staff. It often felt like a kind of adversarial, "us versus them" mentality, as though we weren't all on the same team.[*]

Somehow I was considered "establishment" by some of the White House staff, and this made me suspect. It often led to my policies—on Title IX and other things—being challenged by the occasional twenty-four-year-old. It didn't seem to matter that I was doing hand-to-hand combat with the forces of the administrative state; that I was seen as the enemy of the department I ran; and that I took continuous incoming from Washington insiders in both parties.

As the process of drafting the new Title IX rule ground on, the split of opinion in the White House grew. Even in an administration ostensibly full of "disrupters," there was significant fear of changing Title IX. Strong voices on the Hill—including staff from Senate Health, Education, Labor, and Pensions Committee chairman Lamar Alexander—warned the White House that the reforms would never withstand congressional review. After the hearings for Supreme Court nominee Brett Kavanaugh began in September 2018, some White House staff argued that we shouldn't do anything our critics could spin as "anti-women." Others shared my view that the discussion about due process relating to Judge Kavanaugh was exactly the right time to launch the rule. In the end, the "delay" faction won, so we waited again. Finally, in November 2018, we released a proposed regulation that protected the safety of alleged victims and due process for the accused.

The rule-making process was extraordinarily careful and deliberative. After we released the proposed rule, we received an astonishing

---

* Some White House staff were uninformed as well. During a routine media training session, an assistant to the president posed as a hostile journalist and demanded that I defend a statement I had supposedly made calling for "gun choice" for school shooters. I thought he was making a sick joke. "I never said that," I answered. My inquisitor insisted, "Yes, you did. I have it right here." My chief of staff demanded to see the clip he was referring to and a young aide handed it to him. It was from the *Onion*, the satirical newspaper. The article quoted me supposedly saying, "It makes sense that a shooter in rural Iowa is going to require a different setup than a shooter in the middle of Atlanta. Instead of trying to solve this with an overly broad and ineffective mandate, we need to be making decisions on a shooter-by-shooter basis." It was not something my worst enemy would have believed, much less a White House staffer.

124,196 comments from the public. Each one had to be answered, though fortunately many of them were form letters from advocacy groups. As the months wore on, staff turnover in the White House meant that proposed changes had to be restarted multiple times with multiple teams. The permanent bureaucracy also did its part to slow the process. Few people know this, but Supreme Court justice Ruth Bader Ginsburg, hailed as an ardent supporter of Title IX, was critical of the due process violations in the Obama rules.[7] She seemed to share my "better way" views as she discussed the issue with Jeff Rosen of the National Constitution Center:

> ROSEN: What about due process for the accused?
> GINSBURG: Well, that must not be ignored and it goes beyond sexual harassment. The person who is accused has a right to defend herself or himself, and we certainly should not lose sight of that. Recognizing that these are complaints that should be heard. There's been criticism of some college codes of conduct for not giving the accused person a fair opportunity to be heard, and that's one of the basic tenets of our system, as you know, everyone deserves a fair hearing.
> ROSEN: Are some of those criticisms of the college codes valid?
> GINSBURG: Do I think they are? Yes.
> ROSEN: I think people are hungry for your thoughts about how to balance the values of due process against the need for increased gender equality.
> GINSBURG: It's not one or the other. It's both. We have a system of justice where people who are accused get due process, so it's just applying to this field what we have applied generally.

When we sought to cite her observations in our new regulation, bureaucrats at the Office of Management and Budget told us we couldn't. We could quote the Supreme Court, they contended, but not an individual justice. Happily, we won that fight.

Finally, almost three years after we'd begun, we issued the final rule on May 6, 2020. Our new rule requires colleges and universities to hold live hearings on sexual harassment cases, and allow cross-examination of witnesses by advisors. It prohibits the practice of a single administrator being both judge and jury. Amazingly, we had to go out of our way to note in the regulation that all the accused had to be presumed innocent until proven guilty—something the Obama rules failed to do.

We gave schools the choice of using the "clear and convincing" standard of evidence or the lesser "preponderance of the evidence" to prove guilt. But there was an important caveat. Whichever standard a school chose, it had to apply it to all sexual harassment complaints, including those against faculty members. Since most faculty's collective bargaining and tenure rules already required the higher standard (just another example of unions putting the interests of adults above those of students), our rule would result in the same standard for accused students.

Lastly, our rule defines sexual harassment using the Supreme Court precedent as our guide. It also includes cyberbullying and dating violence as categories schools needed to consider, something that became much more important during the COVID-19 pandemic.

In short, *justice* was the goal of our Title IX enforcement, something you would think law enforcement officials would respect. But lamentably, eighteen Democratic attorneys general immediately filed a lawsuit against the new rule. Fortunately, a federal judge quickly dismissed their claim.

When I went in to seek the president's approval on the final rule, I presented it as a victory for due process. President Trump congratulated me and my team, noting he had twice been falsely accused of sexual misconduct. Once again, he seemed to only be able to understand the issue through the lens of his own experiences, but he said the words I needed to hear: "It's so right. Go ahead and do it."

We knew that what we had achieved was important. It was a hard-fought win and we had the scars to prove it. No secretary of education had ever issued a new regulation under Title IX. We were the first. And it was a big victory for justice for everyone.

I f federal policy can be created—and law effectively be made—by simply writing a letter, very few bureaucrats will be able to help themselves. They will abuse the practice. In 2014, the Obama OCR and Department of Justice issued yet another "Dear Colleague" letter. This time they unilaterally changed the way students are disciplined in American K–12 schools under federal civil rights law. It was another directive written by unaccountable, unelected bureaucrats that extended more coercive federal power into our schools. As always, the authors of the edict, far removed from the daily realities of schools, tried to hide behind the fiction that the letter was simply "guidance." But that was not true. Their rules were binding on public schools everywhere.

Within four years, the Obama administration's act of regulatory letter writing would run headlong into one of the worst school disasters in our history. What role it played in the disaster is disputed. But one thing is not disputed: It did nothing to stop it.

A s part of the Trump administration's regulatory eradication, I reviewed—and eventually retracted—hundreds of DOEd regulations and guidance letters in addition to the Title IX sexual harassment rule. The 2014 school discipline letter was begging to be retracted from the very beginning.

To be fair, the Obama discipline guidance was aimed at a real problem. Across the spectrum of race and gender, there are differences in suspension levels of students. For example, African-American students are much more likely to be suspended from K–12 schools than white students. Black students make up about 15 percent of public school students but represent around 39 percent of suspensions.[8] These suspensions, in turn, result in lost days of education, which lead to higher dropout rates, which result in lives lost to crime and incarceration—what is known as the "school to prison pipeline."

This is a reality in our schools that desperately needs to be addressed. But, as was their pattern, the Obama OCR took a misguided, top-down approach. They attempted to remedy this disparity by focusing on statistics rather than individual students.

The 2014 school discipline rule was modeled on a program begun in Broward County, Florida, by the school superintendent, a man named Robert Runcie. Runcie was a college pal of Obama education secretary Arne Duncan. He implemented a program called PROMISE (a burdensome acronym I won't try to repeat). PROMISE tackled the "school to prison pipeline" in Broward County by sending students who had committed misdemeanor offenses temporarily to alternative schools, where they could receive counseling instead of being suspended or arrested. Fans—like President Obama and Secretary of Education Duncan—hailed the program for involving fewer minority students in suspensions and the criminal justice system. Critics thought it let dangerous students off the hook and tied teachers' hands when it came to student discipline.

Like the PROMISE program, the Obama OCR letter mandated what is called "restorative justice." It directed schools to find nonpunitive ways of dealing with student misbehavior. Just like in Broward, instead of suspending the student or notifying the police, schools were told to send students to counseling or behavior support.

The new policy eliminated teachers' agency by forcing them to count by race when deciding what kind of discipline a student should receive. The language of the letter was positively Orwellian. A school would be found in violation of federal civil rights law if a policy is neutral on its face—meaning that **the policy itself does not mention race**—and is **administered in an evenhanded manner** but has a *disparate impact*, i.e., a disproportionate and unjustified *effect* on students of a particular race." (bold emphasis mine)[9]

In other words, if schools disciplined black and Hispanic students at higher rates than white students, they were in violation of federal civil rights law. Period. The rule did not encourage schools to root out acts of discrimination but to produce the right statistics. If the student body of a school was 25 percent African-American but 35 percent of the students being punished for misconduct were African-American, the school was "guilty." The "correct" rate of discipline for black students at the school, according to the rule, was the proportion of the student body that was black: 25 percent.

And, as ever, the penalty for being found in violation by OCR was death—the end of federal funding—for a school.

The unstated premise of the new policy was that the only thing that accounts for the disparity in discipline between white and minority students is the racism of teachers. It was the *teacher's discriminatory actions*, not the family circumstances, past trauma, or the quality of the education, that led to more African-American students being suspended or arrested. By taking the decision-making away from teachers, the rule implied, the racial disparity would be taken care of.

The Obama OCR set out to ensure schools knew they meant business by launching hundreds of systemic reviews of schools and school districts to ferret out violations of this new rule. Finding "guilty" schools was easy. All they had to do was look at the numbers. Schools with the wrong statistics were presumed to be in violation of federal civil rights laws. They were not exonerated until they adopted the Obama OCR's new discipline quota system.

Schools reacted to this heavy-handed approach in predictable ways. Teachers reported being under pressure not to "write up" minority students for discipline infractions. They complained about being forced to look the other way when certain students misbehaved. Violence increased and teachers reported feeling unsafe in classrooms. One teacher was pressured to ignore multiple threats from a student until the student acted on his threats and assaulted the teacher. Another teacher reported that a student who assaulted a classmate so violently that the victim was sent to the hospital was allowed to remain in school and get "counseling."

Then, on February 14, 2018, the unthinkable happened.

_____

That Wednesday morning, an eighteen-year-old walked into Marjory Stoneman Douglas High School and killed seventeen people with an AR-15 style semiautomatic rifle. I won't dignify him by using his name.[10] Marjory Stoneman Douglas was in Parkland, Florida, the heart of Broward County. The killer, who had been expelled from the school a year earlier, had a long record of violent behavior. Going back to middle school, he had repeated citations for fighting with classmates, being obsessed with guns, and other threatening and bizarre behavior. Broward Schools superintendent Robert Runcie initially denied that the killer had been part of the PROMISE program but later admitted that he had.

We were reviewing the Obama discipline letter long before the tragedy at Parkland. The loss of seventeen students and faculty added both controversy and urgency to our task. As more details came to light about the killer's troubled background, the tragedy put a national spotlight on the Broward County discipline program—and the Obama OCR policy it was based upon.

I did not wish to interfere in a community that was in pain and mourning, so I waited to visit Marjory Stoneman Douglas. When

I did go, on March 7, I purposefully kept a light footprint. I didn't want anyone in the school to feel like they were forced into conversation or engaging in any way. I tried to be respectful, but the mood was brittle. A few students thanked me for coming. Others shared haltingly about the pain they were navigating. Still others looked at me with hostility in their eyes.

The tragedy had already split the community into opposing camps. One contingent of students and parents blamed the Parkland event on the availability of guns. Others blamed what the South Florida *Sun Sentinel* called "a culture of leniency" in Broward County schools, in which "teachers are expressly told or subtly pressured not to send students to the administration for punishment."[11]

In an effort to clarify what had gone wrong and what could be done about it, President Trump asked me to head up a federal school safety commission. Attorney General Jeff Sessions, Secretary of Labor Alex Azar, and Secretary of Homeland Security Kirstjen Nielsen joined me on the commission. We were charged with seeking input from students, parents, teachers, school safety personnel, administrators, law enforcement officials, mental health professionals, school counselors—anyone who could help identify and elevate solutions to keeping schools safe.

As before with the transgender bathroom policy, Attorney General Sessions was intent on simply rescinding the Obama "Dear Colleague" discipline letter. Rather than work with and through the commission to include addressing the issue in the final report, he wanted to short-circuit the process.

"Betsy, I'm not gonna serve one more day with the daggum policy on my books!" the attorney general told me. As before, I argued that this was another emotionally, racially charged issue. We needed to take time to explain to the American people why we were taking—or not taking—action. It was the model that we were following with Title IX, and it was working.

This time, we prevailed. In a series of deeply painful meetings, I met with the parents of students killed at Parkland. One of them—Andrew Pollack—ended up writing a book on this topic.[12] We went across the country consulting with law enforcement and school officials who had been involved with previous school shootings.

We also met with teachers to hear what their classroom experiences had been and to get their input. Astoundingly, the national school union bosses supported the Obama policy. I wondered if they realized that the policy was premised on their members being conscious or unconscious racists. The local teacher unions, on the other hand, were more interested in keeping their members safe. One after another, teachers told us that "restorative justice" wasn't working in their classrooms. Conditions were getting more dangerous, they said. And minority students weren't getting the kind of support many of them needed.

The commission also studied what had been learned about other students who commit mass shooting in schools. The one thing that stood out like a flashing neon light was that all these young men had been widely known as potential threats to their schools and communities. In every case, there had been warning signs. It was a fact that our laws and regulations simply had to come to grips with.

The process of compiling the *Report of the Federal Commission on School Safety* was made more complicated than it should have been by internal administration issues. The final report wasn't published until December 18, 2018, when everyone was busy and distracted by the coming holidays. Despite the problems, the report turned out to be a valuable collection of best practices for schools to consider.[13]

We did not issue mandates—no one plan or approach will keep all schools safe. The report focused on policy recommendations, like expanded mental health services, strengthened background checks, and a tip line for students to anonymously report worrying behavior. It called on states to adopt "red flag laws" that prohibit individuals who pose a threat from possessing or purchasing firearms. It also recommended rescinding the 2014 school discipline letter, and acknowledging the importance of actually following civil rights law and not simply counting by race and ethnicity. We rescinded the letter three days after the report was released. Unfortunately, apart from the fact that we withdrew the Obama letter, the commission's extensive work never got the attention it deserved.*

We did more—much more—to defend civil rights and the rule of law than just curb the excesses of the previous administration. We solved civil rights cases, not only more judiciously but more quickly. We resolved 25 percent more cases "with change" (meaning requiring a school to take corrective action) than the Obama-Biden team did over a comparable time period, including resolving 78 percent more Title IX cases. We cut the pending case backlog by two-thirds.[14] While they had spent years building "systemic" cases against schools, we actually brought justice to more individual victims. We levied a record $4.5 million fine against Michigan State University for failing to protect its female athletes from sports doctor Larry Nassar. We resolved the nearly decade-long investigation into Jerry Sandusky's crimes at Penn State, for which a court had convicted him eight years earlier. We held Chicago public school officials accountable for decades of failure to respond to hundreds of sexual harassment complaints—many of them committed by adults on students. Chicago didn't even have a Title IX coordinator on staff.

In short, we put seeking justice back at the center of the Office for Civil Rights mission.

---

* You can read the full report at https://www2.ed.gov/documents/school-safety/school-safety-report.pdf.

CHAPTER SEVEN

THE HIGHER ED HIGHWAY

I t is an inconvenient fact for opponents of education freedom that the United States already has a robust policy of private education choice. It has produced an education system that is consistently ranked the best in the world. It has created American schools that are more sought after than schools in any other country.

I am referring, of course, to the U.S. higher education system. Students can take "public" money—Pell Grants, the GI Bill, or federal student loans—to any college or university they choose, regardless of whether it is public, private, or religious. The fact that they do this is uncontroversial. I didn't hear a single person criticize higher education choice while I was in Washington. Freedom of choice is what helped make our colleges and universities the best in the world.

Meanwhile, our elementary and high schools, which lack choice, lag behind those of our competitors.

Why it's fine for government funding to go to Notre Dame University but not Notre Dame Prep has never made any sense to me. But there is a lot about the way government works—or doesn't— that doesn't make sense.

Having school choice in higher education, so to speak, is the good news. The bad news is it's still largely a one-size-fits-all model. Go to college, sit through the right classes, get the requisite number of credits, and receive a degree. Our system of higher education is unrivaled. But the single-minded adherence to this educational approach has crowded out many other effective options and alternatives for post–high school learning. This problem has been exacerbated in recent years by the push for everyone to go to college, and the not-so-subtle message that those who don't are "less than."

This message has come from the highest levels. In his first address to Congress, President Barack Obama made a pledge to the youth of America. "We will provide the support for you to complete college and meet a new goal," he said. "By 2020, America will once again have the highest proportion of college graduates in the world." His education secretary, Arne Duncan, called producing more college graduates the administration's "North Star."

Obama's goal was tied to the growing cultural belief that a college degree was the only route to the middle class. More than that, the implication was clear that a college degree was the only route to *respectability*. It was the thing smart people did. As a result, Americans increasingly looked down on vocational education or associate's degrees. Anything less than a four-year degree was seen as second-rate.

Dr. Virginia Foxx, the Republican chair of the House Education and Workforce Committee, explained the damage of this message as well and as passionately as anyone else. She often repeated the mantra, "All education is career education." She was right. She added, "Whether an individual acquires a skill credential, a bachelor's degree, a postgraduate degree, or anything in between, it's all education. We need to think about the words we use and why we use them if we are to break the stigma around all forms of education. If we don't, we will never overcome the abiding sense of inequality and unfairness that so many Americans feel."[1]

This unfairness has for decades been rooted in how the elites denigrate the value of craftsmanship, of working with your hands, of imagining and building the companies that keep America running. Perhaps I'm biased because I come from a manufacturing family in a manufacturing state. Michigan is the place that put the world on wheels. I know firsthand that there is value and dignity in all work.

Rich or poor, black or white, eventually everyone needs a plumber, an electrician, an auto mechanic, a nurse. You would think we would celebrate those who find a path to a well-paying career without taking on as much burdensome student loan debt. But we really don't. Our leaders, our policies, and our culture continue to treat going to college as the be-all and end-all.

A vicious cycle of bad incentives followed this bias toward four-year degrees. More students than ever headed to college—many who would have done as well or better without a four-year degree. Student loans skyrocketed, fueling increases in the price of college, as there was no governor on what schools charged for their services. Federal loan forgiveness programs encouraged students and parents to take on even more debt, which fed the top-line revenues of colleges and ballooned individual students' tuition, which fed the need for more loans, and so on and so on. A self-perpetuating cycle of more federal loans feeding rising education costs developed. *Wall Street Journal* reporter Josh Mitchell dubbed this phenomenon "The Debt Trap," arguing that student loans have become a national catastrophe as Congress and previous administrations "ignored red flags."[2]

All the while, few of our leaders took the time to examine whether or not what they were saying was correct: Is a four-year degree really the better path to the middle class? According to compiled Federal Reserve data, the answer is no. The Fed reports that the cost of college grew *eight times* faster than wages did from 1989 to 2016.[3] It's hard to secure a better life when the price of doing so far outpaces what you might earn.

Just to be clear, suggesting that some students might be better off pursuing other options is not a proxy argument for saying some students should be excluded from higher education. This is the kind of race-and-class-tinged warfare that the education establishment loves to peddle. Everyone who wants to go to college should have the opportunity. Colleges and universities should be doing *more* to be accessible, especially to lower-income and first-time students.

But the fact is, despite all their talk of inclusiveness, higher education is limiting options for less-advantaged students today. Colleges and universities are doing away with screens for the academic capabilities of students in the name of openness, but their more substantive actions are making American higher education less accessible and less inclusive. Much of that starts with the runaway cost of a college degree, but it extends to the lack of tolerance for divergent opinions and the outright canceling of professors and speakers who don't parrot the liberal dogma of ivory tower academia.

———————

My experience with higher education policy as education secretary underscored something I've known for a long time: There is a fundamental disconnect between our system of education and our economy.

Going to college has always been seen as a good thing because the credential earned—a four-year degree—sent a previously valuable signal to employers. And that's still true for lots of students. But the return on investment for college simply isn't as pronounced as many proclaim. While there is clear correlation between receiving a college degree and earning a higher income, it is not as clear that there is causation. Those who go to college often have other

attributes, including parental educational attainment and household income, that also make them statistically more likely to achieve
success.[4]

We need to reconsider whether all these credentials match what
students and employers need today. Too many students graduate only to
learn that their degree is an expensive—and unnecessary—mismatch.

Today, across states and industries, there are 6 million–plus job
openings. There are an estimated 30 million "good" jobs that don't
require a bachelor's degree.[5] The "blue-collar" jobs of yesterday have
morphed and proliferated into the "take your pick" or "gig" jobs of
today. Coding is an increasingly necessary skill, much like riveting
or stamping was a few decades back. But employers report that there
are not enough Americans qualified and prepared to fill these myriad
positions. The skilled jobs of today require specific preparation and
customized certification. American higher education is simply not
readying students for these kinds of careers.

In today's reality, it is also less and less likely that a single degree
will sustain a thirty-plus year career or that someone will stay in the
same career for their productive lifetime. Lifelong learning opportunities should continue to become the rule rather than the exception.

President Trump clearly understood something President Obama
didn't: There is more than one way to be successful in America. Not
everyone needs to go to college. However, our culture, driven by
traditional higher education, considers career and technical education
something less than "real" education. The system silos these opportunities off from liberal arts or STEM degrees like they are consola-
tion prizes. But these education pursuits are as valid and important
as other pursuits of study.

I long suspected that this career and technical education stigma
was reflected in the career advice high school students were receiving. To test my theory, we convened a meeting of guidance counselors from around the country to discuss college and career pathways

for students. I was disappointed but unsurprised to hear that very few of them had offered many resources to students on options other than going to college. Choices like apprenticeships, for instance, were rarely mentioned. To their credit, most of the counselors left the meeting with a desire to improve and expand the array of options they presented.

Other parts of the world embrace a more holistic approach to education. We visited Switzerland in 2018 to learn about the highly integrated way they approach lifelong education. We learned about how commonplace apprenticeships and other "earn and learn" opportunities are for high school students.

Nearly three-quarters of Swiss high school students participate in education and training programs that combine school learning with learning in the workplace—in other words, apprenticeships. And unlike in the United States, where apprenticeships are uncommon outside of building trades, in Switzerland they encompass everything from trades skills to health care and finance. Both the CEO and the chairman of the Swiss global financial giant UBS started their careers at the bank with apprenticeships.

I met a young woman from Minnesota who started an apprenticeship in high school at Bühler, a Swiss manufacturing company with operations in Minneapolis. She continued working with Bühler after high school and by the time we met she had her own home, her own car, and a retirement account. She was still in her early twenties and had just accepted a promotion with the company for a position in Switzerland. She was the poster child for the power and possibilities of apprenticeships.

One notable lesson for America from Switzerland is that business and community leaders there don't ask for approval from government to partner with educators. They just do it. They identify needs and proactively take steps to fill them by creating new apprenticeships and preparing students to be professionals. As someone who thrives on hands-on learning, I would have loved those opportunities when I was in school.

President Trump and his daughter Ivanka had a genuine interest in creating more apprenticeships in America as accredited alternatives to traditional four-year degrees. This was an important part of the mission of the Council for the American Worker, which Ivanka chaired. After I went to Switzerland, I visited a community college in Northern Virginia that partnered with Amazon to create a technical apprenticeship for military veterans. Like the Swiss, they simply took the initiative. They identified a need and created the program.

Valencia College in Orlando does something similar. They meet first-generation students where they are, giving them the chance to take colleges classes and earn associate's degrees while they're still in high school. When a student completes one of Valencia's associate degree programs with a qualifying GPA, they gain automatic admission to Florida's state universities to complete a four-year degree if they choose to pursue that avenue.

Valencia makes learning relevant to real-world jobs for students. They have a semitruck trailer that houses large construction equipment simulators. It's mobile, so students at all of their campuses can access them. I couldn't pass up the chance to take a turn on a simulator for a front-loader. It was great fun!

I also had the opportunity to give the commencement speech at Butler Tech Career Center in Ohio. Butler Tech high school teams up with local employers to educate students in health care, engineering, cosmetology, automotive engineering, aviation, and the list goes on. Butler students are in high demand.

Their career-readiness is reflected in their commencement ceremony. When students finish the program at Butler Tech, they have a "signing day" in which graduates announce the company with which they're going to work. When I attended signing day, I watched as the graduates of Butler Tech ceremoniously put on the hats of the businesses they've chosen—and that have chosen them. It's a celebratory occasion, with lots of proud families in the audience.

Butler Tech's graduation tradition is a play on how student athletes have a "signing day" to announce which college they've chosen to attend. Students who have prepared to go to work in construction, health care, or cosmetology should be valued as highly as those who have prepared to play football or basketball. They all merit celebration. It was a high honor for me to be there that day and help widen the aperture on who all "signs" after finishing high school.

But these kinds of programs are still outliers in America today. At the Department of Education, we worked with the Department of Labor to create something called IRAPs—industry-recognized apprenticeship programs—to help scale up these opportunities. IRAPs encouraged businesses to create programs and "credential" graduates with a certificate or a degree that showed the student had met the industry standards for employment. It was a great idea that labor unions effectively killed in its infancy.

However, that didn't stop us from trying to connect employers with students. We worked with Congress to update the federal Perkins career education law to accomplish the same end. The Perkins Act gives states and communities federal grants to use for career and technical education. We removed all the federal strings and freed state and local leaders to use these funds in the way they deem best based upon their state's unique opportunities. Colorado, for instance, has used its funding from the Perkins law to create its own Swiss-style apprenticeship program. Any governor or mayor with a clear view of their respective state's or city's situation and a creative idea can do the same today.

Ultimately, to expand higher education opportunities, we need to expand our thinking about what education actually is and what it is for. The goal, at all times, should be to provide a multitude of pathways to quality education. Anyone who wants to better himself or herself should have that opportunity. I've always imagined careers to be like highways, not one-way or dead-end streets. Students should be able to exit the highway easily to learn something new, then reenter the highway at an on-ramp of their choosing. They should be able to change lanes when they want to. But the route to a traditional four-year degree can't be smooth pavement while the roads to other options are rutted gravel.

The federal government has a much more significant role in higher education than in K–12 education. This is overwhelmingly due to one thing: federal student loans. The federal government has insinuated itself into higher education under the cover of "helping" Americans pay for colleges and universities. What has resulted hasn't been good for students, their pocketbooks, or their future employment.

The Obama administration backed up their ambitious rhetoric on increasing college graduates by doing something that hasn't gotten nearly as much attention as it should: They executed a complete federal takeover of the student loan system.

Previously, student loans were issued by private banks and backed by the federal government. But in 2010, the federal government became the sole lender of student loans. Interestingly, it was Broward County school superintendent Robert Runcie's brother, James Runcie, who oversaw the Obama student loan takeover. James Runcie was the head of federal student loans for the department when I became secretary. Early on in my tenure, when Congress held a hearing on improper payments in the federal student loan program, I asked him to testify. He refused. Then I required him to testify. Rather than appear before Congress, Runcie resigned at midnight the day before the hearing.

After the takeover, the Department of Education became responsible for the largest direct loan portfolio in the entire federal government. Federal student loans are the second-largest source of consumer debt in America, just behind mortgage debt. Americans take out more student debt than credit cards or car loans.[6] Overnight, the department was essentially one of the nation's largest banks.

The government's rationale for making itself the sole provider of federal student loans sounded appealing at first (as rationales for government intervention almost always do). The Obama administration claimed that having the government grant the loans instead of paying private banks to do so would save money. Those savings, in turn, would be used to expand aid to low-income students and pay for Obamacare. It would be a win-win. That was the intention. That was the theory.

Well, good intentions absent sound economics just don't work.

It took more than forty years—from 1965, when the federal student loan program was created, until 2007—for the federal loan balance to reach $500 billion. It took just *six years*—from 2007 to 2013—for that balance to double to $1 trillion—that's $1,000,000,000,000. By 2018, when I was secretary of education, $1.5 trillion in federal student loans was outstanding. By the time repayments were halted because of the COVID-19 pandemic in March 2020, the federal government had extended $1.6 trillion in student loans.

Of course, student loans aren't just financial products. Each one represents a student with dreams. Families with hopes. Better and brighter futures.

More cynically, for the people in charge in Washington, these loans represent *voters*.

The politicians couldn't help themselves. The student loan portfolio was now wholly owned by the federal government, and they had *plans* for it. After encouraging students to borrow more, President Obama immediately introduced ways for them to repay less. Instead of the usual ten-year, fixed payment plan, students were given a new choice of a repayment plan based on how much they made after graduating. The feds would take anything from 0 to 10 percent of a graduate's income for up to twenty-five years as repayment. The payment period was just ten years if the graduate was employed in "public service," that is, working for the government or a nonprofit policy organization. Whatever was left of the loan after that period would be forgiven.

The Obama administration's calculation that federalizing student loans would be a moneymaker was based on only a small percentage of borrowers choosing the income-based repayment option. But—surprise!—borrowers flocked to these programs in numbers far outpacing their projections. The administration's math had always been too good to be true. When government makes loans and then tells the borrowers they don't have to pay them all back, there is going to be a shortfall. And *someone* pays.

In 2018, the nonpartisan Congressional Budget Office (CBO) projected that, instead of producing a surplus—"making money"—the federalization of student loans would *cost* the taxpayers $31 billion over the next decade.[7] I, along with friends in the administration like National Economic Council director Larry Kudlow, had always strongly suspected that the Obama administration's calculation was overly optimistic. In fact, most of the deficit was the result of income-based repayment. The Obama administration's effort to appeal to young voters with cheaper student loans was working—to the detriment of the taxpayers. Less money was being repaid by the borrowers, so costs to the Treasury continued to go up.

The politicization of student lending didn't stop with income-based repayment. Candidates for the Democratic presidential nomination in 2020 competed with each other to see who could promise more student loan forgiveness. Bernie Sanders, Elizabeth Warren, and, eventually, Joe Biden, all started talking about making college "free."

President Trump was not immune to the politics of student loans. But behind the sunny rhetoric of free money for young Americans is a complicated system of incentives and disincentives that the president did not take the time to understand. As the campaign for the 2020 election intensified, he was more and more tempted to pander to borrowers by promising loan forgiveness. At one point, I worried he would end up supporting a congressional effort to overturn a rule we had developed to curb abuses of a student loan forgiveness program. Fortunately, he did not.

————————

"Free college" may be a nice-sounding campaign promise. In practice, it's really bad policy with myriad, layered problems.

"Free" college tuition, while not actually free, would also not be free of government control. It would amount to a government take-over of higher education. After all, that which government funds, government controls.

Recall Obamacare and President Obama's now-infamous quote: "If you like your health care plan, you can keep it." It was named the "Lie of the Year."[8] People all across the country lost access to the doctors and their health care plans because of the federal takeover. Why would anyone believe a takeover of higher education would end differently? We've already seen what the K–12 system has become while under monopolistic government control.

If the federal government takes full control of higher education, it is almost certain that, before long, the "school choice" American college students enjoy would be eliminated. Rationing of degrees likely wouldn't be far behind. Politicians would argue that redirecting students from the degree they are interested in to the one "most needed," or just plain available once the rationing sets in, is in the public interest, and the public is paying the bill. At best, government control would eliminate, rather than expand, the diversity of choice that makes U.S. higher education sought after today.

Free college via mass loan forgiveness is just a more complicated route to government-controlled higher education. As I write this,

Democrats like Senate Majority Leader Chuck Schumer want the
president to unilaterally forgive an astounding $50,000 per borrower,
despite the fact that 60 percent of borrowers owe less than $20,000.[9]
At a total cost of more than $1 trillion, the Democrats' plan would be
double the amount taxpayers have spent on Pell Grants for low-income
students during the past twenty years.[10] President Biden has said
he is unsure if he has the authority to abolish student debt without
congressional buy-in. But his hesitancy seems to have affected only
the *amount* he will promise to forgive. He has committed to forgiving
"only" $10,000 per student, a paltry $373 billion escapade. The more
"modest" Biden plan would cost taxpayers more than the cost of
providing free and reduced breakfast and lunch in every school in
America for twenty years.[11]

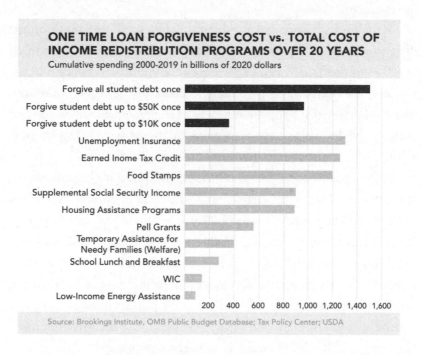

**ONE TIME LOAN FORGIVENESS COST vs. TOTAL COST OF
INCOME REDISTRIBUTION PROGRAMS OVER 20 YEARS**
Cumulative spending 2000-2019 in billions of 2020 dollars

Source: Brookings Institute, OMB Public Budget Database; Tax Policy Center; USDA

Mass student loan forgiveness isn't money that President Biden
has to spend. The inability or unwillingness of some politicians to

acknowledge this fact is another example of the disconnect between Washington and the people whose money they play with. These student loans have been issued by American taxpayers. We're all picking up the tab when they are not repaid.

The media would have everyone believe that student loans are primarily held by the poor. That would be, to borrow a phrase, fake news.

According to data from the Federal Reserve, the highest-earning 40 percent of households owe nearly 60 percent of the total outstanding student loan debt. More than half of the outstanding debt is from households with graduate degrees, which comprise only 14 percent of total American households.[12]

On top of that, less than one-third of Americans pursue a four-year degree or have a student loan in the first place, leaving the other two-thirds—including those who didn't need a college degree for their chosen career, who saved, or who already paid off their loans—to foot the bill.[13]

In sum, this means mass student loan forgiveness is a reverse Robin Hood—a transfer from the poor and middle class to the rich.

Elizabeth Warren was reminded of this when she was running for the Democratic presidential nomination in 2020. She had the kind of encounter with a taxpayer we would soon see more of when angry parents confronted school board members over school closures and anti-American curricula.

A father came up to Senator Warren at an event in Iowa and said her plan to forgive student debt would "screw" people who paid for college by themselves.

"My daughter is getting out of school. I've saved all my money. She doesn't have any student loans. Am I going to get my money back?" the man asked Warren.

She said no, he wouldn't.

"So you're going to pay for people who didn't save any money and those of us who did the right thing get screwed," the man replied. He was right.

Politicians, take note. Americans, it seems, understand economics better than you do. And they can't all be bought off by promises of free money.

I asked every college president I met where they spent most of their time, and almost every single one replied "development" (read: fundraising). Despite the ever-rising cost of tuition, there never seems to be enough cash on campus.

One factor is an amenities arms race that has gripped residential schools. Enrollment decisions have become less about academic quality and more like picking a cruise ship or resort, sorting out which school has the nicest pool, the biggest bathrooms, and the best climbing wall. It's hard to find a campus where a new building isn't under construction. The construction crane is the symbol of a campus whose tuition is—literally—on the rise.

None of this does much to improve academic outcomes, of course. It doesn't ensure that the programs offered are relevant to the job market and economy. Or that faculty are challenging and encouraging students. It doesn't guarantee that ideas are debated and debate is welcomed.

In fact, too little of higher education is actually about education at all. It's a problem exacerbated, in part, by the sweetheart deal schools enjoy. Students take out the loans, but the colleges take their cut first. In fact, the Department of Education's Federal Student Aid office actually issues the loan disbursement to the school, which then sends a "refund" check to the student for any excess funds after tuition and fees. After taking out all this debt, students suffer economically if they aren't well prepared for the workforce, but the school is never held accountable. Students are evaluated based on academic achievement to earn admission, but there is no type of cumulative assessment to gauge what a student learned in college in order to receive the degree.

Even the core measure of higher education attainment—the credit hour—is centered on the enrichment of adults. (Students, if you're noticing a theme, you're right.) Most people assume a credit hour is a reference to the hour-long course the student has taken. In fact, it is a credit the professor receives toward his or her pension for having taught for the hour.[14]

That's right: The core unit of measurement for study at a university isn't actually about student learning at all. The credit hour system, popularized by Andrew Carnegie, came about at the turn of the century (*last* century)—another outdated education model that limits students today. The idea that the amount of time spent learning is somehow a proxy for *what* is learned defies logic, but it dominates all our education structures. K–12, which typically requires 180 school days per year, is hardly different.

Some have sought to challenge this antiquated notion. You may have heard of Western Governors University (WGU). It is a nonprofit online university that was formed by governors of western states. As the school became more popular, it expanded eastward.[15] WGU has long enjoyed broad, bipartisan support because their results have been exceptional. Among a number of things that makes them different, they use a competency-based (or mastery) education model. Instead of moving a student through a course in a defined time period (that is, the credit hour), WGU students move at the pace at which they demonstrate command of the subject matter. As a result, students who "get it" can move through their courses more rapidly, while those who need more time to learn a concept can have it.[16]

It makes good sense, but it challenges the higher education orthodoxy. So, naturally, it comes under attack.

The Department of Education has an inspector general (IG) that is meant to be a watchdog, auditing grantees and holding government accountable. But like everything else in Washington, the IG is far from independent of politics. And in the federal government, the politics is devoted to protecting the status quo.

When I came to office, the Education Department IG was investigating WGU. They claimed the school didn't provide sufficient professor-student interaction, based on an interpretation of regulations developed before the internet came of age. The IG recommended hitting WGU with a $713,000,000 fine, which was about the total yearly budget of the school.[17] Such a fine would effectively have been the "death penalty" for WGU, a successful competitor to traditional, nonprofit higher education. So we intervened. We painstakingly took apart the inspector general's faulty findings, leaving them little choice but to concur with our decision.[18] No fine was issued, and WGU continues to provide a quality education option today.

There's another problem with money in higher education that doesn't get enough attention.

Section 117 of the Higher Education Act requires colleges and universities to report gifts from foreign sources totaling more than $250,000.[19] It's a pretty cut-and-dried provision intended to bring transparency to foreign influence on our schools. The problem? No one was complying.

The issue came to the public's attention initially because of the Confucius Institutes, the Chinese Communist Party–controlled and funded education programs that were popping up at schools across the United States. They were represented as cultural exchanges, but it quickly became clear that there was no freedom of academic inquiry for any topic critical of the Chinese government at the institutes.[20]

We launched an investigation to see just how much foreign money had silently crept into our universities. A review of just twelve schools yielded $6.5 billion in previously unreported foreign donations. Subsequently, sixty schools that had *never* reported a single foreign donation filed a report for the first time.[21]

In reports filed in the summer of 2020, donations originating from Qatar, China, Saudi Arabia, and the United Arab Emirates totaled $1.05 billion. There's good reason to believe many of these countries, especially our global adversaries, are attempting nothing short of espionage via higher education institutions.

Consider the case of Professor Charles Lieber, formerly the chemistry and chemical biology chair at Harvard, who was convicted of concealing his work with the Chinese government.[22] Lieber, who was secretly on the payroll of a Chinese program designed to gather strategic military intelligence, was also the recipient of more than $15 million in U.S. research grants, many from the U.S. Department of Defense.

None of this deterred the higher education lobby. They wrote us, saying "it is now impossible for institutions to know how to comply" with their Section 117 requirements.[23] It was inexplicable that a group of prestigious academics and lawyers, most with advanced degrees, couldn't understand how to report the foreign funding they received. You would almost think they wanted to keep it a secret.

Despite all the headwinds, we made real progress in improving the federal student loan system for both borrowers and taxpayers. One area that desperately needed cleaning up when I became secretary was the consumer—or the student—facing side of the process. There were eight different repayment plans for students to choose from, each with different eligibility requirements. There were more than thirty variations of deferment and forbearance options. There were fourteen forgiveness options. And unbelievably, all this information was handled by eleven different servicers, all with totally separate websites and platforms, phone numbers, and forms.

My expectations of government efficiency and effectiveness are not high, but I was shocked to discover that, in 2017, there was no single, accessible website that students could load onto their tablet or phone to use to manage their student loans. The average student had 4.8 student loans. That meant he or she could have as many as five different servicers to connect with in order see how much they owed. Five different sets of forms to complete. Five different numbers to call and wait on hold to know if their last payment had been received.

Students have lots of reasons to not pay their student loans, some good and some not so good. I didn't want woefully outdated communications technology to be one of them. So we transformed the system. We brought all federal student loan services behind one digital gateway. In the private sector, what we did would not be considered groundbreaking. But in government, it was revolutionary. We created a one-stop resource for borrowers, an app called myStudentAid. There, for the first time ever, students could apply for student loans, check balances, view past payments, and receive notifications on their phone for future payments.

What's more, we significantly expanded the data that the government provides to students before they take out loans, called the College Scorecard. We broke down data for each school by department and field of study. Students can use this information to determine how much they will be expected to pay and what they can expect to earn once they graduate from a particular program or field of study. Previously, this information was obscured by "average" or "median" income earned by graduates of an entire institution. Averaging together the salaries of a doctor and a newspaper reporter does not exactly yield a meaningful data point. If student loans are going to be controlled by the federal government, I was determined to administer them with transparency and responsibility.

Another significant change was to the federal work-study rules. Students used to have to work on campus, in the cafeteria, the computer lab, or the bookstore to participate in work-study. Most of those jobs were not relevant to what they were pursing educationally.

We changed the rules to enable them to work off campus in any job in their field of study.

We also worked to free up the higher education marketplace. Competition among colleges and universities had long been suffocated by accrediting agencies that protected existing schools from any innovative newcomer. We changed this process to end federal government micromanagement and give more accreditors more flexibility to approve new schools and new approaches to learning.

Importantly, we also implemented meaningful reforms to help marginalized students access higher education. I was honored to give the commencement address at a maximum-security prison in Oklahoma that partnered with Tulsa Community College (TCC) on what they called the Second Chance program. Around fifty inmates were receiving high school diplomas, certificates, associate's degrees, and even a bachelor's degree. TCC provided both in-person and online teaching at the prison. The room was filled with families, mentors, and friends cheering for someone who had completed the program. It was a very moving—and intense—experience.

We acted to foster more of these "second chance" programs for prisons. The 1994 Clinton-Biden crime bill made it illegal for incarcerated people to qualify for federal student aid, effectively ensuring that none of them had a chance to pursue education. President Obama worked around that by starting a pilot program to allow inmates to qualify for grants through the Second Chance Pell program. We expanded the pilot program and made it permanent in federal law.

While the cost of higher education climbs ever higher, everything else seems to be going downhill.

Institutions that were built on advancing knowledge and fostering rigorous debate have become emaciated shadows of their former selves. Assaults on free speech and academic freedom that were once infrequent transgressions have become daily occurrences. And for conservatives on campus, the environment has deteriorated from uncomfortable to unacceptable. I won't recite or catalog the many attacks on free speech, free inquiry, and academic exploration that rot the learning experience on all too many campuses, for they are well documented.*

All of this tends to get dismissed in the corporate media as Republican whining. But what's going on is far more serious than that. When institutions limit what students can learn or debate—when they censor what they are exposed to—they shrink students' horizons and stunt their growth. In short, they don't deliver a true education.

It's becoming commonplace now for university administrators to shut down lectures or research that is deemed "hateful" or "offensive." This is patronizing to students, built on an assumption that they can't—or, more accurately, *shouldn't*—learn from, respond to, and wrestle with ideas with which they disagree or that are objectionable. To the contrary, institutions of higher education *should* be presenting the widest array of views to empower students to form their own views on life's questions.

That's not to be confused with ensuring learning remains the pursuit of truth. There are and should be divergent opinions on things like politics, philosophy, and culture. But schools have an obligation to students to not lose sight of the fact that there are absolute truths, whether one acknowledges them or not. Too many colleges and universities today are caught up in the idea of "finding your own truth"—and why would you spend tens of thousands of dollars to do something you could do on your own? Discovering your truth is an innocent-sounding thought—maybe even a worthwhile endeavor. But for an education institution, such an approach is highly deceptive and

---

* Consider, among other sources, the Foundation for Individual Rights in Education's annual report: https://rankings.thefire.org/.

destructive. It is an attempt to dismiss the fact that some people are simply wrong, that some theories have been disproven, and that some ideas just will not work.

Colleges and universities today are creating more and more intellectual forbidden zones. Some censor themselves and their students based on ideology; some do it out of fear. Today's professor cannot verbalize views that are out of the "accepted mainstream" without fear of retaliation or so-called canceling.

There was an alarming example involving University of Pennsylvania law professor Amy Wax. Professor Wax wrote an op-ed describing her belief that the cultural values of midcentury America—strong families, hard work, civic-mindedness, and charity among them—led to the significant advances the country enjoyed.[24] The response? Widespread calls for her termination.[25] There was little effort expended on rebutting Wax's arguments or presenting an alternative hypothesis.

Or take the case of Dr. William "Ajax" Peris, a political science lecturer at the University of California, Los Angeles and a veteran of the U.S. Air Force. While teaching a class on racism, Dr. Peris read aloud the words of Dr. Martin Luther King Jr.'s "Letter from a Birmingham Jail"—including Dr. King's use of the "N" word. This prompted outrage from students and an investigation of Dr. Peris by UCLA.[26] No one discussed whether censoring historical documents, no less the very words of Dr. King, would have been a better and more effective way to teach the lesson.

I could fill the rest of this book with such examples. They're lamentably common. What is less common is an acknowledgment that all of this is lunacy. And it's tearing apart the very fiber of what makes higher education work.

In 2020, Abigail Shrier wrote a book called *Irreversible Damage: The Transgender Craze Seducing Our Daughters*. For daring to question the nature of transgenderism in the West today, and to point out the danger of children taking puberty blockers and cross-sex hormones,

Shrier's book was banned from the shelves at Target. Amazon would not let her publisher run ads for the book on their website. The American Civil Liberties Union—the "civil libertarian" group that used to defend the free speech of Nazis—called the book "a dangerous polemic"—that is, dangerous speech.[27]

Shrier has been held up as a prime example of a victim of the "cancel culture"—and rightly so. She was punished by much of the tech world, social media, and the mainstream media for stating beliefs they disagreed with. After coming through that onslaught with her principles intact, Shrier gave a speech to students at Princeton that thoughtfully pointed out to them who are the real victims of today's war against free speech: students at institutions like Princeton. They are slowly being robbed of their freedom and their free will by what she called the "force-fed falsehoods we are all expected to take seriously." Then she listed some examples:

"Some men have periods and get pregnant." "Hard work and objectivity are hallmarks of whiteness." "Only a child knows her own true gender." "Transwomen don't have an unfair advantage when playing girls' sports."[28]

This last lie, that it's fair for transgender women to compete on girls' and women's sports teams, is something we grappled with when I was in office. It is a growing threat to women's sports that we would have likely spent a lot of time on in a second term. The issue came into national focus in early 2022 when Penn swimmer Lia Thomas, who had previously competed on the men's team, joined the women's team and began smashing records.

For me, the issue of transgender women competing on women's sports teams was different than the issue of bathroom access. My strong, federalist sense with regard to school bathrooms is that schools and districts should have the latitude to develop policies that ensure the privacy and safety of all students. The Obama directive that schools had to allow students to use the bathroom of their perceived gender prohibited those commonsense solutions.

But in the case of women's sports, there can be no policy developed by the school or the district that ensures fairness to all students while allowing transgender athletes to compete on women's teams. In Connecticut, two transgender sprinters—who competed on the girls' team thanks to state policy that allows biological males to compete on girls' teams—were obliterating female track records in the state. Several members of the team sued the state over the policy. One of the plaintiffs, Chelsea Mitchell, was ranked the fastest female in the 55-meter dash in Connecticut. But she had lost two state championships and multiple other races to the transgender runners.

"That's a devastating experience," she wrote in *USA Today*. "It tells me that I'm not good enough; that my body isn't good enough; and that no matter how hard I work, I am unlikely to succeed, because I'm a woman."[29]*

For me, the legal question was straightforward. Title IX explicitly forbids discrimination on the basis of "sex." It also allows for the segregation of men's and women's sports on the basis of sex. But when sex is replaced by the idea of a subjective, changeable gender, Title IX becomes unenforceable. And one of the main things the law helped protect—women's athletics—becomes a thing of the past. We resolved the complaint in favor of the young women athletes in Connecticut, arguing that drafters of Title IX clearly meant biological sex when they cited sex in the law. If the state wanted a different meaning for Title IX, they had to ask Congress to amend the law.

At its core, this dispute goes far deeper than different interpretations of the law. It goes to the difference between the truth and a lie. Do we timidly and compliantly parrot what we know is a lie, or do we understand and acknowledge what is true? Are we people who are willing to sacrifice freedom and free will for a falsehood, or people

---

* Throughout her op-ed, Mitchell referred to the transgender runners as "male." After publishing the piece, and without notifying Mitchell, *USA Today* changed all references to the runners to "transgender." They apologized for the "hurtful language."

who are determined to speak the truth and accept the consequences? We were determined to side with the truth. The Biden Education Department reversed our decision almost immediately upon coming into office.

These fights remind me of what Nebraska senator Ben Sasse, a former college president, wrote in his great book, *The Vanishing American Adult*: "The generation now coming of age is going to need even greater grit and resilience . . . critical thinking, the thoughtful contesting of ideas, and individuals willing to stand up for what they believe, even when challenged."[30]

We embrace far too little of that these days. Principled stands are replaced with virtue signaling. Our rising generations are the casualties.

In September 2020, Princeton's president, Christopher Eisgruber, wrote a letter outlining his school's history with "systemic racism."[31] He wrote that "[r]acist assumptions . . . remain embedded in structures of the University itself." He was quite unabashed in his criticism of Princeton's racism and the harm it had caused to minorities.

Title VI of the Civil Rights Act requires that schools not deny anyone access to education based on their race. Princeton annually affirmed, in writing, that they do not discriminate. You cannot on the one hand say that you do not discriminate, that you are not racist, and then on the other hand produce a letter full of verbal vomit to tell the world that you are systemically racist. Eisgruber's mea culpa required us to take action, so my team sent a letter to Princeton asking for more details about its self-reported history of racism.[32] His response was filled with the kind of mental gymnastics only a cadre of university professors and lawyers could create. Our point was made.

CHAPTER EIGHT

THE EDUCATION FREEDOM AGENDA

"We were told: 'Just go home. Let us do what we do.'" That sentence still haunts me every time I hear my friend Tera Myers say it. She and her son, Samuel, who has Down syndrome, were in a struggle with their assigned public school in Ohio. Samuel was being bullied. He wasn't learning the way Tera knew he could. When she complained to the school, they told her in patronizing words that they didn't think she should be telling them how Samuel could and should learn. "This is all you get—like it or not," they added.

But to parents, these are fighting words. And Tera fought back.

She and other school choice advocates twice succeeded in getting Ohio legislators to pass a scholarship program for special needs students like Samuel. And twice, Democratic governor Ted Strickland vetoed the bills. Tera was beginning to think that education freedom wouldn't happen for Samuel in his lifetime. Then she saw opportunity when Republican John Kasich was elected governor in 2010. He signed the special needs scholarship law, and Tera almost single-handedly created a program at a local private school that would meet the needs of students like Samuel.

Nothing can stop a mom on a mission.

Annette "Polly" Williams was a Milwaukee mom and Democratic Wisconsin assemblywoman. When her daughter was turned away from a majority-white school because it had already filled its racial quota, Polly was incensed that she couldn't determine where her daughter went to school. She rejected the idea that African-American kids had to be bused to majority-white schools to get a decent education. Her daughter deserved a quality education as much as any other.

Polly devoted her adult life to pursuing quality education for poor and minority kids. She worked with a governor of another race and another political party—Tommy Thompson—to accomplish what neither of them could do alone. Polly became "the mother of school choice" when the nation's longest-lived private school voucher program was created in Milwaukee in 1990.

That's right. The oldest private school choice program in the country was started by a Democrat. The first charter school law was as well. And both programs had bipartisan support.

In Washington, DC, another single mother of a fifteen-year-old son, Virginia Walden Ford, took on the DC Democratic machine to create the DC Opportunity Scholarship Program. They lived in a tough neighborhood in DC that was run by gangs and drug dealers. That extended to the school Virginia's son, William, attended. She worried he would not succeed, and maybe not live, if he stayed in that environment.

Virginia knew she had to get her son out. She took on a third job in an attempt to be able to pay the tuition at a nearby Catholic school. But even with giving literally everything she had, Virginia couldn't make it work.

That's when it hit her how unjust government-assigned education truly was.

And that's saying something. Virginia had known education inequality in her life. She was among the first students to integrate Little Rock Central High School in Arkansas following the landmark

Brown v. Board of Education decision from the U.S. Supreme Court in 1954. She had endured and overcome a racist governor trying to stop kids like her from going to better schools.[1]

She wasn't about to let what was happening to William stand, either. Virginia went door-to-door to rally support. She rallied parents to attend school board meetings, where they were condescendingly dismissed as being "problem parents" (sound familiar?). She walked the marble halls of Congress until her feet wouldn't take her any farther.

Finally, in 2003, powerful people started listening. District of Columbia mayor Anthony Williams and Councilman Kevin Chavous, both Democrats, took a courageous stand to back Virginia's plan for a scholarship program.[2] The plan had friends in Congress, including Texas congressman Dick Armey, who bluntly addressed the situation from his committee dais: "We walk away from these kids in every regard. We never fix these schools."[3]

The scholarship plan had another powerful friend in education-minded president George W. Bush. Momentum really grew when Democrat senators Joe Lieberman of Connecticut and Dianne Feinstein of California joined other champions like Arizona senator Jeff Flake and Ohio congressman John Boehner. In December 2003, Virginia Walden Ford's dream became law, creating new educational opportunities for thousands of DC kids.[4]

Her story was turned into a beautiful movie, *Miss Virginia*, in 2019. Hollywood did its best to pretend the movie didn't exist, but thankfully the streaming services brought it to living rooms across the country. It's a film every family and every policy maker should make the time to watch.

These are some of the women who inspired me to devote more than three decades to education freedom before I became the secretary of education. Like them, my passion for school choice started as a mother of young children. But my experience was the opposite of these women's. My children were able to enjoy the benefits of education freedom because I was blessed with resources to afford it. These moms had to fight the system. And their battles created opportunities for thousands of kids. I joined their fight, not because I'm a hero like Tera, Polly, or Virginia, but because I felt angry and frustrated with the injustices I observed.

I fight because I'm an American who's always taken seriously the notion that each of us is equal in God's eyes, and we should all have the same opportunity to live and thrive in freedom. Seeing children robbed of their potential because of the zip code they were born in makes me mad.

So what is school choice, anyway?

One thing I learned in Washington that I hadn't fully appreciated before is that many people know the term *school choice*, but far fewer understand what it actually means or entails. Part of that is because its opponents have been so relentless in attacking the term and its associated concepts.

Early on, we used the word *vouchers* to describe what we were fighting for. That worked at the time. In places like Milwaukee, students get vouchers—direct aid, something like a check—from the government to spend on the school of their choice. The government gives out vouchers for lots of other things. You may be familiar, for example, with Section 8 vouchers, which help lower-income families access housing.

The problem with calling this education support a voucher, beyond the untold millions the unions have spent to demonize the term, is that the word implies dependency. It sounds like the recipient is getting a handout from government. To me, school choice has always been about empowerment, not dependency. Taxpayers have already made the commitment to fund the education of every child, so there is no handout; every student has already been allocated a share of government funding. School choice is really about who gets to decide how and where that money is spent: the government or the family.

School choice is the power to choose the right school for your child, not just accept the one the government assigns to you.

But the term *school choice* doesn't even capture this movement completely. It makes it sound like we're simply talking about schools—buildings, infrastructure. The movement is really something much bigger than that.

I use the term *education freedom*. While that might sound a bit like a catchphrase or slogan, it's actually a vision for what education could be, versus what it is today. Education freedom starts from the premise that every student is unique and every student learns differently. This is something every parent knows. Yet we have a school system that essentially treats children as if they were all the same.

At the core, my vision for American education is to ensure that all children have the freedom to learn in their own way. It's to give parents freedom to find the best option and fit for their children.

Education freedom will give rise to new kinds of schools and new ways of learning we can't even begin to imagine today. There is no limit to the new ways that will be created to inspire children to learn.

Critically, education freedom also means giving teachers freedom to meet their students' needs in many different learning environments. As it stands, public school teachers have very limited choice in where they teach and in how they teach. What's more, the COVID-19 crisis has been very tough on teachers. At a time when fewer and fewer college students are choosing to become teachers, education freedom would bring an entirely new dynamism to the teaching profession.

The difference between education freedom and school choice is broad and deep. Education freedom is disruptive. It broadens the categories in which most Americans are used to thinking about education. When I was secretary, it often took multiple conversations with elected officials to help them understand the various school choice mechanisms (charters, vouchers, tax credit scholarships, education savings accounts), much less the distinction between school choice and education freedom. During one of my early conversations with President Trump about proposing an "education freedom" tax credit he asked me, "What do you mean, education freedom?" I told him it was a broader way to talk about school choice. He objected. "No one knows what the hell that is. We have to call it school choice."

Donald Trump is an instinctual communicator—he knew how to get his point across. But I was firm on this one. If Americans weren't sure what education freedom was, then it was up to us to put in the hard work to explain it.

Part of the logic to talk about education freedom versus school choice was to highlight the range of opportunities American parents (should) have to exercise their education freedom.

Consider public charter schools, for example. As I mentioned before when I described the charter school Dick founded, the West Michigan Aviation Academy in Grand Rapids, lots of Americans think charter schools are private schools (they are not), that they have selective enrollment—that is, that they "cherry-pick" (they do not and cannot), and that they won't serve students with disabilities (they not only do serve students with disabilities, they want to serve more). All these beliefs are categorically false, yet members of Congress regularly repeated them to me as if they were facts.

Others allege that school choice, and my motivation, is about wanting to "privatize" education. That's just not true. In actuality, I'm for *personalizing* education, not privatizing. I'm for customizing, not standardizing. I'm for freeing kids from a centuries-old, one-size-fits-all educational model. I'm for recognizing and embracing their inherent uniqueness. I'm for ensuring that every single child in America has an equal opportunity to benefit from a world-class education and can unlock every educational option. The truth is I don't really focus on the "type" of school—the adjective they put in front of the word school (public, charter, private, religious, and the like). My focus is on ensuring that the best interests of students are always put first.

Before we dive more deeply into the notion of education freedom, it will be helpful to have a proper and shared definition of its various expressions and funding mechanisms as we know them today:

- A *public charter school* is, first and foremost, a public school. It is taxpayer-funded, tuition-free, and open to anyone who wants to attend. There are usually many more students who want to attend charter schools than there is space to accommodate them, in which case an enrollment lottery occurs. Charter schools receive funding roughly the same way traditional assigned public schools do, though they usually receive less funding per student than those schools. The key difference is a charter school is independently run, freeing it from much of the burdensome school bureaucracy and some of the regulations. This autonomy makes room for more creativity and improved outcomes.
- *Public school choice* allows families to send their children to a different public school than their government-assigned or zoned school. Some states allow families to pick only from schools within the district where their home is, while others allow them to choose any school in their region or state. In both forms, most schools institute caps on how many nonassigned students they will accept.
- A *magnet school* is a public school structured around a theme or convening principle, like the STEM fields or the performing arts. Like charters, magnet schools are tuition-free public

schools. However, magnet schools typically have enrollment criteria, like academic performance. In their earliest days, magnet schools were designed to help racially integrate public schools. The idea was simple: If families pick a school based on what it offers, not where it is geographically located, kids will identify based on their shared interests, not their skin color. In this way, it was thought, magnet schools will naturally become integrated.

- A *homeschool* is exactly what it sounds like: a school run at home. Parents use curriculum and experience-based learning to help their children learn. Increasingly, homeschooling involves multiple families working together to advance their children's education, including going on field trips or meeting in a community venue to learn together. Families bear all the costs of this education themselves.

- A *tax credit scholarship* involves a two-step process to facilitate students being able to choose a school for which they need to pay tuition. First, individuals or businesses make donations to an education nonprofit, known as a 501(c)(3). To encourage more donors to participate, the contributions are treated like taxes paid, meaning the donor's tax bill is lowered by the amount they donated. That does not reduce how much the donor pays overall. It simply means they decide to redirect a portion of their tax bill to help other people's children choose a school that's right for them. In the second step, the nonprofit organization provides scholarships to families so they can pick the right school for their children, including private schools. They usually have criteria for who can receive scholarships; most commonly they are families who have lower incomes. Some scholarship programs are designed to benefit students with disabilities or gifted and talented students.

- An *education savings account*, or ESA, is the newest (and my favorite, thus far) mechanism to facilitate education freedom. With ESAs, funds are deposited into an account that a family can use to pay tuition and a variety of other education-related expenses. They maximize freedom of choice because families can use their ESAs at a variety of providers, thus "unbundling" or customizing school. ESAs can be funded by a government or by individuals who receive a tax credit for their donations.
- A *voucher* is a direct payment from the government to a student for their education. The student can use the voucher to pay for education at any school of their choice. This works similarly to SNAP (food stamps) or housing vouchers.

These, in abbreviated form, are the "hows" of education freedom. These are the mechanisms parents can use to educate their child in the way they see fit. In my experience, we spend way too much time arguing about the "hows" of education freedom. The "why" is much more important. Let me paint a word picture of why education freedom will help everyone involved.

For students, it would lead to a system where no child is a misfit in his or her school. As families seek new education options to meet their children's needs, providers will respond. It might look something like this: If your child needs more time to learn a concept or lesson, he or she takes it. If he or she needs less time, they move on to the next concept. If your child wants to study a language or any subject that his or her school building doesn't offer, they can learn it somewhere else. If he or she doesn't like to study at a desk and learns better in a lab or in a garden or between skyscrapers, they can learn there. If he or she wants hands-on experiences to help guide their learning pathway, they can access those. Every child should be free and empowered to learn in any way and in any place that works for them, making their learning a delight, not drudgery.

For teachers, education freedom could look like this: If you want to try something new in your classroom that you think will better help your students, you can. You would be able to choose to teach at a variety of different types of schools (maybe a school located in a lab, a garden, or between skyscrapers), based on where you think you'd be most successful and fulfilled. If you want to mentor, coach, or develop other teachers, you can do that, and you should be rewarded for it. If you want to control your professional development and career path, you would have the power to do so. You would be properly paid for your success rather than being tethered to an inflexible schedule tied to seniority.

Finally, parents, education freedom for you could look like this: If the government-assigned school isn't working for your child, you can take him or her anywhere else. And if your school is working for your child, you can stay put. Another parent's freedom to make a choice doesn't mean you have to make the same choice. If you want to home-school your children for part of the week and send them to a classical academy the rest of the week, you can do that. If one type of learning or instruction is best for your son and another is better for your daughter, you have the flexibility to make those choices. If a school closer to your work is a better fit for your family, that's your choice. You should be free to make the decisions that work best for your children and your family.

As parents of four, and grandparents to ten, Dick and I know firsthand that kids are not "one size fits all." Our children are each very different in personality and interests and they learn in different ways. Our two daughters, Elissa and Andrea, homeschooled for three years together during a stretch for which it worked particularly well for both of them, but for completely different reasons. Son Ryan mastered his spelling words and other memory exercises shooting baskets, the physical activity helping make the mental learning stick. Son Rick was never without a journal to capture his many ideas that didn't fit neatly into any given school subject. These are examples of the many ways we helped them embrace their personal preferences and innate curiosity. But each of them, ultimately, still had to achieve most of their education in a system that is based on the factory production-line model.

It doesn't have to work that way. We can make personalized learning a reality for every child if we start funding the student, not the system.

The positive, aspirational vision for education freedom is this: Students are empowered to find places to learn that maximize their potential rather than be trapped in government-assigned, zoned schools. Every child has the opportunity and the resources to learn and to become a fully productive member of his or her community. Education freedom honors this vision. It puts the student, rather than the system, first.

This alone—making children the center of our education system—is reason enough to advance this cause for every child. But when you consider the state of American education today—how poorly our schools educate to maximize the potential of every child—the case for education freedom is undeniable.

For decades, many, many well-meaning reformers have tried to improve our public schools without changing the system. We've seen valiant and laudable efforts from Republicans and Democrats, liberals, conservatives, philanthropists, volunteers, and everyone else imaginable.

Reformers have added new standards and new tests. They've bused kids across town. They've added new government regulations. Mostly, they've spent or "invested" more money—*lots* of money—to hire more and more adults. Per-student funding has tripled from $4,893 in 1965 to nearly $15,000 today—in inflation-adjusted dollars.[5] And it is

nonclassroom hires—managers, data analysts, HR directors, central
office staff—that account for most of the new spending, *not* higher
salaries for teachers. While student enrollment stayed basically flat
between 2001 and 2019, the number of teachers rose by 7 percent and
the number of district staff members increased 79 percent.[6]

This nation spends more than $750 billion on K–12 education
each year. This number is from before COVID-19. The amount is
much higher now. Most education spending—90 percent or more
in most states—comes from state and local taxes. But the federal
taxpayer kicks in as well. Since 1965, annual federal spending on
K–12 education has increased tenfold, from $4.5 billion to more than
$40 billion, in constant dollars. The U.S. Department of Education
was created in 1979; since then, federal taxpayers have sent well over
$1,000,000,000,000 (one trillion dollars) to K–12 schools, in addi-
tion to all the spending at the state and local levels.[7]

And what has this bought us?

The National Assessment of Educational Progress (NAEP),
better known as the Nation's Report Card, provides the most comprehensive view of the state of American education available. Beginning
in 1992, it gives us a longitudinal record of where our students are,
and a pretty clear idea of where they should go. The NAEP gives
America's parents, teachers, and leaders a detailed picture of student
achievement—or, in frighteningly too many cases, a lack thereof.

After some increases in the 1980s and '90s, math and reading
achievement levels for nine- and thirteen-year-old students have flat-
lined or declined according to the Nation's Report Card, particularly
since 2012. These are the results of the NAEP Long-Term Trend
study released in 2021.[8]

But perhaps most concerning is what is evident when you break
down this data. Opponents of school choice constantly attack it as
a threat to the most vulnerable students. Instead, the opposite is
true: It is the current system that is failing these kids. American

students who were already low-achieving are worse off today, while our best-performing students have plateaued. And those in the bottom 10 percent—our most vulnerable—have fallen even further behind.

The long-term NAEP data shows two lines—one showing higher-achieving students essentially staying flat, and the other reflecting students who are struggling trending steadily downward. Between 2012 and 2020, the achievement gap in math between black and white thirteen-year-olds grew by 7 points.[9]

The explicit purpose of the federal Title I program, which accounts for most of the trillion dollars the U.S. Department of Education has spent, was to close the achievement gap between the richest and poorest students. But the most comprehensive study of the topic, conducted by researchers at Harvard and Stanford, concluded the gap hasn't closed one bit.[10] And an analysis from the Brookings Institution found that most of Title I money has been spent on ineffective efforts.[11]

Let me pause here to say a few words about accountability and testing.

I've always believed the strongest form of accountability for a school is being accountable to its students and families. Nothing can compete with the accountability that comes from a family being free to leave a school that isn't meeting their needs. Of course, until that's universally true, we need other measures of accountability. Transparent data, gleaned from the kinds of test results cited here, gains us much of that desired accountability.

Testing is imperfect, and there are lots of perfectly valid reasons to criticize it. But its necessity is a result of the nature of the system. The *reason we use standardized tests* in this country—which admittedly are the best of the bad options currently available to measure student achievement—is that we have a standardized education model. You measure outputs based on inputs. In the kind of educational future I envision, a mastery or competence-based approach, you wouldn't need standardized tests because every student would have a customized education. You would *always* know how they were doing, what progress they were making, and their entire experience would be oriented around ensuring that they achieved excellence.

It's easy to understand that declining scores are bad, but it's most alarming to understand what that means in context. According to the NAEP, "basic" in reading is defined as the ability to understand words and answer simple questions about factual information in the text. In 2019, 34 percent of our nation's fourth graders were what the NAEP calls "below basic" readers—meaning they did not comprehend a basic, grade-level reading assignment; many can't read at all and even more cannot understand what they read.[12] Among those fourth graders who qualify for free and reduced lunch—low-income students—nearly half are "below basic."[13]

The NAEP term *proficiency* is defined as "solid academic performance." In other words, not great, but not bad. When the test uses the word *proficient* to describe student achievement, it means "the goal for what all students should know."[14]

Viewed in this way—the context of what our schools *should* be ensuring students know—the outcomes for American K–12 students are even more alarming.

Just 24 percent of high school seniors are proficient or better in mathematics. Among eighth graders, one in three are proficient or above. In science, 22 percent of seniors—just one in five—know what they are expected to know.[15]

In the face of these depressing statistics, the education establishment continues to believe that more spending is the way to reform education. The Obama administration poured $7 billion into a program called School Improvement Grants (SIGs). It was the largest federal investment ever made to improve low-performing schools, and it failed. A review by the Obama Education Department (good for them for being so transparent) found that test scores, graduation rates, and college attendance were unchanged in the schools that received the extra funding.[16]

It makes me wonder what it will take for the establishment to learn that more spending isn't the answer. Taxpayers are paying more and more and we are getting less and less from our schools.

The results within our borders are cause for grave concern. When you compare them across the globe, they should set off an ear-piercing alarm. And they eviscerate the education establishment's claim that we could have world-class public schools if we just spent more money on them.

Among all the advanced, industrialized nations in the world— that is, the countries that are like us—the United States spends more per student on education than just three countries: Luxembourg, Austria, and Norway. But we're not even in the top ten—not even close—in terms of educational achievement. We're 37th in math, 13th in reading, and 18th in science in the world.[17] In math, we're outpaced by big competitors like Germany, France, and the United Kingdom, by global foes like China and Russia, and also by countries like Estonia, Finland, and the Slovak Republic. Is this okay with you?

Imagine for a moment what the response would be if America had the 37th best economy in the world. Or if our athletes didn't place in the top ten in any sport at the Olympics. The outcry would be deafening. The outcry about where we stand in educating our rising generation should be no different.

An important and still-relevant report commissioned in 1983, called *A Nation at Risk*, summed it up quite clearly: "If an unfriendly foreign power had attempted to impose on America the mediocre educational performance that exists today, we might well have viewed it as an act of war."[18] That report set off the massive taxpayer infusion of funds. And that was nearly forty years ago.

PISA 2018: TOP RATED COUNTRIES
Sum of mean science, reading and mathematics scores from the OECD PISA Results 2018*

China**	1736
Singapore	1669
Estonia	1576
Japan	1560
South Korea	1559
Canada	1550
Finland	1549
Poland	1539
Ireland	1514
United Kingdom	1511
Slovenia	1511
New Zealand	1508
Sweden	1507
Netherlands	1507
Denmark	1503
Germany	1501
Belgium	1500
Australia	1497
Switzerland	1494
Norway	1490
Czech Republic	1486
United States	**1485**
France	1481
Portugal	1476
Austria	1473

1300   1400   1500   1600   1700   1800

* PISA= Programme for International Student Assessment ** Beijing, Shanghai, Jiangsu and Zheijang
Source: OECD
                                                                    19

It's the sum total of these significant spending increases, objectively dismal results, and the unending train of excuses from the education establishment that is at the core of why I fight so hard for education freedom. We've spent more than half a century playing with inputs to our government-run public schools and our kids are the victims. It is way past time to dismantle the system itself.

———————————

The moment is indelibly etched on my mind. I was walking out of a brick schoolhouse in Milwaukee on a humid September day in 2019. I had just visited with children, teachers, and parents at a high-achieving school in a lower-income neighborhood. The faces of the families I had met were black and brown.

Across the street, I saw a group of protestors. They didn't like the fact that the children were at St. Marcus thanks to vouchers funded by the state of Wisconsin. These folks were angry and they were shouting. The overwhelming majority of their faces were white.

An African-American father who was dropping off his two daughters at the school turned to the protestors and said, "You're debating someone else's child." I bet he would have loved for some of the protestors to walk a mile in his shoes.

I will always remember that dad and that moment.

Inside St. Marcus Lutheran School, I sat in circles with curious young kids, talked with grateful parents, and watched dedicated teachers. It was an experience of hope, expectation, and achievement; an experience that shouldn't be controversial in America. For the families I met, going to St. Marcus was the opportunity to learn and thrive that all parents want for their children.

But then I walked outside and saw the protestors. The head of the Wisconsin teacher union was there. The chairman of the Wisconsin Democratic Party was there, along with other local Democratic politicians. They were visual reminders that there are people who don't think St. Marcus students should have the opportunity to choose a great school. They booed and hissed and chanted "Go home, Betsy!" That didn't bother me in the least.

What *did* bother me was that the protestors were there advocating for adults—politicians, unions, and bureaucrats—not children. St. Marcus is in a poor neighborhood. Students in surrounding schools had math and reading proficiency rates in the single digits. But the protestors weren't likely from the neighborhood—if they had children, they had exercised school choice by moving to the safe, white neighborhoods surrounding Milwaukee. They had taken advantage of *their* opportunity to choose. Now they were protesting that opportunity for someone else's child.

Polly Williams was on my mind on this visit to Milwaukee. I called the city "the birthplace of education freedom." As I've noted, Milwaukee has the nation's oldest private school choice program. And while the idea of school choice has some of its roots in free market theory, in practice, vouchers serve a higher cause in Milwaukee and in dozens of cities across the country. My friend and cofounder of the Black Alliance for Educational Options, Howard Fuller, was one of the forces behind the Milwaukee program. Howard has said that his support of school choice was never just about free markets. "It was a social justice issue." In my view, it's both-and.

I didn't have the opportunity to speak to the protestors in Milwaukee that day, but if I had asked them if they believe in social justice, I'm confident the vast majority would have said yes. They probably would have agreed with the idea that our government-controlled education system is systemically shortchanging black and minority kids. But what I bet they wouldn't—or couldn't—see was the role they play in perpetuating this historic injustice.

Many of the same adults who stand in the way of systemic change for black and brown children offer up fashionable education theories that do nothing but further diminish learning for minority students. "Reforms" such as not requiring students to hand in assignments on time, ending advanced courses, pronouncing math "racist" and merit a form of "white privilege"—all these dangerous ideas are enacted in the name of antiracism. But their real effect is deepening the systemic racism of the education system.

President George W. Bush famously called out "the soft bigotry of low expectations." Students are being challenged and inspired less and less in our schools and minority and low-income students are bearing the biggest brunt of this trend. NAEP data confirms that fewer students are taking more advanced math classes. The number of thirteen-year-olds who took algebra declined 9 percentage points since 2012. The movement away from reading—the number of thirteen-year-olds who reported they rarely or never read for pleasure—grew a whopping 21 points, from 8 percent in 1984 to 29 percent in 2020.[20]

Lowering standards for certain students is an ominous sign for the future of a country that is divided politically, economically, culturally, and racially. Americans don't have a common ethnicity to unite us. We don't come from the same race or religion. What makes us a nation is the set of ideas America was founded upon. But I'm concerned we no longer share a vision for and understanding of what these ideas are and where they came from. Our schools are altogether failing to teach children these ideas. Only 24 percent of high school seniors have a reasonable knowledge of civics—the rights and duties of citizens of our republic.[21] *And just 15 percent are proficient in American history.*[22]

Our democratic system of government was designed for and predicated on an informed citizenry. We will not long survive as a republic if we fail to teach our children what to expect from government and what their responsibilities are as citizens. Either we will teach children to be responsible participants in self-government, or we will lose self-government.

E ducation freedom is morally just. It also works. Students who are empowered to exercise education freedom and make choices have better outcomes.

An extensive study conducted at the University of Arkansas concluded that "higher levels of education freedom are significantly associated with higher NAEP achievement levels and higher NAEP achievement gains in all our statistical models."[23]

In Arizona, ranked highest in education freedom with several strong school choice programs, fourth-grade students gained 8 points in math between 2009 and 2015, while the national average showed no gain, nil. In reading, the same students were plus 5 versus a minus 1 national average. In science, plus 11 versus plus 4.[24]

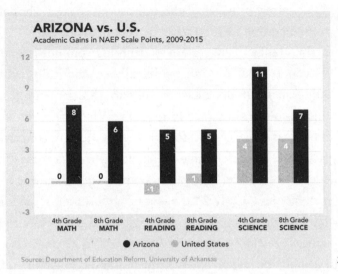

The same study found that Florida's students, more than half of whom choose schools other than their assigned public school, saw similarly impressive gains. Those gains were most pronounced for the lowest-income students, and the improvements shown by students with disabilities were off the charts (so to speak).

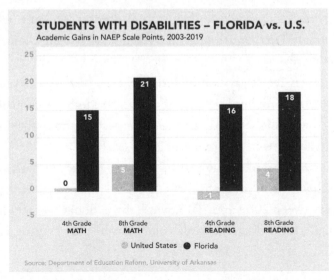

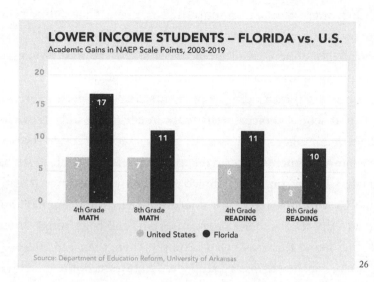

LOWER INCOME STUDENTS – FLORIDA vs. U.S.
Academic Gains in NAEP Scale Points, 2003-2019

Source: Department of Education Reform, University of Arkansas

26

The truth is that, despite what you hear in the media, almost every study ever conducted on private-school choice programs, across a wide array of measures, has shown it improves student outcomes.

FINDINGS OF PRIVATE SCHOOL CHOICE RESEARCH STUDIES

		THE SCHOOL CHOICE PROGRAM HAD:		
OUTCOME STUDIED	NUMBER OF STUDIES	ANY POSITIVE EFFECT	NO VISIBLE EFFECT	ANY NEGATIVE EFFECT
Program Participant Test Scores	17	11	4	3
Educational Attainment	7	5	2	0
Parent Satisfaction	30	28	1	2
Public School Students' Test Scores	27	25	1	1
Civic Values and Practices	11	6	5	0
Integration	7	6	1	0
Fiscal Effects	70	65	4	5

Source: EdChoice

27

One interesting and important finding is that public school students' achievement levels rise when there are nearby private school choice options. And again, the results were most pronounced among—you guessed it—lower-income students.[28]

Because of these findings, opponents of education freedom rarely argue that school choice doesn't work in educating kids; they claim instead that it takes money away from public schools, or, in the words of so many opponents, "privatizes" public education. In fact, we have enough data now on school choice programs to determine that they actually save money. The pro-education-freedom group EdChoice studied forty school choice programs from their beginnings through 2018 and found that they saved taxpayers more than $28 billion—or $7,500 for each participating student. That works out to a savings of approximately $2.80 for every dollar spent on expanding educational options.[29] It's difficult to argue that school choice will defund public schools when it costs less to begin with.

The totality of these studies confirms that when students and families are empowered to make choices about their education, achievement and results improve. School choice is simply common sense; it's economically rational and it's socially just.

I was in Milwaukee that day in September to promote a plan that would fundamentally change our education system by taking power away from the protestors out on the street and giving it to parents who want their children at a school like St. Marcus. A few months earlier, I proposed legislation that was a first for the Department of Education: a federal charitable tax credit for donations to support state-based K–12 education scholarships. We called them Education Freedom Scholarships (EFS).

A federally supported school choice program was one of just a handful of specific campaign promises President Trump made in the 2016 election.[30] This promise was a big reason I had agreed to join the administration. Beyond the pledge and the funding level he put on it—$20 billion—there weren't many specifics. But the promise was enough. It was more than enough. No administration had ever pledged to put forward a concrete legislative proposal to create a nationwide school choice program. We had a historic opportunity. I wanted to help ensure it happened.

Education Freedom Scholarships fall under the "tax credit scholarship" heading in the education choice mechanisms I listed before. People or businesses would receive a tax credit when they redirect part of their federal tax bill to scholarship-granting organizations in the states. States would then use this voluntarily donated money to create their own scholarship program based on local needs and goals. When we began work on Education Freedom Scholarships, nearly twenty states had tax-credit-funded school choice programs of varying kinds. I had worked with most of these states in creating these programs, and they were working well. Most of them, however, were very modest in size and scale. What they needed was rocket fuel to propel their growth and ability to serve more students.

The only federal involvement in the Education Freedom Scholarships plan was a change in the federal tax law. No new federal mandates, no new federal bureaucracies were required. The plan didn't create a new federal "Office of School Choice." And it didn't entangle schools with federal strings or stifling red tape. What's more, Education Freedom Scholarships didn't take a single dollar from public school students. And they didn't spend a single dollar of federal money.

Our proposal required only one thing: Students and parents must be empowered to make the decisions. States could design programs where Education Freedom Scholarships could only be used for private or parochial school tuition. Or, more like ESAs, they could also let families use them to access apprenticeships, career training programs, dual credit programs, or transportation to attend schools outside of their home districts. The range of ways in which the scholarships could be used was only limited by the creativity of those who would implement their use. Each state would have the flexibility to determine which students were in most need of the scholarships, most likely students at the lower end of the income or achievement ladders, including students with disabilities.

Education Freedom Scholarships would be transformative for kids. Now we just had to convince Congress to pass them.

The State of the Union address is every president's principal platform to promote his or her policy priorities. To my delight, President Trump's first speech (which was not technically a "State of the Union") to a joint session of the House and Senate early in 2017 was strong on school choice. He called it, as other presidents had before him, "the civil rights issue of our time." And he urged Congress to "pass an education bill that funds school choice for disadvantaged youth, including millions of African-American and Latino children. These families should be free to choose the public, private, charter, magnet, religious, or home school that is right for them."

The president didn't give any specifics in 2017 of how he might implement this policy, but close watchers of the speech got some insight with a visitor who was sitting with the first lady in the gallery. Just the way it was planned.

Denisha Merriweather grew up in poverty with a teenage mother on the east side of Jacksonville, Florida. Denisha failed third grade twice and regularly got into trouble at school. She wore the scars of her older siblings, and the school wrote her off as "another Merriweather," meaning another problem child unlikely to succeed. She was left to assume they were right. Her ambition was to survive school and get a job at McDonald's.

But Denisha's godmother wasn't going to have that. She found a small faith-based private school where she thought Denisha might do better. But she knew that neither she nor Denisha's family would be able to afford the tuition costs to attend there. Fortuitously, the school introduced her to the Florida Tax Credit Scholarship—one of the programs started by Jeb Bush when he was governor.

The Florida program allows businesses to direct a small amount of their state taxes to a scholarship organization called Step Up for Students. Denisha qualified for a scholarship and she was able to go to the small school her godmother had found. Within a few days, she knew her life was on a completely new trajectory. She went on to become the first member of her family to graduate from high school. When President Trump introduced her to the nation that night in the Capitol, she was not only a college graduate; Denisha was earning her master's degree.

In 2019, the State of the Union address was scheduled right before we planned to unveil the Education Freedom Scholarships. It was more important than ever that President Trump use the State of the Union to promote school choice.

The process of writing a State of the Union address is very much a group effort. It begins months before the speech is delivered, and all the cabinet agencies fight for their initiatives to be included. In my opinion, this process generally makes for a bad speech but an important statement of policies.

We fought hard early on and managed to get a full paragraph in the speech touting education freedom. When the final draft of the speech was distributed the day before the address, however, the paragraph was gone. There was no mention at all of school choice or Education Freedom Scholarships. I called the president, but he couldn't be convinced. The speech was already too damn long, he said. So we called in help. Kellyanne Conway and Mercedes Schlapp, key allies inside the White House on school choice, went to work.

They suggested we get another education freedom advocate to plead our case to the president: Vice President Mike Pence.

Pence went into the Oval Office, our paragraph in hand, with the hope of getting the whole thing reinstated. After a bit, he came out and reported that the president wouldn't agree to the whole paragraph, but he would include one line: "To help support working parents, the time has come to pass school choice for America's children."

It was a victory, of sorts. And just to be sure the words got back in the speech, Kellyanne and Mercedes went to the White House speechwriting office and watched as the line was entered into the final text.

Despite the sausage-making process of the speech, we were excited to watch it. There was just one more physical hurdle. I had broken my pelvis a few weeks before while road biking in Florida. I hit a patch of soft sand and was ejected from my bike directly onto my hip. The accident and subsequent surgery left me in a wheelchair for a couple of months. The sergeant-at-arms was more than reluctant to permit one of my staff to push me into the House chamber. But, like the line in the speech, we made it in.

Then came President Trump's potentially last State of the Union address in 2020. By the time the White House began preparing the speech, working with lead sponsors Texas senator Ted Cruz and Alabama congressman Bradley Byrne, we had secured the support of dozens of members of Congress for the EFS legislation—notwithstanding the fact that Chairman Alexander declined to schedule a committee hearing on the bill. Thanks again to the help of Kellyanne, domestic policy council head Brooke Rollins, and others, the speech was written to deliver a full-throated endorsement of Education Freedom Scholarships.

Once again, President Trump wanted to have someone in the first lady's viewing box to add a visual to his remarks. The notion was to identify a young person who wanted or needed to go to another school but couldn't because his or her state didn't have a scholarship program. The student's presence and example would underscore to Congress the importance of passing the EFS bill.

The search to find that student commenced. As far as I was concerned, it was a huge win that the president was making a pitch for our program. Whomever he showcased was not nearly as important as the call for choice. But the White House folks were after a certain look. They went through several different candidates until they found one they liked. Finally, they settled on a girl who had both the right story (our criterion) and looked the part (the White House's).

Janiyah Davis was a bright, adorable fourth grader from Philadelphia who loved art and math. Janiyah's presence at the State of the Union would not only highlight the Education Freedom Scholarship proposal; it would also illustrate the obstacles that school choice faces in many statehouses—obstacles that the availability of a federal program could overcome.

The year before, Pennsylvania governor Tom Wolf vetoed a bipartisan bill that would have doubled the available tax credits for the state's tax credit scholarship program, the Educational Improvement Tax Credit (EITC). His decision was driven purely by school union politics. The existing program had provided millions of dollars in private, charitable donations for low-income children in Pennsylvania. There was a 40,000-child-long wait list for the scholarships. Businesses had already donated more than $105 million that was just waiting to be dispersed to students. But Wolf, who himself had attended a $61,000-a-year private feeder school for Princeton, sided with his union benefactors over poor kids and their families, denying them the opportunity to choose private schools with a fraction of that tuition.[31] He was the poster boy for the raw interest group politics that education freedom faces in too many states.

In his speech, President Trump planned to present Janiyah with an "Opportunity Scholarship" to highlight the fact that Governor Wolf refused to expand the Pennsylvania program. There was just one little detail. There was no such thing as an "Opportunity Scholarship" on the federal level—not yet at least. So the White House asked if I would be willing to personally pay for Janiyah's scholarship. I was happy to do so. I dedicated part of my salary, which I was already donating entirely to charity, to Janiyah's schooling.

Addressing the joint houses of Congress, President Trump noted that eighteen states already had school choice tax credit scholarships, with tens of thousands of students on waiting lists. One of those students, he said, was Janiyah Davis, and he gestured toward the gallery. The president mentioned Governor Wolf's veto of the expanded tax credit program in Pennsylvania.

"But Janiyah, I have some good news tonight," he said. "Your long wait is over. I can proudly announce tonight that an Opportunity Scholarship has become available. It is going to you. And you will soon be going to the school of your choice."

A look of genuine surprise came over Janiyah's face and she looked at her mother to make sure what she was hearing was real. The chamber thundered with applause.

It was an effective moment of political theater. More than that, it was a substantive gesture of support for an important piece of legislation. But the evening and the speech weren't over yet. In a moving moment about midway through the speech, Trump presented radio personality Rush Limbaugh with the Presidential Medal of Freedom. The day before, Rush had announced that the lung cancer he was suffering from was terminal. There, in the gallery, First Lady Melania Trump placed the medal around the ailing broadcaster's neck.

I joined millions of Americans in being deeply touched by the president's surprise recognition of Rush that night. The next day, it dominated the media coverage of the president's speech. There was little, if any, mention of his call for Education Freedom Scholarships. It was intensely frustrating—and entirely foreseeable. As deserving as Rush was, his award was a one-day event. EFS has the opportunity to change the trajectory of millions of Americans for decades.

We spent a lot of time advocating for Education Freedom Scholarships and looking for a must-pass piece of legislation to attach the plan to. I made the rounds on Capitol Hill, in the states, and with industry groups to build support. At one of these meetings, a speech to the National Conference of Mayors at a hotel near the Capitol in 2019, I first met Joe Biden. I was in my wheelchair after the biking accident. My trusty assistant, Sarah Delahunty, was pushing me around—literally. The ramp up to the stage for the speech was so steep, Sarah had a hard time muscling me up and then very nearly dealt with a runaway situation going down.

After the speech, Sarah and I were waiting in the "back of the house" area of the hotel ballroom for the freight elevator to take us to the ground floor when former vice president Biden came barreling out of a side room. He must have heard about my accident because he came directly up to me.

"How are you doing?" he asked. "Do you have any hardware?"

I told him I had a very fine three-inch screw as the result of my accident.

Then, this casual encounter turned into something totally unexpected and uncomfortable. Biden leaned down, put his hands on my shoulders, and pressed his forehead to mine. He lingered. As I tried to figure out how I could roll the wheelchair and myself away, he said, "I have nine screws in my shoulder. But everyone thinks they're in my head." Then he stood up and strode off.

When we got down to the car, Sarah asked, "Is he a good friend of yours?"

I told her I had never met him before.

"Well," she said, "that was gross." Yes, it was gross, and it was also a feeble attempt to intimidate me. I think about that encounter every time I hear Biden talk about dismantling our reforms of Title IX.

For too many Republicans, education freedom is an issue they agree with philosophically but don't take seriously because of politics. This is proof, in my opinion, that the school union bosses have been spectacularly successful. They have convinced politicians that staking out this ground is too painful to bear. They're doggedly disciplined at making sure the "destroying public schools" alarm is sounded any time education freedom enters the discussion. So many politicians— elected or wannabes—who might otherwise support education freedom view it as a political loser. Not to mention the fact that union bosses have big campaign war chests, while parents are on their own.

The unions deserve a great deal of the blame for why our education system is so calcified. But they alone don't account for the failure of our schools to improve. They've had help—critical help—from government. The cycle goes like this: The union takes money from classroom teachers, who get paid by taxpayers, and use it to elect and lobby the politicians, who then increase the funding for schools and thus the union coffers. Elected officials ultimately do the real work of preserving the union bosses' monopoly and fighting against education freedom.

Armies of aides and administrators have been added to manage the sprawl of the system. As a matter of fact, since 1970, the number of adults employed in schools has grown at a rate nine times faster than the number of children who go there to learn.[32] Looking at 2011–16, the number of teachers alone grew by 13 percent while the number of students grew by only 2 percent.[33] As I've detailed, all this new staff costs taxpayers more to support and it also swells the union rolls and funds their monopoly control.

The current system, however, doesn't serve most teachers any better than it serves children.

Think about the incentives that good teachers have today. Teachers are not treated like the professionals they are in our public schools. The union-created system treats, and compensates, extraordinary teachers the same as ordinary ones. Teachers have no pathways and no incentives to advance professionally in their important teaching roles. The system is designed for them to move from year to year, rung to rung, up the same, automatic compensation ladder, regardless of ability or impact. Everyone is treated the same, because in this union system, everyone *must* be the same. Everyone, that is, except for the union bosses, some of whom get paid more than $500,000 a year.[34]

Great teachers challenge the way things have always been done, which tends to challenge and even embarrass those who don't. Our education system does everything it can to drive away great teachers. It's no surprise that they too often leave the classroom for fulfillment and reward elsewhere.

Teachers aren't the issue. Our failed public education system survives because of the people who *lead* the unions. These leaders have made an unholy alliance with elected officials—at great expense to the children in school and the taxpayers who pay the bill. Public school unions—like all public employee unions—are the only option in town. They have well-funded, extremely powerful political operations. And if they strike or "sick-out," there is no school for most American kids. As long as this reality defines our system, union bosses will have the power to make elected officials do their bidding. As importantly, they will keep receiving the resources from the taxpayers to reward these same elected officials with help getting elected and reelected. It is pure quid pro quo.

The COVID-19 school shutdowns, rise of critical race theory and divisive curriculum, and other education scandals opened American parents' eyes to the self-serving nature of the school unions. Many parents feel helpless in the face of the union monopoly, but there is an effective way to fight back. It's important to keep in mind that it's *elected officials* who make the laws and regulate the schools. *Politicians* have continued to throw money at problems that won't be solved by money. *Politicians* have gone along with overpopulating schools with administrators and bureaucracy. *Politicians* have agreed to contracts that award teachers tenure and reward them based on seniority, not effectiveness. At the union bosses' request, *politicians* signed off on making it all but impossible to fire school personnel who have harmed children. *Politicians* have cocreated a system that actively works against the thousands of talented public school teachers who do what they do because they want to help children.

Politicians and union bosses can't acknowledge this part out loud. They can't honestly defend the system they preside over. Instead they try to demonize anyone who wants to empower families with education freedom.

Meanwhile, politicians, union bosses, and many who are employed by "the system," send their own children to private schools or "good" suburban schools. As Cory Booker put it before he abandoned his principles, "People in the suburbs want to preach to us in the inner cities about what we need to endure so they can have the present system. It's not a system to defend."[35]

The Democratic Party–teacher union alliance is formidable, but it is not insurmountable. Candidates are running for office supporting education freedom and winning. One timely example is the 2018 Florida gubernatorial race. Voter data shows that "school choice moms" made the difference for the victory of Republican Ron DeSantis.

DeSantis ran for governor vowing to protect and expand school choice. He referred to the Florida Tax Credit Scholarship by name, vowing, "I will protect these scholarships. I will stand with these families." His Democratic opponent, Tallahassee mayor Andrew Gillum, an African-American, explicitly ran against choice. In the end, DeSantis's full-throated support for education freedom appealed to a faithfully Democratic constituency: African-American women. He attracted 18 percent of the African-American female vote compared to the national average for Republicans of 7 percent. One hundred thousand black women crossed political party lines to vote for DeSantis over an African-American candidate.

Writing about this in the *Wall Street Journal*, education and civil rights activist William Mattox concluded that "in an election decided by fewer than 40,000 votes, these 100,000 black women proved decisive." The reason for their support was DeSantis's advocacy of the Step Up for Students scholarship, which is funded by a tax credit. DeSantis's support for school choice also attracted the support of 44 percent of the state's Latino population. This result, Mattox wrote, should encourage more Republicans to run on education freedom and "prompt Democrats to rethink their blind allegiance to teachers unions."[36]

When we showed the president the article arguing that school choice supporters delivered the governor's office to Ron DeSantis, Trump replied, characteristically, "*I* delivered the governor's office to Ron DeSantis."

There was probably truth to both assertions, but I think the president got the important part of the story. His campaign team quickly confirmed that their polling showed education freedom to be a very popular and effective administration policy.

Over the course of my time in Washington, I found that receptivity on Capitol Hill to education freedom was also growing. One Republican who had long been a principled skeptic of school choice started warming to the conversation.

Susan Collins of Maine was one of the two Republican votes against my confirmation in the Senate. At the time, she didn't believe school choice was a good fit for her rural state. But Susan was always honest and open-minded. In one of our phone conversations, she told me about a rural school on Deer Isle, about three hours north of Portland. The island's only high school, called Deer Isle–Stonington High School (DISHS), had been struggling on every front. Students were uninspired and low-achieving, and many were on the brink of dropping out. They saw no relevance in their lives to what they were required to learn at school. Deer Isle is home to a thriving lobster industry and in which most of the students' families work.

So a team of DISHS teachers, staff, and community members decided to try to engage the kids by completely reorienting the school around lobstering. Students learned through projects and hands-on work in the town industry. They learned math through navigation and figuring out the market price for the day's catch. They learned to write through essays on fishing tactics and government regulation. Before long, students were attentive and engaged with learning. It became relevant for them. DISHS had only graduated 58 percent of its students before the changes—the worst results in the state. Four years later, 91 percent of DISHS students graduated.[37]

Senator Collins was excited about this story and what it meant for the students. I said, "Yes, this is a great example of what I've been advocating: tailoring education to meet students' needs, not forcing them into a one-size-fits-all model." I think it was an "aha" moment. Something changed in my relationship with Senator Collins that day. There was new understanding and trust. It was evident when she started to seriously question the way Maine's schools were handling COVID, and how forceful the unions were acting in keeping them closed.

By the early months of 2020, Education Freedom Scholarships were gathering momentum. The president's advocacy and our hard work were having an effect. Our bill had more than 110 cosponsors in the House and 16 in the Senate, making it the most widely supported federal school choice proposal in history.

Then the coronavirus crisis hit. Schools across the country shut down. Washington, DC, shut down, too. But we quickly found a silver lining in the shutdown: It was actually an ideal time to talk to families about having education options for their children. Congress went to work on a bill with emergency funding for families and businesses impacted by the shutdown. The initial COVID package included $31 billion for an "Education Stabilization Fund," split nearly evenly between K–12 and higher education.

The legislation came together at light speed by congressional standards. It was passed by the end of March. There wasn't enough time to include Education Freedom Scholarships in the bill, but we could ensure that the emergency funds went to *all* students, whether they were at public, private, or parochial school. We argued the obvious: All children were impacted by the pandemic, no matter where they were educated. And the emergency funds were intended to help mitigate the impact for everyone. Not surprisingly, however, districts didn't want to share the funds. Several lawsuits followed, and kids in nongovernment schools lost out.

However, that was just an opening skirmish. As months ticked by and the schools stayed shuttered, the opportunity to gain support for Education Freedom Scholarships continued to grow. The president recognized before anybody else did the political salience of schools remaining closed. Families were growing frustrated. And we made sure they knew education freedom could help solve the problem.

In late August 2020, I wrote a "back to school" letter to the nation's parents.

"You tried your best to step up to the plate by becoming a full-time teacher yourself, in addition to keeping your day job—all the while worrying about your family's health and safety. Now, as we approach fall, you're told that you may have to go it alone—again. It's a lot. But it doesn't have to be this way," I wrote.

President Trump and I were fighting for more options for parents who felt like they had no options.

"Every family needs to be able to do what's right for their child," I assured parents. "Our schools exist because you pay for them, and you should be empowered to put your money to better use if your school isn't meeting your needs."[38]

A month earlier, Chairman Alexander and South Carolina senator Tim Scott had joined forces with Senator Cruz and us to reintroduce EFS in a bill that would not only make the scholarships law, but would also provide one-time emergency funds to scholarship-granting organizations in the states. These funds would go directly to parents to use however they chose during the pandemic. The companion legislation in the House was authored by Representative Byrne and was sponsored by Congressman Dan Lipinski, an Illinois Democrat. Congressman Lipinski's views, which reflected his Catholic faith and included support for school choice, had led the school union bosses to spend heavily to support his challenger in the Democratic primary earlier in the year. Lipinski lost, but he spent his final months in Congress fighting for education freedom.

The Cruz-Alexander-Scott-Byrne-Lipinski bill, titled the School Choice Now Act, had a realistic chance of being included in the second COVID-19 relief package under negotiation in Congress that summer and fall. As the presidential election approached, President Trump regularly mentioned school choice at his campaign rallies—and regularly got an enthusiastic response. Education freedom was prominently featured at the Republican National Convention in August. As schools failed to open, parents began removing their children from remote-only classrooms. Polling showed growing support for charter schools, school choice, and education freedom.

In September, support for the issue was tested in a Senate vote on a COVID relief bill that included the School Choice Now version of EFS. Fifty-two senators voted yes—every Republican except Rand Paul of Kentucky, but his vote had nothing to do with school choice, which he supports, and everything to do with who Rand Paul is generally. The vote was largely ceremonial because the Mitch McConnell–led Republican package was declared dead on arrival in Nancy Pelosi's House. Still, seeing a majority of the U. S. Senate vote "aye" for a bill with the first federal effort to encourage education freedom nationally was an important measure of support for empowering families.

———————

As fall turned to winter, it became increasingly clear that the second COVID-19 relief bill was the "must-pass" legislation EFS needed to be part of. And after President Trump lost to former vice president Biden in the November election, there was no longer any doubt that this would be our only opportunity. It was that bill or no bill at all.

The pandemic was making the case for EFS stronger with each day that passed. Low-income families without internet access and child care options were genuinely suffering. Countless students weren't participating in Zoom classes and were being lost to the system altogether. Hundreds of tuition-dependent private schools in poor and working-class communities had already closed and more were under extreme financial pressure as families could no longer pay the tuition.

The Democratic leadership in the House and Senate were hearing all this from concerned constituents and thought leaders. Cardinal Timothy Dolan, archbishop of New York, communicated to Senate Minority Leader Chuck Schumer that New York, like everywhere else around the country, was losing Catholic and Jewish schools to the pandemic. House Speaker Pelosi had the same problem in California. The two Democratic leaders certainly didn't become fans of school choice, but they appreciated the uniqueness of the moment. Despite their loyalty to the school union bosses, many of their Democratic voters attended private and parochial schools. They were hurting. What to do about closed schools was a growing, albeit unspoken, concern of Democrats.

The situation was creating a tiny crack in the Democrat–teacher union alliance. It was getting harder for Democrats to ignore the voices of their constituents in favor of the school union bosses. Schumer and Pelosi were more open to the conversation than most people realized.

But just when it looked like we had a chance, the White House gave up the fight after the 2020 election loss. The president was consumed with contesting the election results. His staff was overwhelmed with either supporting his crusade, or putting out the fires he started in pursuit of it. No one seemed to notice—or care—that a deal was possible with the Democratic leadership. So Secretary of the Treasury Steve Mnuchin and Chief of Staff Mark Meadows preemptively abandoned the fight for the School Choice Now provision. The Senate passed a big mess of a spending bill—without any provision for education choice, emergency or not—on December 22. The moment was gone.

Counterfactuals are always tricky. We can't know for certain if Education Freedom Scholarships would have been passed by Congress in the last days of 2020. What we do know, however, is that a growing opportunity was squandered by a dysfunctional White House focused on all the wrong things.

CHAPTER NINE

THE GREAT PARENTAL AWAKENING

The father at the microphone at the Loudoun County, Virginia, school board meeting was mad. It was late January 2021, nearly a year into the pandemic, and Loudoun schools were still closed. His voice rose in frustration. The people who collect his trash, he said, take more risk than anyone who teaches his kids. Then the man stopped looking down at his notes and stared straight ahead at the officials seated in front of him.

"You're a bunch of cowards hiding behind our children as an excuse for keeping schools closed," he said.

The video quickly went viral, and for good reason. During the pandemic, a surging number of parents were learning—no pun intended—just how the people who run their schools view their kids. Long after it was safe for their children to return to school, the schools remained closed. Parents like the father at the school board meeting were waking up, and they weren't liking what they saw.

America's students have never before experienced anything remotely like the COVID-19 pandemic. No single event in United States history has disrupted their education more deeply and

231

more suddenly. During the course of a single month—March 2020—the number of American students whose schools closed due to the pandemic went from zero to 55 million. A year later, many of these schools had yet to reopen. Most schools still relied on remote learning, and fully a third of 4–8th graders received two hours or less of remote instruction a day. As we know now, the impact of this great educational disruption was toughest on those students who could afford it least. A full year after schools closed in 2020, only 28 percent of black students and 33 percent of Hispanic students were attending school in person full-time.[1]

As of this writing, more than two years after schools closed for COVID-19, we are still coming to grips with the massive learning losses and the social and psychological harm American children have suffered. In an early report on the effects of the closures, the management consulting firm McKinsey & Company found that, on average, students completed the 2020–21 school year four or five months behind where they should have been. For students in poor and minority communities, nearly an entire year was lost.[2]

Even more troublingly, some students were actually lost. And not just a few. Estimates suggest more than three million students were unaccounted for by their schools during the spring of 2020.[3] That's the equivalent of every school-aged child in the state of Florida just disappearing from the radar in one semester. In Boston, as just one example, it was estimated that 1 in 5 students never logged onto virtual school.[4] It remains to be seen how many of these students will ever be found.

What has become even clearer as time goes on is the psychological and emotional damage the school shutdown inflicted on students. In October 2021, child-health experts declared a "mental health state of emergency." Suicide attempts among girls aged 12–17 were up more than 50 percent. Emergency mental health visits to doctors and emergency rooms increased by 24 percent among younger students and

31 percent for teenagers.[5] The *New York Times* ran a sobering report on Christmas Eve 2021 about the state of students at a Bethlehem, Pennsylvania, high school. Violence, anxiety, depression, and what the principal called "blunt and flagrant disrespect" ran rampant through the school. Students wore their pajamas to class and walked around with their faces in their phones like they were still on an extended Zoom session.[6]

The depth and breadth of the damage to students won't be known for years. This generation will almost certainly be known as "Gen-COVID."

The impact that school shutdowns had on parents is easier to see. Parents who could afford it pulled their children away from the control of the public school system entirely. Preliminary federal government data released in the summer of 2021 showed a 3 percent drop-off in K–12 public school enrollment in 2020–21 versus the previous year. Out of a total public school population of 51.1 million, 3 percent works out to 1.5 million students. And among children just starting their education, the drop was much more precipitous. The number of public preschool and kindergarten students declined by 13 percent. These numbers will undoubtedly grow as more data comes in.[7] Parents with younger children put off enrolling them in public schools by keeping them home or sending them to private kindergartens.

Some 8.7 million families changed where their children went to school between the 2019–20 and 2020–21 school years.[8] At least 240,000 of these students moved to public charter schools, which saw an enrollment increase of 7 percent.[9]

Homeschooling rates—including families getting together in educational "pods"—more than doubled.[10] Notably, the number of Hispanic families homeschooling doubled, and the number of black families *quintupled.* And that's only what is voluntarily reported.

As of this writing, there is no official data on how many students made the transition from government-run to private and faith-based schools due to the pandemic closures. But the anecdotal evidence is everywhere. Parents who have the financial means sought schools that would be dependably open. As the public education establishment proved it couldn't be agile and committed enough to open classrooms and put kids first, parents who could sought out private and religious schools that did.

––––––––––––

Long before "two weeks to slow the spread" became another two weeks, and then another two weeks, and then another . . . I could see that COVID-19 was going to be a disaster for education. No one knew much about this new threat in those early days, but I knew this: A virus this highly contagious would certainly affect the millions of students who congregate every day in classrooms. Schools would shut down; there was no getting around it.

On January 20, 2020, the Centers for Disease Control and Prevention confirmed the first case of COVID-19 in the United States. By mid-February, schools in Washington State and New York began to close temporarily for deep cleaning to combat the virus. On February 27, Bothell High School in Washington State became the first school in the country to shut down due to a COVID-19 infection. A relative of an employee had tested positive for the coronavirus.

The impact I knew the virus would have on schools was beginning. But at that point at least, the White House was focused elsewhere. In late January, the president announced the creation of the White House Coronavirus Task Force, headed up, initially, by Secretary of Health and Human Services Alex Azar. In addition to the public health officials and White House staff on the task force, there were representatives of the Departments of Health and Human Services, State, Homeland Security, and Transportation. Education was nowhere on the list.

We made several attempts to encourage the White House to get ahead of the impact on students. We were being deluged with

calls from governors, state school chiefs, college presidents, superintendents, and local education leaders. They could see the problems
ahead, I said. Schools and students would unquestionably be deeply
impacted by the coronavirus. "We should be on the task force," I
argued. One assistant to the president didn't even try to argue the
point. "Oh crap," she said. "You're right." It was a laudable admission. Still, the White House never corrected the oversight, though
I was often invited to participate (and when a problem popped up,
I invited myself).

We had set up our own coronavirus task force within the Education Department in February to get ahead of the storm we saw rolling in. Diane Jones, our undersecretary, deserves much of the credit;
her husband works in the health field and Diane has a science background as well, so she was keeping very close tabs on the news that
was emerging out of China.

We didn't announce the task force or make it a big deal, but
during a House Appropriations Committee hearing, Congresswoman
Lois Frankel, a Democrat from Florida, asked what we were doing
about the pandemic. I think she thought it was going to be another
YouTube-worthy "gotcha" question. I shared that the Education
Department had already created a task force to deal with the antici-
pated challenges occurring in American schools. Frankel looked a lot
like the proverbial deer in the headlights. I have to assume the next
question her staff had given her to read was a strong criticism of me
that she was now unable to deliver. She yielded back.

Some White House staff, on the other hand, weren't particularly
pleased. They thought we had gotten out in front of them, but I knew
we had to be proactive. Governors, superintendents, and principals
across the country were being forced to make decisions about whether
to shut down their schools. These decisions were theirs to make,
but the confusing and conflicting guidance from federal health
officials wasn't helping. Neither was the panic-and-fear-inducing

media coverage—nor the doomsday scenarios from the union bosses, especially in America's major cities.

One of our first substantive actions at the department was to delay federally mandated standardized tests that were scheduled to begin in the next few weeks. The last thing students and teachers needed to worry about at that moment was a test, let alone the administrative nightmare it would have caused as schools were shutting down. So we made it easy for states to opt out of the testing. If students weren't in school—as growing numbers weren't—they couldn't take the tests anyway. Not to mention the fact that the data probably wouldn't be very useful. Students had a lot of other things on their minds.

Our next, immediate concern was for college students who may have their lives upended while living far from home and those with student loan debt who might not be able to continue payments because of pandemic-induced job loss or hardship. In contrast to the issue of schools as a whole, doing something about student debt sparked the White House's interest.

Chief of Staff Mark Meadows and White House Counsel Pat Cipollone called midday on March 20. The president was planning on announcing a sixty-day, penalty-free suspension of student loan payments that evening, they said. We had until 4 p.m. to figure out how to "turn off" student loans.

We scrambled and succeeded in suspending payments for millions of federal student loan borrowers. President Trump made the announcement at the White House Coronavirus Task Force press briefing that evening. We provided immediate relief for borrowers and set the interest rate on their loans at zero percent. We stopped federal wage garnishments for students and families in default and we stopped collection agencies from harassing borrowers with calls and emails.

Looking back, these were the easy things to do. They were areas where the federal government had clear control. The harder—and more pressing—task was to help students transition to remote learning. I made it my priority to emphasize something that should have been obvious but wasn't: Adults had to do everything we could to ensure that children continued to learn when schools closed. Many teachers, principals, and superintendents acted heroically to do just that. We urged state and local officials to work creatively to find solutions, not just throw up their hands and say it couldn't be done. Many responses went way beyond setting up Zoom sessions.

The solutions were different based on geography and needs. And frankly, they varied based on the intentionality of leaders to problem-solve. New Hampshire education commissioner Frank Edelblut deployed statewide technology tools to help students stay connected to learning and leveraged federal COVID relief funding to allow parents to hire tutors or go to a camp if they felt their students were falling behind because of distance learning. In remote Colorado mountain towns without internet connectivity, teachers put weekly learning packets together and held office hours by phone to help their students when they were stuck.

South Carolina deployed three thousand buses with mobile Wi-Fi hotspots to help kids in remote areas access learning. Public television stations across the country broadcasted at-home learning programs and lessons.

But too many school districts failed to teach students even close to adequately once schools closed—worse yet, too many of them just didn't try. One study found that in the first months of the shutdown, just one in three school districts even *expected* teachers to interact directly with all their students. Fewer than half of them expected teachers to collect student work, grade it, and include it in final course grades. These numbers were much worse in poor and rural districts.[11]

The best use of my office, I believed, was to support and encourage the school leaders who did think outside the box to keep educating children. Our critics in Congress—led in large part by the stolid Senator Patty Murray—constantly demanded that there be "a plan" to tell schools what to do. They must have thought it was one of their most effective lines of attack, because they said it all the time: *Where is your plan?* But central-planned "plans" wouldn't work. They *couldn't* work. There was no top-down edict that could ensure that students in the thousands of very different school districts could continue to learn. There was no one plan I could develop—there were hundreds of plans that would come together in schools and districts if people made the effort. My job was to help teachers and parents find and implement the ones that worked for them.

Some accused me of trying to exploit the COVID-19 crisis to impose my education views. But they got the causality backward. I wasn't imposing anything. Out of necessity, parents, teachers, and administrators across the country were awakening to a new vision for what makes a school and how kids can learn in different ways.

When buildings were suddenly taken out of the equation, schools began to be understood as collections of *people*—students, teachers, and families—that work together to educate kids. The pandemic—not I—was making this case. The industrial model of education that most American public schools had imposed on students for more than a hundred years was suddenly no longer possible. There were no classrooms and no desks lined up in a row filled with passive students. Teachers were forced to reach students who were scattered to the four winds. Parents were forced to be teachers. The idea of what makes a school was changing. Assistance from the federal government needed to change with it.

In April, after schools had been closed for about a month, I proposed that the federal government support the parents, teachers, and principals who were thinking creatively and proactively to educate kids in this new environment. I offered a solution the education establishment typically welcomes and even insists on: money.

My proposal was to create federal "micro-grants"—a small amount of money given directly to an individual—for disadvantaged students and students with disabilities. Families could use the new grants as they saw fit—to pay for a computer to learn at home, tutoring for their child, or a learning pod for group learning and/or therapy. They could use this money for any number of services, private and public, that would help their child continue to learn. Teachers who were working hard to pivot to new ways of communicating with students would receive the grants. College students who were entering a newly difficult job market could also use them.

I proposed that the micro-grants be funded by using 1 percent of the nearly $31 billion allocated to the Education Stabilization Fund in the first COVID relief act passed by Congress in March—around $300 million. *One percent.* One dollar out of every $100 would go to empower parents and teachers to immediately help students.

Members of the education bureaucracy had the predictable responses. "Where is her plan to push for the tens of billions of dollars that educators, governors, superintendents, and stakeholders know is needed to close budget gaps that will quickly emerge?" NEA president Lily Eskelsen García said.[12]

It was all too predictable. Eskelsen García didn't want to help parents and teachers find new ways for children to learn during the pandemic. She just wanted a *plan* that had exactly one element: more money for the same old system.*

As the spring of 2020 gave way to summer, it was increasingly clear that schools could begin to safely reopen. It was also increasingly clear that students were being harmed by not being in school. At the White House Coronavirus Task Force meetings, the medical experts reenforced my belief that schools should be reopening.

---

* It's worth noting: our team worked day and night to deliver the $30 billion Congress had appropriated to the states within 30 days. The career staff said it was the fastest the Department had ever gotten funding out the door.

Behind the scenes, there was rare unanimity on the task force. Dr. Anthony Fauci of the National Institute of Allergy and Infectious Diseases cautioned that it was prudent that schools not open in areas with high COVID-19 transmission, and that made obvious sense. But everywhere else, they should be open. Administrators just had to use common sense. Everyone agreed with this.

Another doctor on the task force, Amb. Deborah Birx, believed that children—particularly in lower grades—should be back in school for their mental health. Debbie was the first person on the task-force to talk about how the risks associated with the virus had to be balanced with the increased risks of depression, suicide, obesity, and other ill effects of school closures on children. At the end of June, the American Academy of Pediatrics called for children to be "physically present" in school as much as possible. Remote learning, the report emphasized, "was detrimental to the educational attainment of students of all ages and worsened the growing mental health crisis among children and adolescents."[13] Dr. Birx approached me with her concern that Washington was turning a blind eye to this issue. She asked me to help her spread the message that, out of a well-intentioned concern for keeping kids safe from COVID-19, we were doing more harm than good.

Dr. Robert Redfield, who was the director of the Centers for Disease Control and Prevention (CDC) at the time, had taken a personal interest in how to keep students both healthy and in school. He was working hands-on with the Archdiocese of Baltimore to evaluate modified mitigation strategies that fit the profile of their schools, including less distance between desks but more use of masks. His view was that while six feet apart was "best," three feet was still "good." He extended that offer to any school that needed help transitioning back to in-person learning. He lamented that the media tended to report CDC guidance as absolutes, as opposed to directional advice. As a result, all nuance was lost.

For me and my team at Education, it was the children who had simply fallen off the radar—estimated to be up to 3 million—that concerned us most.[14] They didn't show up for Zoom sessions or engage in any way. Children with disabilities and children suffering from abuse and neglect were also of grave concern. Many of these were children whose only lifeline was school; it was the only place they ate well and the only place they felt safe. All of these children were constantly on my heart and mind. But parents who were leaving their children alone to fend for themselves all day, either out of necessity or neglect, were not going to identify themselves. They were largely nameless and faceless, but every day that schools remained shuttered was a day these kids suffered more harm.

Despite this, it was appalling to see how many school districts and entire states dithered all summer in preparing to reopen schools. Whether these officials were incompetent or complacent or were just holding out for more money and benefits, it was all the same to their students. We clearly knew by then that kids were falling further and further behind, even as the case for opening the schools safely in the fall got even stronger.[15]

Washington, rightly, wasn't making the call as to which schools would open and which wouldn't—that was best left to states and communities. But Washington wasn't very constructive, either. Too few people in the nation's capital fully recognized the hardships parents faced with schools remaining closed—and the future political consequence it would have. Too few gave credence to the fact that children were suffering and falling behind.

In August we circulated a memo to our administration colleagues pressing the need to respond to both parents' desire to open schools and their desire to keep their children safe. It wasn't a binary decision—the solution wasn't either making all kids go back to school or keeping all kids home. The answer boiled down to education freedom.

"To escape the black-and-white debate of open schools versus safety, we must return to our core policy ideals of school choice," read the memo. "Rather than allow the Left to characterize our efforts as a federal mandate for every child to attend school in person, we must forcefully advocate for giving every American student the power—and the resources—to make the right choice for their situation."

The administration's message should have been clear and unambiguous: Students who wanted to should get back into the classroom and schools should not use excuses to keep them home and isolated. But on the question of schools and COVID-19 during the summer of 2020, the messaging was inconsistent, conflicting, or just plain missing.

As outsiders looking in to the White House Coronavirus Task Force, it was clear that a potent combination of distrust and political posturing among its members severely undercut its ability to communicate a consistent message. President Trump didn't trust Dr. Fauci, and it was just generally difficult to work with Fauci to help get schools opened. The vice president's staff didn't seem to trust Dr. Birx, so it was difficult for us to coordinate openly with her. On top of that, Dr. Fauci and Dr. Birx frequently disagreed over the unfolding science and what it meant for education. Dr. Fauci could be counted on to take the narrowest and most virus-centric position possible, while Dr. Birx's was often the voice that called for considering all the factors that impacted students: physical, mental, and emotional.

All the internal task force machinations coupled with the real-world implications for students compelled the White House to eventually lean further into the education issue. The vice president, who chaired the task force, asked me to host a meeting of the group at the Education Department. I willingly obliged. We needed to emphasize everything the administration was doing to help students and to urge educators to get back to in-person learning.

But the meeting was not all smooth sailing. The communications problems that plagued the Trump White House reemerged and muddled our message. The morning of the meeting, President Trump first raised the prospect of cutting off funding for schools that don't reopen. The president had an important point. Congress had passed billions of dollars in emergency education funding for schools, yet many of them were not open and had no plans to reopen. The public had a right to question the wisdom of this. The schools that were working hard to keep kids learning obviously needed funding. But what about the schools that weren't trying at all?

I agreed with the president's goal, but his means were typically blunt and unnuanced. First, he made the call to deny funding of schools that wouldn't open in the context of the election.

"The Dems think it would be bad for them politically if U.S. schools open before the November Election, but is important for the children & families. May cut off funding if not open!" he tweeted.

Second, President Trump was broadly perceived as saying that every child had to go back to school in person for a school to qualify for pandemic relief money. That was never the intention, but it wasn't getting through in the administration's messaging. I believed parents should have the choice of whether to send their children to school or to learn remotely. But if a school wasn't offering in-person instruction, it didn't make sense that it needed funding for in-person mitigation efforts.

When I was asked about the president's comments, I hedged because we didn't yet know if the federal government could legally withhold funds from schools that wouldn't open. I did, however, confirm that we were looking at the question "very seriously." Later in the week I was able to clarify our position. The solution to the problem of reopening schools was to be found, not in defunding schools, but in giving parents control of the funding.

"American investment in education is a promise to our students and families and if schools aren't going to reopen we're not suggesting pulling funding from education, but instead allowing families to take that money and figure out where their kids can get educated if their schools are going to refuse to open," I told Fox News' Sandra Smith.[16]

Sadly, all that got through the media filter was that we wanted to punish schools that wouldn't reopen. And for some people, if President Trump was for it, they were automatically against it. One of those people was Randi Weingarten.

"Our teachers were ready to go back as long as it was safe," she said, combatively, in September. "Then Trump and DeVos played their political bullshit."[17]

Our "political bullshit" was evidently our call for schools to safely reopen. But if the school union bosses were ready to return in the fall, how did the president's words change that? The issue that supposedly was preventing the unions from supporting reopening schools was the safety of teachers—that wasn't changed by the president's tweets. I wondered: Was it possible the union had a plan for teachers to return in the fall that they abandoned when the president began to call for schools to be opened? I didn't know. But that seems to be what Weingarten was saying. Her "political bullshit" comment suggests that it was the political struggle, not children, that mattered most.

As 2021 began, scientists looked at schools that had been fully or partially open in the fall 2020 semester and concluded that keeping schools closed was not supported by the data. Multiple studies showed that COVID-19 transmission was not affected by school openings.[18] Three researchers from the CDC published a paper in the *Journal of the American Medical Association* reporting that "there has been little evidence that schools have contributed meaningfully to increased community transmission."[19]

The evidence became even clearer that it was safe to go back to school. Countries like Denmark, Sweden, South Korea, and Japan had already opened their schools. I consulted with the British education minister, who was very aggressive about reopening schools after the pandemic hit. In the Netherlands, schools were closed for only eight weeks. Danish elementary school students were only out of class for a month before Denmark became the first European country to reopen its schools in April 2020. Most European schools, in fact, were opened by May.[20] Closer to home, many private and charter schools had safely reopened, along with district schools with less of a union stranglehold.[21]

But the school union bosses in the United States doubled down on their refusal to allow teachers to come back to school. Parents who wholeheartedly supported their schools at the start of the lockdown began to change their minds. Teachers weren't the problem, but the union leadership increasingly was.

In Montclair, New Jersey, the union stepped in and blocked a district plan for students to return to in-person education in January. It turned out, the mayor of Montclair was the number two official in the New Jersey Education Association.[22]

In Chicago, the teacher union threatened a strike if they were asked to return to the classroom. In January 2022, nearly two years into the pandemic, they did just that, leaving kids out in the cold for days. Chicago's Mayor Lori Lightfoot said the union had taken children "hostage."[23]

In California's two largest school districts, San Diego and Los Angeles, the school unions refused to conclude a months-long negotiation on the conditions under which their members would return to school.

In Fairfax County, Virginia, the union demanded their members be moved to the front of the line in early 2021 to receive the newly developed COVID-19 vaccine. But as soon as they were, the union announced that they would not support a return to in-person education *even in the fall of 2021.*

In West Virginia, the union sued the state to stop the resumption of in-classroom learning.

The union bosses in Oregon's five biggest school districts refused to reopen schools.

School unions in Newark, Philadelphia, Massachusetts, Minneapolis–St. Paul, Broward County, Manchester, Ohio, Maryland—and the list goes on and on—resisted plans to return students to the classroom, all citing COVID-19 safety concerns. And all despite the increasing volumes of scientific data—in the United States and around the world—showing opening schools was safe.

Even the *New York Times* concluded that "educators are using some of the same organizing tactics they employed in walkouts over issues of pay and funding in recent years to demand that schools remain closed."[24]

Meanwhile, Vice President Pence, Dr. Birx, and I toured the country visiting schools that had figured out how to safely have students back in person. We also met with parents who were desperate to have their children back in school. One woman, a retired teacher and the mother of a child with Down syndrome in South Carolina, told me that every day her son was out of the classroom he fell further behind—academically and emotionally. Another parent in North Carolina told me with tear-filled eyes about her daughter, a rising senior in high school. She had become worrisomely dark and depressed throughout the spring when her school was closed. But once she enrolled her daughter in a private school that had reopened, she saw a 180-degree turnaround in her daughter after just one day.

Her child has only one chance to grow up, the mom told me. She didn't have time to wait for the school union bosses to negotiate their ransom.

Few school districts more clearly demonstrated the recalcitrance of the school unions—and the compliance of the government officials they controlled—than the Los Angeles Unified School District. Home to more than 600,000 students, LA's is the second-largest school district in the country. On March 16, 2020, the district closed its schools to all K–12 students. Like districts across the country, the plan was to shut down for two weeks while schools figured out how to respond to the pandemic. That was the plan. Full-time, in-person learning did not return for Los Angles public school students until the fall of 2021—seventeen months later. The union controlled the process from start to finish.

Even at the outset of the pandemic, United Teachers Los Angeles (UTLA) boss Cecily Myart-Cruz was intent on using the school shutdown to benefit her members. As schools elsewhere scrambled to set up Zoom classes and other remote learning, Myart-Cruz insisted that her members wouldn't teach remotely for more than four hours a day, even though they would collect a full day's pay. Myart-Cruz was able to hold out until the next fall—September 2020—before Los Angeles teachers were obligated to provide any live, online instruction instead of prerecorded material.

The LA union was determined to come out of the pandemic with more than just new benefits. In the summer of 2020 the UTLA put out a "research paper" demanding that schools not reopen until federal, state, and local government stop prioritizing "plutocrats" over "pupils."

The UTLA demanded socialized medicine (Medicare for All) before schools would open. They called for defunding the police, additional wealth taxes, and a moratorium on charter schools. It was a thoroughly political wish list that had nothing to do with getting kids back in school. What's worse, their demands ended with a totally baffling statement of who stands to gain—and who stands to lose—from reopening schools. "As it stands," the UTLA concluded, "the only people guaranteed to benefit from the premature physical reopening of schools amidst a rapidly accelerating pandemic are the billionaires and the politicians they've purchased."[25]

The LA union bosses couldn't have been more wrong—nor more deceitful. It was poor, minority students—the people they claimed they were trying to help by eliminating inequality—that had the most to gain from schools reopening. Four days later, district officials went along with the union and announced that LA public schools would not reopen in the fall.

As the new school year began, negotiations dragged on and schools stayed closed. In February 2021, the union came out with a new list of demands. All school employees must be moved to number two in line—just behind health care workers—to receive COVID-19 vaccinations. In addition, communities had to achieve a level of COVID-19 transmission *lower* than the one California governor Gavin Newsom had called for. Again, like choreography, the schools superintendent announced that LA schools would not reopen until more employees were vaccinated and COVID-19 transmission rates matched the union's demand.

While all this was going on in Los Angeles and other districts nationwide, Washington was literally overwhelming school districts with new funding. In the three COVID bills, Congress passed nearly $200 *billion* in "Elementary and Secondary School Emergency Relief (ESSER)" aid for public schools. For context, in any given year, the federal contribution to K–12 education is around $40 billion.

There was initially a legitimate need to help schools navigate the COVID-19 pandemic. Schools needed to set up remote learning. Food had to be provided to children who relied on schools for meals. We regularly heard from schools about their need to clean and to upgrade ventilation systems before they could open.

The aid came in three massive infusions from Congress. The first relief bill, passed in March 2020, included $13.2 billion for K–12 schools. The second passed that December with more than $54 billion for K–12. Finally, under the new Biden administration, Congress showered an amazing $128 billion–plus on schools.

In November 2020—when Congress had passed just $13 billion of the $200 billion it would eventually appropriate to K–12—the Education Department unveiled a data "portal" that tracked the emergency money spending. *We found that only $1.6 billion of the initial $13.2 billion appropriated to schools in March—just 12 percent—had actually been spent by September 2020.*[26]

In February 2021, as Congress was poised to allocate the final and largest pot of new funding, the Congressional Budget Office estimated that government-run schools were so inundated with new money they would be able to spend only $6.4 billion of the $128 billion in fiscal year 2021. The CBO predicted it would take until 2028 for all the extra funds to be spent—years after anyone believed we would still be dealing with a COVID-19 emergency.

When the COVID-19 money was calculated by students in each state, the median amount allocated per student was $2,800. But the amount individual districts received varied wildly. Utah received $1,300 per student while Detroit received the highest amount among the large school districts: more than $25,000 per student.[27] When I saw that data, I recalled a conversation I had with the Detroit schools superintendent after the first round of COVID-19 funding had been passed. After he got Detroit's share of the initial $13.2 billion, he told me he didn't need additional money. He had bought everything he needed to safely reopen schools.

Congress's allocation of "emergency" pandemic relief was so excessive that the *Wall Street Journal* editorialized, "Democrats are using the banner of 'Covid relief' not to increase student learning but to reward a Democratic constituency at taxpayer expense."[28]

It's hard to argue with that conclusion. Schools and teachers deserved to have the resources they needed to educate children, especially in a once-in-a-lifetime pandemic. But at some point in 2020–21, Washington went beyond funding schools to funding political allies. They showered a system that was already failing students and families with the single largest infusion of federal cash in the nation's history. In doing so, they made a broken system even more entrenched.

Another example of the school unions' and their allies' willingness to play political games—even in the middle of a national emergency— was how they proposed addressing the needs of students with disabilities. Many of these students require specialized services and therapies that can only be offered in person.

Members of Congress—particularly Democrats—were in a quandary. On the one hand, they wanted to be responsive to the desires of the school lobby and unions, who had been arguing hard for waivers from having to meet the IDEA requirements for students. Fulfilling the IDEA mandates, they argued, was "impossible."[29] On the other hand, Congress didn't want to take the blame for shortchanging students with disabilities. So they punted it to me. They gave me thirty days to decide if there would be a waiver on meeting the requirements of the IDEA.

But it wasn't deference to my office. I deeply suspect they thought they had laid a clever trap.

Members of Congress quickly suggested that their *own idea* for a waiver was something I had asked for (I hadn't) and that I might use it to disenfranchise students with disabilities (I wouldn't). Predictably, they ginned the media machine up, with the *New York Times* breathlessly writing: "Tucked away in the $2 trillion coronavirus stabilization bill is a provision that allows Education Secretary Betsy DeVos to seek congressional approval to waive parts of the federal special education law while schools combat the coronavirus pandemic. *How she might use that authority scares parents . . .*" (emphasis mine).[30] Most preposterously, but not surprisingly, some members of Congress saw fit to demand I not use the authority *they* gave me—of course making no mention of their role in the whole thing.

Congress thought they could outsource the blame onto me while giving their financial backers the win they desired. But the whole episode was just more proof they never understood what motivated me. I was always going to do what's best for kids, and that meant refusing to waive educational rights for children with disabilities. It wasn't even a decision we had to think twice about.[31]

Meanwhile, in Los Angeles, all the goal-shifting and foot-dragging of the UTLA paid off. In March 2021, they finally agreed to *partially* reopen LA public schools. Better late than never, I guess you could say. At that point, almost 60 percent of students in the country were attending full-time, in-person schools. And 88 percent of students nationally were attending some in-person schooling.[32]

But for the UTLA, the long struggle was worth it. Sure, children stayed home for a full year. Full-time, in-person instruction didn't begin again for a year and a half. But the union walked away from the bargaining table with all their demands met—plus $8,363 per student in extra federal funding.[33]

When the history of American education during the coronavirus pandemic is written, it will record that when schools closed, parents were awakened to their powerlessness in the face of the education establishment. That feeling of powerlessness was amplified by what they saw on their children's screens at home.

A short history of the Loudoun County, Virginia, school board tells this story. Loudoun County has the highest median income of any county in America. Not coincidentally, it is located less than fifty miles from Washington, DC. It's an increasingly diverse community that voted for Joe Biden for president in 2020 by more than ten points.

Before COVID, Loudoun County school board meetings were sleepy, sparsely attended affairs. They occurred twice a month at the high school and nobody much cared about them. All that changed as the schools entered their eighth, ninth, tenth, and eleventh months being closed to in-person instruction during the pandemic. Organizations called Fight for Children and Loudoun Parents for Education quickly organized online and took their grievances to the Tuesday night meetings. They began to crowd the school board meetings. Concerned parents spilled out into the parking lot. Many held signs advocating for the recall of school board members.

Then an interesting thing happened. Seventeen months after they were closed, Loudoun County schools opened to full-time, in-person instruction. But the crowds at the school board meetings didn't fade away—they got bigger.

———————————————

The murder of George Floyd in Minneapolis in May 2020 set off a racial reckoning in the United States. The issue of race and how it is perceived and experienced in our country was suddenly everywhere. Much of this national soul-searching has been a long-needed corrective. It has opened many Americans' eyes to the experiences of their fellow Americans. It has shown us that life for some of our countrymen and women is marked by injustice and inequality. It has taken us back to the dream of Dr. Martin Luther King Jr., who called for the promise of the American founding—of life, liberty, and the pursuit of happiness—to be guaranteed to *all* Americans.

But this reckoning has also called forth a poisonous ideology that rejects the belief in the fundamental goodness of America held by Dr. King. It is an ideology that writes off America as irredeemably racist—founded on the exploitation of minorities, especially African-Americans, and dedicated to their continued exploitation. This America is divided into oppressors and the oppressed. White people are racist simply because they're white. Other groups are automatically victims by virtue of the color of their skin, their sexual orientation, or their perceived gender. Far from being rooted in judging people by the "content of their character," the America portrayed by this ideology is divided and at odds. And it can't be healed. It can only be torn down and remade.

"Critical race theory" (CRT) became the catch-all phrase for all the racialized, divisive ideas about race being taught. Parents of all political persuasions and races were alarmed by what they saw. Their children, they believed, were being taught to hate their country and themselves. The education establishment responded to parents' growing concern with condescension, denial, and technicalities. Defenders of the new teaching, from President Biden, to the school union bosses, to members of the Loudoun County school board, told parents they were seeing things. What they claimed was on their children's computer screens wasn't there because, they said, CRT is not being taught in elementary or high schools. It's a "decades old" theory taught only in colleges and law schools.

That was and is a complete evasion. It may be true that CRT is taught in colleges and law schools, but that doesn't mean the racism that animates it hasn't found its way to elementary and high school classrooms. It has.

In 2019, an audit of Loudoun County schools by a consulting firm called Equity Collaborative concluded that the district's public schools were a "hostile learning environment" for minority students and teachers. The county then paid the same firm almost $400,000 to create and implement a "Comprehensive Equity Plan." Loudoun County High School changed its mascot from the "Raiders"—which was linked to confederates in the Civil War—to the "Captains." They produced a video apologizing for segregation. Teachers were required to undergo training for "cultural sensitivity."

One of the training programs the Equity Collaborative offers teachers is called "Introduction to Critical Race Theory." It defines CRT as centered on "the permanence of racism" in America. It is embedded in our system and even in the beliefs we hold. To overcome this internalized racism, teachers and, therefore, students, must reject tenets of liberal democracy such as "color-blindness, the neutrality of the law, incremental change, and equal opportunity for all." These ideas function, the program continues, not to protect the inalienable rights of all, but to "allow whites to feel consciously irresponsible for the hardships people of color face and encounter daily and also maintain whites' power and strongholds within society."[34]

In other words, the foundations of liberal democracy only perpetuate racism and injustice. But what were teachers supposed to do with this information? Keep it to themselves? Teach it in a law school class? No. The prompt for the final breakout session of "Introduction to Critical Race Theory" asked teachers to contemplate "How might you use CRT to identify and address systemic oppression in your school, district, or organization?"

Some Loudoun County teachers complained about a chart used in their training sessions that broke down Americans into two groups, one that "experiences privilege" and the other that "experiences oppression." Christians were listed among the privileged, while non-Christians were deemed oppressed.[35]

None of this stopped Terry McAuliffe, the Democrat candidate for Virginia governor in 2021, from claiming it was *I* who had "made up" CRT.[36]

The outrage expressed by parents wasn't confined to Northern Virginia. School boards across the country were inundated by parents of students in schools infected with the racism of the new education ideology.

In Cupertino, California, third graders at one school were asked to create an "identity map" describing themselves. They were told to list their race, class, gender, religion, and other traits. Then the teacher told the students they live in a country with a "dominant culture" of "white, middle class, cisgender, educated, able-bodied, Christian, English speaker[s]," which uses its dominance to oppress other people.[37]

In 2019, as part of its effort to promote "equity, inclusion, and diversity," Seattle Public Schools developed a "Math Ethnic Studies

Framework." The method purports to teach math by introducing divisive and unrelated concepts. For instance, the framework asked students to "explain how math dictates economic oppression" and to "explain how math has been used to exploit natural resources." Students could also find math useful in "identify[ing] the inherent inequities of the standardized testing system used to oppress and marginalize people and communities of color."[38]

In Lexington, Massachusetts, fourth graders were taught to "articulate what gender identity is and why it's important to use nonbinary language in describing people we don't know yet." They learned about "gender identity," "gender expression," "sexual orientation," and "sex assigned at birth" by applying sticky notes to a "Gender Snowperson" drawn in Magic Marker.

These may not technically be examples of "critical race theory." But in the minds of increasing numbers of parents in the summer of 2021, CRT was just a shorthand for the racism and inappropriate sexual material being taught in their schools without their knowledge or consent. And it wasn't just happening in public schools.

The Grace Church School in New York is an elite private school that adopted the practice of routinely separating its students into groups based on race, gender, and ethnicity. One day a math teacher at the school was with a "white identifying" group of students when a diversity consultant hired by the school proclaimed that objectivity and individualism were "white supremacy" concepts. The teacher, Paul Rossi, confronted the consultant.

"Human attributes are being reduced to racial traits," he said. The consultant responded by asking Rossi if he was having "white feelings."

Some of Rossi's students shared his condemnation of the racism of the exercise with their peers. When word of it got back to the school administration, Rossi was publicly shamed for his questioning. He was offered to stay at the school only if he agreed to "restorative practices" for the minority students he supposedly harmed. He resigned from the school instead.[39]

Another parent of a child in an expensive New York City private school, the Brearley School, wrote a scathing letter to fellow parents as he withdrew his daughter from the school in disgust. Andrew Gutmann's open letter to the Brearley community is worth quoting at length because it captures the dismissal of and disregard for the opinions of parents in the new educational ideology, even at a $54,000-a-year New York private school.

> I object, with as strong a sentiment as possible, that Brearley has begun to teach what to think, instead of how to think. I object that the school is now fostering an environment where our daughters, and our daughters' teachers, are afraid to speak their minds in class for fear of "consequences." I object that Brearley is trying to usurp the role of parents in teaching morality, and bullying parents to adopt that false morality at home. I object that Brearley is fostering a divisive community where families of different races, which until recently were part of the same community, are now segregated into two. These are the reasons why we can no longer send our daughter to Brearley.[40]

Defenders of the politicization of curricula claim that these are "cherry-picked" stories that paint a false picture of schools. But these are just a few of literally hundreds of examples that have come to light as parents and teachers feel more comfortable exposing the truth about what's happening in schools.

And truth is what is desperately needed in our schools today. America's past is stained by slavery and Jim Crow. Racism lingers in their wake. Any and all American history curricula should deal honestly and forthrightly with these facts. Certainly, Loudoun County,

Virginia, has its own troubled racial past. But the "woke," CRT-infused ideology in our schools goes far beyond teaching the facts of our history or even acknowledging the ongoing challenges of our present. In the name of "antiracism," *racism* is being taught to American children. Fundamental facts of our country and its founding principles are at best being overlooked and at worst being distorted and denied.

Perhaps most damaging to the education of children is the fact that the solution often advocated for achieving "equity"—reducing the gap in academic performance between races—is to lower expectations and standards for everyone, not to raise the achievement of lower performers. Even though schools are awash in new funding thanks to the COVID-19 relief bills, many are simply giving up on learning standards and an aspiration for excellence. Instead they rationalize their surrender with the twisted logic of critical race theory.

In the summer of 2021, Kate Brown, the Democratic governor of Oregon, quietly signed a law doing away with a requirement that high schoolers in Oregon demonstrate that they can read, write, and do math before they can graduate. The problem was that the graduation rate of African-American students lagged that of white students in Oregon schools. So the solution, according to Governor Brown, was to make everyone "equal" by eliminating standards. Without any apparent understanding that she was demeaning the groups the governor purported to want to help, the governor's spokesman said the elimination of the test will benefit "Oregon's Black, Latino, Latina, Latinx [*sic*], Indigenous, Asian, Pacific Islander, Tribal, and students of color."[41]

There is nothing more antithetical to achieving equality between individuals of different races than defining standards, merit, and hard work as "racist." Lamentably, this toxic message isn't just being spread in government schools. In 2020, the Knowledge is Power Program (KIPP) charter school chain announced that it was abolishing its traditional slogan, "Work Hard, Be Nice," in an effort to tackle systemic racism. Apparently the phrases "work hard" and "be nice," in the KIPP leadership's eyes, "supports the illusion of meritocracy."[42] By exposing that "illusion," the once-great KIPP schools signaled to parents of all races that they no longer cared about the achievement and success of their students. But what parent wants to send their child to a school that believes rewarding accomplishment is an "illusion"?

———————

President Trump had a tendency to call at random times and places. Most of his calls were unscheduled, whenever he was inspired to pick up the phone. Such was the case one weekend in the summer of 2020 when the president called me to do something about the 1619 Project.

The 1619 Project was a production of the *New York Times* that was explicitly intended to "reconsider"—critics would say revise—American history in light of the existence of slavery. The date in the name of the project, 1619, is believed to be the year that the first African slaves arrived in the colonies of the New World. The central assertion of the 1619 Project is very much in line with the principles of critical race theory. The real date of the American founding, it argued, is not 1776 but 1619. America was founded on slavery and slavery was responsible for America becoming a great power. In fact, the 1619 Project asserted, slavery was the *purpose* of America. The Revolutionary War, it says, was fought to preserve slavery.

The most respected scholars of American history lauded the series for focusing on slavery in America's history but noted that many "facts" it asserts—including the central fact that the United States was founded to preserve and protect slavery—were flatly wrong. In fact, one of the Project's own fact-checkers felt compelled to publicly share the factual edits the *New York Times* team refused to make.[43] But that didn't stop the series from being made into a podcast, a book, and—alarmingly—a high school curriculum.

President Trump's purpose in calling me that particular weekend was to rant about the pernicious inaccuracies in the 1619 Project—an opinion I very much shared—and to ask me about the feasibility of simply banning it from American schools. I had to remind him that the United States does not have a national curriculum, and for good reason. The federal government can't ban the 1619 Project, I said. The states have to stand up and fight this fight. But we could and should use our bully pulpit to talk about how distorted and divisive the project was.

President Trump said he understood, but it clearly wasn't the answer he wanted to hear. The White House then came up with the idea to create a curriculum to push back against the 1619 Project. As the election approached in September 2020, the administration created a 1776 Commission to support what the president called "patriotic education." We argued that it was completely appropriate for a private sector entity to create a curriculum that corrected the revisionist history of the 1619 Project, but the federal government cannot and should not create a national curriculum. If you opposed Common Core, we argued, you have to oppose this. A better use of our time and resources, we contended, was to advocate for a return to teaching civics in American public schools, something that has been almost completely abandoned.

In the end, it was the Biden administration, not the Trump administration, that politicized the teaching of American history. Almost immediately after they came into office, the Biden Department of Education changed the criterion for schools to receive the department's largest grant for teaching American history and civics. They cited the 1619 Project and critical race theorist Ibram X. Kendi in announcing that programs that "incorporate racially, ethnically, culturally, and linguistically diverse perspectives" would be given priority in receiving the grant. The ensuing uproar forced the administration to withdraw the criterion several months later. No wonder.

More than two-thirds of adults oppose schools teaching students that America was founded on racism.[44]

This lack of support for racist ideology in our schools stands in stark contrast to the avowed views of the school unions. Last year, in the middle of the parent uprising at school board meetings, the National Education Association voted to support school curricula "informed by academic frameworks . . . including critical race theory." It also committed tens of thousands of dollars to not only promote this toxic ideology, but also to conduct opposition research against its critics.

About the same time, Randi Weingarten told educators at the American Federation of Teachers annual conference that parents are "bullying teachers" with their opposition to CRT. She also claimed that the anti-CRT ferment was part of a political effort to influence the 2020 elections (never mind that the AFT transferred more than $10 million to Democratic politicians in 2020 alone). The NEA and AFT proceeded to create two different funds, the first to promote the value of teaching CRT and the second to defend teachers who were criticized for teaching CRT. But at the same time, they continued to argue that schools *weren't teaching* CRT.[45][46] Incredibly, the legacy corporate media never caught on that these two actions were irreconcilable.

The entire history of the pandemic school shutdown is testimony to the power imbalance between parents and the unions. Contrary to the spin of their spokespeople, it's school union bosses who are the bullies. Most parents didn't want to fight with their local school boards. They spoke out because they care about their kids, and they were tired of government-run, union-controlled schools imposing their version of what's best for them.

Understanding America requires understanding the sins of our past, slavery very much included. But it also requires appreciating the ways generations of Americans have worked together to form a more perfect union. It requires teaching the *whole* of our history, with an eye toward appreciating what's good about America. A thoroughly self-loathing account of our history is poisonous. It's also wrong.

The answer isn't to ban critical race theory in schools, as many state legislatures have tried to do. Ideas can't be banned, even noxious ones. And reflexive anti-Americanism is going to continue to be present in some schools no matter what state legislatures decree.

The answer is for American parents to have schools that reflect *their* values, not the NEA's. The answer is to force the government school monopoly to be responsive to the people it's supposed to serve. Who doubts that public school leaders would be a lot less likely to jam political and social agendas down the throats of young students if they knew parents had the power to enroll their children elsewhere?

Parents—especially many minority parents—just want their children to be educated, period. If union activists want to look for systemic racism in this country, they need look no further than the government-assigned schools they so crassly and stridently defend. Our current education system is the definition of systemic racism—it is designed to hold poor black and Hispanic children hostage to the agendas of those who run it.

Among many other things, education freedom is the idea that students should be free to learn wherever, whenever, and however works best for them. That includes being free from forced indoctrination by the adults who run their schools. Our kids deserve to be challenged, not brainwashed.

CHAPTER TEN

WHAT'S A PARENT TO DO?

Imagine with me, for a moment, that the year is 2030. You're the parent of an ambitious middle schooler, and together you are charting out the mix of courses your daughter will take next. It's summer, but that doesn't mean she's on summer break. It doesn't make a whole lot of sense for an ambitious child—or really any child—to take a three-month break from learning simply because that's how it's always been done.

Instead she started her morning in a virtual Hindi immersion course taught by one of the finest dual-language instructors in Mumbai. She's not only learning the language—a course your assigned government school doesn't offer—but has made friends truly the world over. She hasn't yet said it, but they're clearly working on a plan to all meet in person someday, somewhere.

Next she'll head to a STEM-focused charter academy nearby for some applied math coursework. There are no math textbooks; instead they learn geometry and algebra concepts hands-on as they program an AI-powered robot. You're hoping today might be the day she trains it to clean up her room, one of the few things in life she does not seem especially interested in.

She'll hop in a ride-share vehicle with a few classmates after math to head to what was known as the elite private school when you were a kid, the one you wanted to attend but your parents could never dream of being able to afford. Today it's simply known as a really great school. There she is taking an integrated course on economics, history, and government. Today they're running a simulation on how tax rates impact new business start-ups.

In the fall, she wants to spend mornings at the school attached to the church you attend, focusing on character development. It's important to all of you for her to stay close to the values your family holds dear. While there, she'll work on her writing skills. She'll be in a classroom, but the teacher won't be. He's the author of last year's must-read teen fiction sensation. He never would have been interested in teaching writing at just one school, but he was intrigued by a proposal to teach fifty classes simultaneously. There will be a coach in the room to help make sure everyone gets any help they need, and the author-turned-educator is planning to visit your daughter's school in person a few weeks into the semester. Your daughter tries to hide it, but she couldn't be more excited.

The cost to you for all of this? Not one cent. Your state passed an education savings account law five years ago. Instead of sending the resources allocated to your child's education to a school building you didn't select, the new law puts them into an education account you control. Your daughter's love of learning has exploded since then. Sure, there are still mornings when you have to cajole her out of bed, but once she's up, she's learning, and there's no stopping her.

Or perhaps you're the parent of a high schooler in a rural area in mid-America. He goes to what most consider to be a pretty good regional public school, and for the most part, he would agree. His teachers care and the classes he can take are fairly engaging.

But they don't have any of the courses he really *wants*. His aim is to become an artificial intelligence machine learning engineer. It's not a common job in his farming community, but he thinks integrating robotics and sensors could really improve crop yields and reduce the amount of water and pesticides required.

He starts his morning on the farm, helping his dad. He's enrolled in the Great Books program at Columbia University and uses the tractor time to listen to the novels. At 9 a.m., he heads to the John Deere factory where he's employed in an apprenticeship, working side by side with some of the best thinkers in the AI field. He's there through lunch, and then heads back home and attends a virtual charter school for his core coursework (which also gives him class credit for the apprenticeship). He's found that the self-paced lessons help him focus better than he did in the classroom, plus he can work through the material much faster than the classroom pace. Five p.m. is football practice. They've shifted to a community-based team versus a school-based team. Previously there was only one school and they excluded nonenrolled students. They realized a couple of years ago that that didn't really make much sense. The team has won a lot more games since then, too.

He, too, does all of this through his education savings account. It doesn't cost his family anything, which is good on a family farm where the margins always seem to be tight. Perhaps his newfound engineering and computer science skills will help improve their fortunes—and everyone else's in town—before long.

Maybe instead you're a single parent living in an urban area. You commute to work, and the hours are long. They don't come close to matching up with the hours your government-assigned school has set. It's a struggle every day just to make sure someone has eyes on your child from when you both hop on the bus in the morning until the evening, when you can get home.

You're concerned about academic quality, but you're especially concerned about safety. The neighborhood seems to be getting worse with each passing year. One day you come across a booth at the YMCA with all sorts of information about school options in the area. You never really had the time to think about sending your child somewhere else; most days you barely have time to think at all. One option catches your eye. It's a dual-language immersion school, and importantly, it's open from 7 to 7. They've brought several community resources and programs together under one roof to provide a safe, nurturing place for kids like yours to gain new skills and expand their horizons, versus enduring what waits for them on the streets.

You marvel at the novel concept of a school that works around parents' schedules, not the other way around. But as a result, you assume there must be a cost that's beyond your means. Much to your surprise, it is covered fully by a tax-credit-funded scholarship program in your state. You enroll your child on the spot.

———————————

This is what education can look like. It's what it *should* look like. Innately curious children following their passions, expanding their horizons, and learning from the best of the best. Educators— both those trained to teach and those who have a lot of knowledge to impart—freed to inspire and engage young minds, not conform to a system controlled by mandates from on high and measured only by a standardized test.

It's a stunning contrast to what education looks like today. It's also a quantum leap from what most of us can imagine education looking like, probably because we've never known another way.

Education reformers call the approach to education I've described above "unbundling." It means what it sounds like. Instead of "bundling" every course into a package provided at a school, unbundled education looks at classes, venues, and learning in pieces that can be mixed and matched to best meet an individual student's needs.

An easier way to understand this concept is to consider a closer-to-home example: your television.

It's hard to guess what your specific setup might look like today. But the odds are high that not long ago you had cable. It delivered the channels the cable company chose. You paid the price the cable company set. If you didn't have a cable outlet in the room you wanted, or even on the right side of the room, you either had to simply accept it, or go through quite a process to run cable to where it needed to be.

Others might have had a satellite dish in the past. And when you think about it, the functionality wasn't all that different from cable. It was just a different way of delivering the same content, still trapped in the same "take it or leave it" dynamic. Except, of course, that with the satellite dish, you would have no picture at all if the weather turned bad.

Or, for others still, maybe cable or satellite was something you only dreamed about—they were more than you could afford. You would have loved to have more choices of things to watch, but it wasn't in the cards. So you readjusted the rabbit ears and got whatever was available over the air. For a long time, that wasn't necessarily bad, since CBS, NBC, and ABC were the content creators of "must-see TV" anyway.

In thinking about the ways we watched television in the past, it didn't really matter if you didn't like the channels you got. Or if there was a channel you wanted to get but didn't. You were stuck with what the system provided and how they provided it. Consumers were hostages to the system, to the way things had always been done. Improvements were incremental, not transformative. The upgrade to an on-screen guide from the printed *TV Guide* was helpful, but it didn't fundamentally change what you could watch.

Now fast-forward back to the present reality. For most, watching television looks much different today. We subscribe to Netflix, to Disney+, to Amazon Prime, to HBO Max. We stream the TV channels we want. And my grandkids are still bemused when they watch something that involves a—gasp!—commercial.

But it's not just the "cord cutters" (or "streamers") who are benefiting. Cable itself has responded to changes in customer demand.

They offer many more packages and options to customize the channels you receive. Satellite does the same. They even offer streaming versions of their traditional product—no physical cable necessary. The delivery mechanisms are not the only things that have changed. Content has improved and multiplied as well. Almost every network or platform has had a breakout original program. There are almost too many good shows to watch.

These changes have also disrupted the movie rental industry (RIP, Blockbuster). You no longer need to "be kind, rewind" or make sure the DVD doesn't get a scratch. The movies you want are available, in your home, on demand.

I could go on with the example, but I think you get the point. It's not just that TV has been disrupted. It's not just different. It's better. Way better. Better for everyone. Higher quality, more options, more control, and less expensive.

We can do the same with education.

E ducation is the least disrupted industry in America. I've made that statement often. People in education still get offended at hearing the word *industry*, but that doesn't make it any less true. Education *is* an industry. It provides a service to the public. It exchanges that service for money, with outposts in every town across the country. Education has vendors, trade shows, whole lines of business set up just to support it, and lobbyists—armies of lobbyists—local, state, and federal lobbyists. Truth be told, there are some classic industries that don't have all of that.

What's more telling to me is that the education establishment doesn't quibble with the "least disrupted" part of the above statement. They can't, because they know it's true. They know education hasn't evolved the way television has, the way everything else we interact with has.

Horace Mann, who originally called American children "hostages to the cause" of our public school system, is often called the "father" of that system. In the middle of the nineteenth century, Mann took a model of education developed in central Europe for the industrial age and brought it to American schools. Students lined up in rows. A teacher in front of a blackboard. Learning was rote. Sit down; no talking; eyes up front. Wait for the bell. Move to the next class. And . . . repeat.

American education hasn't really changed from the basic framework Mann created 175 years ago. Think about that in this context: Horace Mann died nearly two decades *before* Alexander Graham Bell invented the telephone. The man who designed the education system that is still structurally intact across almost all of the United States never made a telephone call. He likely didn't even dream of such a thing.

It took a century—one hundred years—from Bell's first call to Mr. Watson before the first cell phone came on the market. And three decades after that Steve Jobs held the first iPhone up to the world. In total, 150 years came and went between "father" Horace Mann's demise and our ability to access information the world over from the palm of our hand. A child entering kindergarten today may very well never see a landline telephone in his or her entire life, or at least not outside of a museum. While that may evoke some nostalgia for those of my generation, it would be hard to argue that the child is worse off because of it.

That's the beauty of disruption. Ideas that stick do so because they make our lives better. They signal progress. They improve the human condition. And that's what makes it nonsensical that so many oppose allowing education to be disrupted—to be improved. Yes, change is scary, but change is also how we make things better.

We've considered how disruption works; how innovation can transform things for the better. Now let's talk about the things that inhibit change. Let's talk about taxis.

For decades, taxis were the only game in town because government mandated it. Government sold expensive taxi "medallions"—licenses—drivers had to have to operate a taxi. This system of government control severely limited options for riders. You had to pay whatever their rate was. You had to endure whatever cabbie you found yourself along for the ride with. The car was the car—usually old, smelly, and not terribly comfortable. And you had to pay cash—it was impossible for them to take credit cards, they said.

Then one day Uber came along.

Suddenly the rider had real choices. There were different types of cars. There were different price points. You could schedule a ride. You could see if the driver was someone you trusted. Payment was handled on the front end, on a credit card—no awkward tip conversation, no scrambling for cash. And it's not just that Uber was a great improvement on a long-standing, entrenched system. It was, but that wasn't the only way Uber improved life for the rider. Uber improved the entire system of automobile transportation. Cabs changed because they had to—their monopoly protection was gone. Suddenly they took credit cards. They had an app. They took quality more seriously. The competition and disruption forced them to become better.

That's what I want for education in America. I'm not just looking for the Uber, the Netflix, or the Amazon Prime of schools, though we desperately need those. I want the spark that will force the whole system to evolve and improve. My mission—truly my calling—is to motivate enough disruption so that we no longer imagine doing education the same old way, because the alternative is so plainly better.

Let me pause here to underscore the obvious: Educating children is not the equivalent of television, transportation, or telephones. It isn't the same. It's far more important. Educating all American children is realizing the promise of America. It's about their future and ours. We all have a very practical—a very unsentimental—interest in seeing all American children educated to their fullest potential.

That doesn't mean education will look the same "new and improved" way for everyone, either. The dynamic vision I shared of a child learning in several different environments, in several different ways, might seem like something that would fit your child well. Alternatively, you may conclude your child needs a more structured environment with robust guardrails in order to learn and grow optimally. You might even conclude that your assigned public school is the right option. And that's great!

When it comes to finding the truth, there are right and wrong answers. But when it comes to how to best educate your child, there is no universally true answer—the true answer is the one that is right for *your* child and family.

No child is average. I don't say that as a predictable cliché; I say it as an empirical fact.

Todd Rose, a professor at Harvard, relayed a story in his important book, *The End of Average*.[1] The U.S. Air Force faced a serious problem following World War II: Planes kept crashing. The problem was there was nothing wrong, mechanically, with the planes. The first thought was it must be "pilot error," but after interviewing the pilots, it became clear that that likely wasn't the case. So the Air Force started looking at the conditions in which the pilots flew the airplanes.

When the Army had first designed the cockpit in 1926, it had done so based on measuring various physical attributes of a hundred soldiers and determining the "average" size of hands, heads, arms, legs, and everything else. One enterprising airman thought that might be the root cause of the problem. They commissioned a much larger study, of 4,063 pilots, to see how many fit within the "average" dimensions. The results were telling. In what became an "aha!" moment, they found that exactly zero pilots fit ten out of ten of the physical dimensions most important to cockpit design.

There was no average-sized pilot.

The Air Force decided to make the needed shift. The plane needed to fit the pilot, not the other way around. Naturally, the military establishment and plane manufacturers balked, said it couldn't be done, and said it would be prohibitively expensive. But the military held its ground, and the aeronautical engineers figured it out. Technology that exists in every car or home today, like adjustable seats and helmet straps, became the norm. As a result, every pilot could easily reach all the instruments and pedals and their gear actually fit. Lo and behold, pilot performance improved. Planes stopped crashing. The problem was solved.

Human beings are individuals. We are all unique, in the Webster's dictionary sense of the word. But Mann's education system isn't about embracing our inherent uniqueness; it's about creating conformity.

H. L. Mencken, one of the preeminent authors and cultural critics of the 1920s, aptly described American education this way:

> The most erroneous assumption is to the effect that the aim of public education is to fill the young of the species with knowledge and awaken their intelligence, and so make them fit to discharge the duties of citizenship in an enlightened and independent manner. *Nothing could be further from the truth.* The aim of public education is not to spread enlightenment at all; it is simply to reduce as many individuals as possible to the same safe level, to breed and train a standardized citizenry, to put down dissent and originality.[2] (emphasis mine)

Mencken's century-old description is not too far off from today. Education is still bound by what Todd Rose dubbed the "tyranny of the average." A "C" is an *average* grade (or it was before grade inflation). Students accumulate a grade point *average*. Parents strive to move to a neighborhood with "above *average*" schools. A teacher, put in a room with twenty-one kids (the national *average*[3]), is left with little alternative but to teach to the *average* student, with few practical ways to help advanced students move more quickly and struggling students get more help.

Curriculum planners determine what an *average* student needs to know. They determine what *average* (which they even more ominously call "adequate") yearly progress needs to be. They give standardized tests to gauge if an *average* amount of learning has taken place. And sometimes they even grade on a curve if the *average* didn't turn out to actually be, well . . . *average*.

Even the very structure of the school conforms to an *average*. Kids of the same age are grouped into the same class, assuming they share an *average* ability based on their shared age. Pause there a moment—how brilliant is that?! Just because two individuals are both ten years old does not mean they have learned the same things in their first nine years of life, nor does it mean they will learn at the same pace moving forward or learn in the same manner. Worse yet, the assumption of *average* is applied across every subject. "The system" leaves no space for them to be advanced readers or struggling scientists. Instead, they are in the fifth grade (assuming their birthday was at the average time of year)—period.

As secretary, I often posed what we called the "why" questions. They went something like this:

- Why do we group students by age?
- Why do schools close for the summer?
- Why must the school day start with the rise of the sun?
- Why are schools assigned by your address?
- Why do students have to go to a school building in the first place?
- Why is choice only available to those who can buy their way out? Or buy their way in?
- Why can't a student learn at his or her own pace?
- Why isn't technology more widely embraced in schools?

- Why do we limit what a student can learn based upon the faculty and facilities available?

My observation was these kinds of questions often get labeled as "nonnegotiable" or put in a category of "things we can't change." I think more commonly, if someone does ask these questions, they get a shoulder shrug and everyone moves on.

There's nothing wrong with different people having different answers to these questions. In fact, that's my very point. If education shouldn't be a one-size-fits-all endeavor, then there shouldn't be a standardized answer to the questions. But these are questions that should be asked and answered. They—and more—*must* be. This is the only way to end the averaging of America's students.

Public education should mean educating the public, not a specific type of school building or school system. Understanding this definition of public education is central to understanding what the future needs to hold. I would argue that any *school* that educates the public is a public school. And any *place* or *person* that educates the public is providing public education. After all, that's the point of publicly funding education—to have the public be educated.

Even to Horace Mann, the reason parents were to give their children as hostages was that he knew a republic composed of uneducated individuals was unlikely to remain a republic for very long. Washington and Jefferson, along with most of their contemporaries, held similar views.

In fact, the first voucher for education in America wasn't actually established in 1989 in Wisconsin. The first one came about much earlier than that—in 1781, to be exact. Thomas Jefferson, while constructing Virginia's school system, realized some students would have the capabilities and interest to pursue higher levels of schooling than what their parents would be able to afford and beyond what the public schools of the day offered. So Jefferson proposed a simple solution: The government would cover the cost of their tuition.[4] Jefferson didn't call it a "voucher," but that's precisely what it was.

I have yet to meet any serious person opposed to education, or to public education—as defined above. That's what makes the union talking point that I and other reformers are "anti–public education" so maddening. One of the most cited but least sensical criticisms of school choice is that it's meant to destroy or defund public schools. In a choice system, the only way a traditional public school loses students, and thus funding, is if a family *chooses* to leave the school. The odds are low that someone would choose to leave a school where their student is learning, growing, and thriving. Students are going to leave schools that aren't working for them. And if a school isn't working for enough of the kids assigned to it, that should be a signal to the leadership that changes need to happen. And if they can't respond accordingly, maybe it should close! Clearly it isn't doing its job.

This is what happens with charter and private schools. If not enough families choose them, they close. Just like Blockbuster closed. There's nothing inherently bad about this. Stores and businesses close every day. New ones open. This healthy dynamic is what continually brings us better restaurants, better grocery stores, better experiences in every other area of life.

The reason public schools don't close is that we've become more attached to the infrastructure than to who is served inside. Defending the system and all of its component parts—its buildings, its traditions, its power, even our nostalgia about our own school experience—has become what matters most. "The system" is the focus of nearly all discussions about K–12 education.

It is worth noting that I've never heard it claimed that giving parents more options is bad for mom and dad. Or for the child. What you hear is that it's bad for "the system"—for the school building, the school system, the funding stream. That tells you a lot about where priorities lie.

Let me posit another hypothetical. Imagine we gave every student in America an education savings accounts with the sum total of the local, state, and federal taxpayer investment that is currently given to their government-assigned school.

What would be the downside?

Kids would still learn. Teachers would still teach. Taxpayers would spend the same amount as they are today.

Of course, I believe—and the research confirms—education would improve. Students would learn more. Teachers would have more autonomy to teach. Taxpayers would get a better return on their investment.

But even if you don't believe all of that, decades of data prove unequivocally that the present system isn't working. Recall the NAEP and PISA scores. We have government schools that are consistently producing middling results—even for the "best" students.

So why haven't we stopped trying to "reform" our education system by doing the same thing over and over? Why haven't we changed our education system to one of education freedom?

As Donald Trump infamously said, though in a different context, "what the hell do you have to lose?"

Terry McAuliffe was wrong. Parents *should* have a say in what their children are taught. Parents *must* have a say. Parents must remain the primary educators of a child, because it is *your* child! The idea that modern families should surrender the education of their children to the experts, as hostages to the cause, is as antiquated as it is alarming.

So what do you do about it? How do you end the hostage-taking of your children? Here's your opportunity—your homework, so to speak.

Reclaim Your Role as Your Children's Primary Educator

Since Horace Mann installed our education system, parents have been told to leave educating to the experts. Parents have been subtly or not so subtly told that they are not qualified to be involved in educating their children. But no one cares about your child more than you do. You have the right as a parent to see that your child receives an education that is not only excellent, but also reflects your values.

You also have the opportunity and obligation to be involved in your child's education. More than just pickup and drop-off, parental engagement actually requires active involvement in what your child learns and doesn't learn. It means taking responsibility and ownership, as a family, for learning. It includes solving problems, not just lodging complaints.

Demand Education Freedom

Here's something you can do right now. Email, call, and write your state legislators, your governor, your members of Congress, even the president of the United States. Tell each of them you want education freedom for your family. You want the power, the control, and the money, to make sure your child gets the right and best education for them.

You can do it easily here: https://www.federationforchildren.org/advocacy/.

You may not believe your voice matters, or that politicians listen, but I can tell you from firsthand experience: They do. Hearing from constituents who feel strongly about an issue can give a politician the courage to vote for education freedom. I've seen it happen many times.

Open a School

This may sound daunting, but thousands of parents across America did it during the past two years. We called them different things— pods, homeschools, micro-schools, and the like. But if a school is a place where students can learn and grow, they all count as schools.

Perhaps you see a need in your community for a school that focuses on kids with a passion for the arts, like Kansas City Academy. Or entrepreneurship, like an Acton Academy. Or actually succeeding at teaching reading, writing, and arithmetic, like Success Academy. Whatever the need is, whatever the passion of the kids is, whatever your skills and gifts are—you can do it! All it takes to start the revolution needed in education is engaged parents who get involved and commit themselves to making a difference.

Be an Engaged Part of Your Child's Learning Journey

Anyone and everyone can start doing this today. There is no barrier to entry. Ask probing questions of your child about what they learned at school today. Find ways to make everyday tasks opportunities to learn about something new. Go on learning field trips together. Even just picking up a book and reading together can have a significant impact.

Be committed to lifelong learning yourself, as well. Model a love of curiosity and growing that your children can emulate. Share with them when you learn something new. If you foster an environment where learning is the norm, it becomes a joy, not a burden.

Ask to See the Curriculum

The quality of the teacher and the rigor of the curriculum are two of the most undeniable keys to academic success. But for too long, too many have tried to obfuscate both. Parents have a right to see what is being taught to their children and doing so can often provide valuable insights into how your school is approaching teaching core subjects. You can start by just asking to see the curriculum. If the school stonewalls you, you may be able to use the Freedom of Information Act (or a similar process in your state) to request a copy.

Additionally, the parental "right to know" requirements of the Every Student Succeeds Act (ESSA; the federal law that governs most of K–12 education) allow every parent to request and receive detailed information about the qualifications of their child's teacher. It also provides many other rights for parental engagement, including frequent reports on your child's progress and the district's plan to ensure that every child can meet the challenging standards the district has set out.[5]

The Protection of Pupil Rights Amendment (PPRA) ensures a school cannot ask sensitive, personal questions of your child, including questions about politics, sex, or religion, without your permission.[6] In addition, the Family Educational Rights and Privacy Act, or FERPA in Washington acronym-speak, exists to help ensure student privacy. It gives parents the right to see their child's education records.[7]

Run for School Board

Like most governmental entities, schools are only accountable when they are held accountable. The most powerful way to hold government schools accountable is to get elected to their governing board. School boards have broad, though certainly not complete, control over what happens within a school system. By joining one, you can be a voice for what's best for the parents and students in your area.

If running for election isn't for you, there are other impactful options: Show up. Ask questions. Provide feedback. Challenge, respectfully, when necessary. Board meetings may not remain the "must-see TV" programming they are today for long, but they are still public meetings where any citizen can go on record and raise issues that require attention. You can also ask to meet privately with school board members.

The same framework applies at private schools. Though they may not have an elected school board, they are still sensitive to the demands of their tuition-paying families. Meet with the head of school to share your views and expectations, or consider forming a volunteer parent advisory committee to make sure your voices are being heard.

Be an Education Voter

Voters are often grouped into categories (like Second Amendment, environment, abortion, etc.). As a result, there is perceived political power in those movements. Education should be the same. Parents should be seen as a force that politicians don't want to cross, just as they were in Virginia in 2021.

Start locally. Find out when your school board elections are and vote. Then move upstream, making sure your state representatives, governor, and members of Congress are willing to support meaningful education reform and freedom. Don't cast your vote for any elected official at any level who refuses to do what's best for your kids.

This certainly isn't an all-encompassing or exclusive list; there are a thousand ways you can start revolutionizing education today. The real key is to get involved, to ask the tough questions, to advocate, to demand better, to have a seat at the table.

The same maxim applies for schools, as well. Parental engagement cannot be viewed as a "check the box" activity. Earnestly caring about what parents think, along with the desire and openness to make changes when expectations aren't being met, must be daily postures. The schoolhouse doesn't exist for its own benefit; it exists to serve those who gather inside to learn.

Fundamentally changing education will begin around dining room tables and classroom tables. It starts with concerned parents and caring educators deciding to make changes—big and small, easy and hard—because they're necessary. Americans can do hard things. We always have.

I thought President Trump captured that idea very nicely when he said, "If we can put a man on the moon, dig out the Panama Canal, and win two world wars, then I have no doubt that we as a nation can provide school choice to every disadvantaged child in America."[8]

Empowering every family with the opportunity to get a high-quality education is nowhere near as hard or complicated as the things he cited. It just requires people, like the airmen who fixed the cockpit in our fighter planes, willing and committed to making changes.

When I was at the Education Department, I met a parent who was desperate for answers. She wasn't someone at a round-table or in a meeting. She was a cashier in the department cafeteria. Her name was Shirley, and we became friendly. I sought her out every time I went to get some lunch. One day, when I asked her how her family was doing, she confided in me that she was really worried about her four children. Most of them were not doing well in their government-assigned school, and she felt powerless to do anything for them. They were uninterested and unengaged and she was afraid they would drop out and they would never reach their potential.

I told Shirley about a lifeline she could grab. The DC Opportunity Scholarship was available for her children. Congress had created it as the only federal school choice program in the country. Shirley could use it to get her children in better schools that better fit their needs. She didn't have to sit helplessly and worry. There was an option for her kids. I sent her the link to the program.

I didn't see Shirley again for several months. Our cafeteria closed down and she was working at another agency. When I did run into her again, she could not wait to tell me about her kids. Her four children were now attending the Cornerstone School—a small, Christian, academically rigorous school in Washington, DC. Her sister's four were attending there, too. They were thriving.

By the grace of God, the DC Opportunity Scholarship was there for Shirley's kids. The school union bosses and their allies have been trying to kill the program since that very determined mom, Virginia Walden Ford, rallied a bipartisan group in Washington to create it.

That they haven't succeeded in killing it is a miracle. The DC scholarship program stands as a testament to what is possible. It was created under improbable circumstances once. It can and must be re-created in other communities.

I don't pretend to have all the answers for parents looking for a miracle for their kids. And I never set out to be a politician, so I don't have a ten-point plan to fix everything that's wrong in America. But I do have countless examples of leaders and schools that are showing us the way to change education for the better—for our children. I've shared some of their stories here.

My hope is that this book will start a conversation about what you can do for your child, your grandchildren, and your community. I hope it has opened your eyes, mind, and heart to thinking afresh about what we must do to change how we educate kids in America. I hope it has given you optimism that change can happen. *Miracles* happen. They just haven't happened in enough places and for enough kids . . . yet.

Instead of doing more of the same things to support the same unsuccessful approach and the same outdated system, let's focus on the children the system is meant to serve. I often use the metaphor of a backpack. Most kids take one to school daily, filled with the things they need for that day. Let's try putting the money that is already allocated for their education into that backpack and empowering their family to make the decision about where to spend that money for that child's education. This approach is already working for kids in places like Florida and Arizona and Indiana and Milwaukee. There's every reason to believe it will work everywhere.

An overwhelming majority of Americans consistently support giving parents more options for where and how their children learn. Public charter schools are wildly popular. More students are home-schooled today than since Horace Mann began taking hostages to his 175-year-old cause. American parents are beginning to take back their children's education.

There is an unavoidable reality that confronts those who stand against fundamental reform and defend the "cause" and the system. They could repeal every voucher law, close every charter school, and defund every choice program across the country, but they couldn't make school choice go away. There will always be education choices for the affluent and the powerful. It's the marginalized who will continue to be left behind. Those who can't afford to move or pay tuition. Those who didn't fit an "average." Those who come from the "wrong side of town."

It's kids like Denisha, Samuel, Janiyah, and hundreds more like them I've met through the years, and thousands more I've never met but who face the same challenges. They aren't hung up on what "type" of school they attend. They don't care about the school choice mechanism or the union steward. They care about learning in a safe and nurturing environment that challenges them, meets their needs, and helps them reach their goals.

During my Senate confirmation hearing, I laid out my vision in very simple terms. I said, "I trust parents, and I believe in our children."[9] That remains my vision today. Indeed, it's my life's work. Our children, *your children*, have been held hostage for too long. So long as I have breath, I'll remain in the fight for them, and I hope you'll join me! Working together with many others who are committed to education freedom for all, we can be the agents for change. Remember, there are more of us: more students, more parents, more reformers, and more concerned citizens than there ever will be apologists for the system.

This is a book about extraordinary, but ultimately *ordinary*, people; people who are motivated by the most common and human of concerns: the welfare of their children. I haven't quoted a lot of eminent historical figures in this book. But there is something President Lincoln said on the eve of the Civil War that fits here. "The dogmas of the quiet past, are inadequate to the stormy present," he wrote to Congress. "As our case is new, so we must think anew, and act anew."

We have an urgent problem. Challenges—even great challenges like the pandemic—will come and go. But educating and preparing the rising generation of a nation is a timeless pursuit. It's also a can't-fail exercise. It's no exaggeration to say that our future hangs in the balance. The world is changing, rapidly. Our economy has changed fundamentally. Globalization demands that we educate our kids to be aware of and know how to handle global foes. Today's children will be tomorrow's national leaders, and we need to give them every opportunity to be successful.

In America, the solution to a problem is always found in freedom. The solution to our future will be found in education freedom. Freedom from centralized control. Freedom from a one-size-fits-all mentality. Freedom from "the system."

The education "dogmas of the quiet past" are truly inadequate today. Parents all over America are awakening to this fact. We must think anew and act anew. We're too great a nation to do anything less, and our children deserve nothing less. A better and brighter future awaits each and every child if we have the courage and the political will to set them free. Only through education freedom will they be *hostages no more*.

EPILOGUE

About two weeks before the father took to the microphone at the Loudoun County School Board meeting to berate the members for "hiding behind our children as an excuse for keeping schools closed," I resigned as the U.S. secretary of education.

Quitting isn't in my DNA. I've often said, "You owe it to your ideas to win." When I take on a mission, I do so to see it through to completion.

The only exception is when there is no other tenable choice. That's been the case twice in my life: once as state party chair in 2000, and then as secretary of education in 2021.

The warning signs had been gathering for some time.

I was concerned about how the president was handling his defeat—or *not* handling it, as it were. He was increasingly isolated in the White House. He rarely left. All the wrong people were whispering all the wrong things in his ear. But to be honest, I didn't have a lot of time to be focused on that. Congress was in the middle of negotiating the second COVID relief bill and all of my attention was on trying to get the School Choice Now bill included. As was always the case, President Trump would do and say what he pleased. I was concentrating on doing the work.

The first time I really paused and reflected on his crusade to overturn the election's results was at a meeting of the 1776 Commission.

The president opened the meeting, but the Constitution wasn't on his mind—the election results were. He spent twenty minutes regaling us with his views on why the election was a fraud. Finally, one member had heard enough. She told the president that the only way he might have any chance of achieving what he wanted was if he humbled himself before the Lord. She slid her daily devotional book across the Cabinet Room table to the president.

The president accepted the book and responded that she might have a point. We got on with the meeting's agenda. But what followed made it fairly clear that the president did not take the message on humility to heart.

I watched with horror what transpired on January 6, 2021. You could see the Capitol very prominently from my office at the department. Though I didn't always like what happened under that dome, the dome itself was a strong and striking visual reminder to me about the fight for freedom. I didn't watch the worst of it from that vantage point. At the insistence of my team, especially the Marshals, I had headed home around lunchtime. They were getting numerous indications it wasn't going to be a good day in DC. But I don't think anyone knew it would end up as badly as it did.

Some believe the president sparked the fire that was lit that day—I'll acknowledge it's certainly debatable. But I'm not sure he really envisioned or wanted what would happen next, either. What is not debatable is that he failed to act to put a stop to it. My breaking point came when President Trump did *not* do what only he could do: call off the mob that was ransacking the Capitol building. My concern became shock when he turned on his vice president—a friend who had been unfailingly loyal to Trump—even as he and his family were forced into hiding by the mob.

To me, there was a line in the sand. It wasn't about the election results. It was about the values and the image of the United States. It was about public service rising above self. The president had lost sight of that.

It was also unclear to me if the president was actually in the mental place to continue to serve as the commander in chief of the most powerful military in the world. His behavior had grown increasingly erratic and unnerving.

The Constitution prescribes very few significant powers to members of the cabinet. The one clear power it provides is through the Twenty-Fifth Amendment, which states that if a majority of the cabinet and the vice president submit "their written declaration that the President is unable to discharge the powers and duties of his office, the Vice President shall immediately assume the powers and duties of the office as Acting President."

The Constitution holds the cabinet responsible, like a board of directors, to remove the president if he is unable to do the job. What exactly constitutes being "unable" is a largely untested legal question, but it was a question I thought we had an obligation to ask. I spent much of the morning of January 7 calling my cabinet colleagues to gauge their opinions. They were mixed, ranging from a desire to convene the cabinet to a need to better understand the legal framework to a desire to remain silent.

Later that afternoon, I reached Vice President Pence, the man who had made me education secretary—twice—and the man who came face-to-face with real threats against his life the day before. I was concerned about him, and I couldn't even begin to imagine the weight and stress he felt. My message was that, as a friend, I was there to support anything he wanted to do. I'll hold the substance of the conversation in confidence, but as Mike Pence has said publicly, he didn't see removing the president from office as the proper thing to do.[1] I respected his decision, but I told him I couldn't just stand by and do nothing. He said he respected that, in kind.

I sent the president my resignation that evening, noting that "there is no mistaking the impact your rhetoric had on the situation, and it is the inflection point for me."

My chief of staff, Nate, had told me about watching his young daughter watch the violence on the television on January 6. The image of a child witnessing the degradation of such a powerful symbol of American democracy as the Capitol stayed with me.

"Impressionable children are watching all of this, and they are learning from us," I wrote the president. "I believe we each have a moral obligation to exercise good judgement and model the behavior we hope they would emulate. They must know from us that America is greater than what transpired yesterday."

I didn't get to speak to the president, and haven't since, but instead received a reply from White House chief of staff Mark Meadows: "Thank you for your service." With that, *my* work in Washington came to an end. But *the* work of freeing America's students to learn and grow carries on.

I had pointed out in my letter: "We should be highlighting and celebrating your Administration's many accomplishments on behalf of the American people."[2] On this point I felt especially strongly, as there were so many good things that had simply gone unreported or uncelebrated.

That was certainly true of the Department of Education. We had reoriented the conversation on education to be about students and their needs, not adults. We had navigated a pandemic that was transformational for our schools. We had restored sanity to sexual harassment cases under Title IX. We had made the student loan process fairer, less costly, and more student-centric. We had gotten Washington bureaucrats and their "guidance" out of the way and empowered students, teachers, families, communities, and states to do what worked best for them.

I am proud of the work our team did. We changed the debate about education in Washington and sparked significant progress in the states. I'm grateful that President Trump gave me the opportunity to serve. The experience made me more hopeful and optimistic than ever about improving the lives and learning journeys of America's future, her children.

ACKNOWLEDGMENTS

First and foremost, I'm grateful to my children and grandchildren for their unwavering love and support. My passion for serving kids has meant my own have not gotten my undivided attention on too many occasions. And to my extended Prince and DeVos families, you've put up with getting mud-splattered because of my work more than once. You have calmly wiped it off and kept going. I'm grateful for your love and support.

My husband, Dick, has been supporter and encourager extraordinaire. His input and perspective on this project were highly valued. Not to mention the fact that even after forty-three years, my heart still picks up pace when I see him.

Writing a book was never on a list of things I wanted to do, but it falls squarely into two categories I embrace: lifelong learning and sharing things about which I'm passionate. It has been far more engaging and cathartic than I had imagined, no doubt because of the people with whom I was blessed to work in the process.

Jessica Gavora was a joy to work with. Her patience, wisdom, and talent with her craft were a godsend. Then there is Nate Bailey. I cannot adequately capture his contributions to what you have (hopefully) enjoyed and been challenged by. He has been like an air traffic controller and pilot simultaneously. I cannot thank either of them enough.

Several friends and colleagues provided timely and invaluable input, most certainly making the read better. Thank you Greg McNeilly, John Booy, Greg Brock, Tandy Champion, Em Wierda, Bill Hybels, Bruce Los, and Bill Payne. I'm grateful for each of your contributions. Bob Eitel and Jim Blew helped recall some of the finer (or more alarming) details of our work at the Education Department.

Dougie Simmons and Liz Hill provided logistical support and helpful research, in addition to the myriad other ways they have helped me do the things I do best. And there was no better support team in DC than those with whom I was privileged to work, including: Sarah Delahunty, Jessica Newman, Allen Ernst, Daniela Garcia, and Nick Hahn. To *every* member of our political appointee team, thank you for the time and talent you invested in the cause of America's students.

I'm also grateful for all the members of the U.S. Marshals Service who protected me at (nearly literally) every step. Dan Vizzi and team—thank you, thank you.

Phil Rosenfelt, Denise Carter, Jason Gray, Tracey St. Pierre, Joe Conaty, and all the folks at ED who came to work each day with the kids we serve in mind—thank you for your commitment. Paul Wood and Joshua Hoover, thank you for all the beautiful photos—and the laughs—along the way. And Officer Newman, I will always remember and cherish your joyful daily greeting.

So many friends were regular sources of encouragement as well. Our Insula group: Jillane and Bill, Sally and Dirk, Leesa and Jon, Linda and Ken, Susan and Clare, Sharon and Dave, Mary and Garth, Sally and Bill, Andi and Frank, Julie and Brian, Meg and Kevin, Val and Mike, Claire and Garry, Marcy and Jerry; our house church: John, Ruth and Jeff, Stefany and Tom; along with Lynne and Bill, Tori and Henry, Kathy and Al, Dee and Jimmy . . . doing life with you is quite awesome.

Alex Pappas, thanks to you and the whole Hachette team for your editorial support and encouragement. Matt Latimer and Keith Urbahn at Javelin, thank you for your help from start to finish.

Finally, a salute to my fellow education freedom fighters on the front lines. There's nobody else I'd rather be in the battle with than the likes of Bill Oberndorf, John Kirtley, and the entire AFC team. To every student, parent, grandparent, aunt, uncle, elected official, or anyone else who has courageously added their voice to the chorus demanding that kids be held hostage no more: thank you most of all.

NOTES

INTRODUCTION: THE QUIET PART OUT LOUD

1. Horace Mann, *Lectures and Annual Reports on Education* (Boston: Lee & Shepard, 1872), p. 210.
2. "NAEP Long Term Trend Assessment Results: Reading and Mathematics," *The Nation's Report Card*, 2020.
3. "Education Expenditures by Country," National Center for Education Statistics, May, 2021.
4. "PISA 2018 Mathematics Literacy Results," National Center for Education Statistics, 2018.

CHAPTER TWO: THE UN-AMERICAN EDUCATION SYSTEM

1. David Broder, "Teachers' Union: Vital Bloc for Carter," The Washington Post, July 2, 1980.
2. Joseph A. Califano Jr., *Governing America: An Insider's Report from the White House and the Cabinet* (New York: Simon & Schuster, 1981).
3. Ibid., p. 284.
4. "History," Children's Scholarship Fund, accessed June 2021.
5. Justice Samuel Alito, concurring opinion in *Espinoza v. Montana Department of Revenue*, Supreme Court of the United States, 2019.
6. June Kronholz, "In Michigan, Amway Chief and Wife Give School Vouchers a Higher Profile," *Wall Street Journal*, October 25, 2000.
7. "Engler Certain That Voucher Plan Is a Loser," *Detroit Free Press*, December 23, 1999.
8. Tim Skubick, *Off the Record* (Ann Arbor: University of Michigan Press, 2003), p. 198.
9. John Agar and John Tunison, "Senator Comes Clean on Trash," *Grand Rapids Press*, July 4, 2002.

CHAPTER THREE: "THE REAL DEBATE ISN'T BETSY DEVOS"

1. "The 123s of School Choice," Ed Choice, April 14, 2021, p. 28.
2. David N. Figlio, Cassandra M. D. Hart, and Krzysztof Karbownik, "Effects of Scaling Up Private School Choice Programs on Public School Students," National Bureau of Economic Research, February 2020.
3. Fred Lucas, "Energy Secretary Granholm's investment in electric vehicle battery company sparks concern," Fox News, May 13, 2021.
4. "Teachers Unions: Long Term Contribution Trends," Open Secrets, accessed September 2021.
5. Emma Brown, "Trump Picks Billionaire Betsy DeVos, School Voucher Advocate, as Education Secretary," *Washington Post*, November 23, 2016.
6. Alyson Klein, "How Many Education Secretaries Have Been K–12 Classroom Teachers?" *Education Week*, February 16, 2016.

7. "Notable & Quotable: Elizabeth Warren on School Vouchers," *Wall Street Journal*, February 8, 2017.

8. Todd Spangler and Greg Toppo, "Betsy DeVos Nomination Clears Senate Committee in Tight Vote," *Detroit Free Press*, January 31, 2017.

9. Rebecca Buck, "How Cory Booker's Past Support for School Choice Could Complicate His 2020 Campaign," CNN Politics, March 29, 2019.

10. Laura Waters, "Analysis: Cory Booker Could Have Run Away from School Reform. Instead, He's Doubling Down on Newark's Education Revival. That's a Smart Move," *The 74*, September 17, 2018.

11. Eric Garcia, "Booker on DeVos: 'I'm Not Saying Anything,'" *Roll Call*, December 2, 2016.

12. Naomi Nix, "Cory Booker Has 'Serious Early Concerns' About Nomination of DeVos as Education Sec'y," *The 74*, December 14, 2016.

CHAPTER FOUR: THE SWAMP

1. Emily Tillett, "Dick Durbin Tells Betsy DeVos Cuts to Special Olympics Get 'Gold Medal for Insensitivity,'" CBS News, March 28, 2019.

2. Erica L. Green and Maggie Haberman, "After Trump Casts Blame for a Special Olympics Cut, Betsy DeVos Flashes Pique," *New York Times*, March 29, 2019.

3. Alice B. Lloyd, "DeVos Calls on Congress to Clarify Title IX," *Weekly Standard*, July 13, 2017.

4. Jessica Bakeman, "After Calling Black Colleges School Choice 'Pioneers,' DeVos to Speak at Bethune-Cookman Graduation," *Politico*, April 30, 2017.

CHAPTER FIVE: THE SCHOOLS OF THE FUTURE ARE HERE TODAY

1. Paul E. Peterson, *Saving Schools: From Horace Mann to Virtual Learning* (Cambridge, MA: Harvard University Press, 2011), p. 210.

2. "New York City Charter Schools Are in Demand," New York City Charter School Center, Spring, 2019.

3. Jamison White, Jessica Snydman, and Yueting Xu, "How Many Charter Schools and Students Are There?" National Alliance for Public Charter Schools, July 19, 2021.

4. "DC's Public Charter Schools," DC Public Charter School Board, July 2020.

5. "City Enrollment Share," National Alliance for Public Charter Schools, September 9, 2020.

6. "Charter School Performance in New York City," Center for Research on Education Outcomes, 2017, Table 7, p. 46.

7. "Charter School Performance in Michigan," Center for Research on Education Outcomes, January 11, 2013, Table 3, p. 15.

8. "Straight Facts About Success Academy and NYC Charter Schools," Success Academy, September 16, 2016.

9. Corey A. DeAngelis, Patrick J. Wolf, Larry D. Maloney, and Jay F. May, "Charter School Funding: Inequity Surges in the Cities," School Choice Demonstration Project, University of Arkansas, November 2020.

10. Corey A. DeAngelis, Patrick J. Wolf, Larry D. Maloney, and Jay F. May, "A Good Investment: The Updated Productivity of Public Charter Schools in Eight U.S. Cities," School Choice Demonstration Project, University of Arkansas, April 2019.

11. Ibid.

12. "Map: Tracking Betsy DeVos' School Visits," *Education Week*, accessed August 2021.

13. Kimberley A. Strassel, "One of America's Remotest States Makes Learning Work," *Wall Street Journal*, May 15, 2020.

14. Phil Hamburger, "Is the Public School System Constitutional?" *Wall Street Journal*, October 22, 2021.

CHAPTER SIX: THERE'S NOTHING CIVIL ABOUT CIVIL RIGHTS

1. Samantha Harris and K. C. Johnson, "Campus Courts in Court: The Rise in Judicial Involvement in Campus Sexual Misconduct Adjudications," *NYU Journal of Legislation & Public Policy* 22, no. 1 (2019): 49.

2. Robby Soave, "Tennessee Student Accused of Sexual Harassment Because He Wrote Instructor's Name Wrong," *Reason*, October 4, 2016.

3. Harris and Johnson, "Campus Courts," p. 49.

4. Rachel Axon, "Feds Press Colleges on Handling of Sex Assault Complaints," *USA Today*, July 14, 2014.

5. *Davis v. Monroe County Board of Education*, United States Supreme Court, No. 97-843 (1999).

6. Sheila Coronel, Steve Coll, and Derek Kravitz, "*Rolling Stone* and UVA: The Columbia University Graduate School of Journalism Report," *Rolling Stone*, April 5, 2015.

7. Jeffrey Rosen, "Ruth Bader Ginsburg Opens Up About #MeToo, Voting Rights, and Millennials," *Atlantic*, February 15, 2018.

8. "K–12 Education: Discipline Disparities for Black Students, Boys, and Students with Disabilities," U.S. Government Accountability Office, March 22, 2018.

9. "Joint 'Dear Colleague' Letter," U.S. Department of Education and U.S. Department of Justice, January 8, 2014.

10. This is in line with one of many important recommendations we made in the Final Report of the Presidential Commission on School Safety.

11. Megan O'Matz and Scott Travis, "Schools Culture of Tolerance Lets Students Like Nikolas Cruz Slide," *South Florida Sun Sentinel*, May 12, 2018.

12. Andrew Pollack and Max Eden, *Why Meadow Died: The People and the Policies That Created the Parkland Shooter and Endanger America's Students* (Franklin, TN: Post Hill Press, 2019).

13. "Final Report of the Federal Commission on School Safety," December 18, 2018.

14. "Annual Report to the President, the Secretary, and the Congress," U.S. Department of Education Office for Civil Rights, January 2021.

CHAPTER SEVEN: THE HIGHER ED HIGHWAY

1. U.S. Representative Virginia Foxx, "Stop Calling It 'Vocational Training,'" *Wall Street Journal*, December 31, 2018.

2. Josh Mitchell, *The Debt Trap* (New York: Simon & Schuster, 2021), p. 9.

3. Camilo Maldonado, "Price of College Increasing Almost 8 Times Faster Than Wages," *Forbes*, July 24, 2018.

4. Paul Fain, "Wealth's Influence on Enrollment and Completion," *Inside Higher Ed*, May 23, 2019.

5. Anthony Carnevale, Jeff Strohl, and Neil Ridley, "Good Jobs That Pay Without a BA," Georgetown University Center on Education and the Workforce, 2017.

6. Adam Looney, David Wessel, and Kadija Yilla, "Who Owes All That Student Debt? And Who'd Benefit if It Were Forgiven?" Brookings Institution, January 28, 2020.

7. Josh Mitchell, "U.S. Student-Loan Program Now Runs Deficit, CBO Estimates," *Wall Street Journal*, May 7, 2019.

8. Angie Drobnic Holan, "Lie of the Year: 'If You Like Your Healthcare Plan You Can Keep It,'" PolitiFact, December 12, 2013.

9. "Should We Forgive All Student-Loan Debt?" *Wall Street Journal*, May 26, 2020.

10. Adam Looney, "Putting Student Loan Forgiveness in Perspective: How Costly Is It and Who Benefits?" Brookings Institution, February 12, 2021.

11. Ibid.

12. Sandy Baum and Adam Looney, "Who Owes the Most in Student Loans: New Data from the Fed," Brookings Institution, October 9, 2020.

13. "Report on the Economic Well-Being of U.S. Households in 2020," Board of Governors of the Federal Reserve System, May 2021.

14. Amy Laitinen, "Cracking the Credit Hour," New America Foundation, September 2012.

15. "The Story of WGU," Western Governors University, accessed October 2021.

16. "We Call It Competency-Based Education—Our Grads Call It the Best Way to Learn," Western Governors University, accessed October 2021.

17. "Western Governors University Was Not Eligible to Participate in the Title IV Programs, Final Audit Report," U.S. Department of Education Office of the Inspector General, September 2017.

18. Hallie Busta, "Western Governors U Does Not Have to Pay Back $713M in Title IV Funds," Higher Ed Dive, January 14, 2019.

19. "Section 117 of the Higher Education Act of 1965," U.S. Department of Education, accessed November 2021.

20. Ethan Epstein, "How China Infiltrated U.S. Classrooms," *Politico*, January 16, 2018.

21. "Institutional Compliance with Section 117 of the Higher Education Act of 1965," U.S. Department of Education Office of the General Counsel, October 2020.

22. "Harvard University Professor Convicted of Making False Statements and Tax Offenses," U.S. Department of Justice Office of Public Affairs, December 21, 2021.

23. American Council on Education Senior Vice President Terry W. Hartle, letter to Acting U.S. Department of Education General Counsel Reed Rubenstein, August 9, 2019.

24. Amy Wax and Larry Alexander, "Paying the Price for Breakdown of the Country's Bourgeois Culture," *Philadelphia Inquirer*, August 9, 2017.

25. Amy Wax, "What Can't Be Debated on Campus," *Wall Street Journal*, February 16, 2018.

26. Chrissy Clark, "University to Investigate Lecturer for Reading MLK's Letter from Birmingham Jail," *Washington Free Beacon*, June 6, 2020.

27. Nick Gillespie, "Abigail Shrier: Trans Activists, Cancel Culture, and the Future of Free Expression," *Reason*, July 7, 2021.

28. Abigail Shrier, "What I Told the Students of Princeton," *Truth Fairy*, December 8, 2021.

29. Chelsea Mitchell, "I Was the Fastest Girl in Connecticut. But Transgender Athletes Made It an Unfair Fight," *USA Today*, May 22, 2021.

30. U.S. Senator Ben Sasse, *The Vanishing American Adult* (New York: St. Martin's Press, 2017), pp. 6–7.

31. Princeton University President Christopher L. Eisgruber, "Letter from President Eisgruber on the University's Efforts to Combat Systemic Racism," Princeton University Office of Communications, September 2, 2020.

32. Assistant Secretary of Education Robert King, letter to Princeton University President Christopher L. Eisgruber, September 16, 2020.

CHAPTER EIGHT: THE EDUCATION FREEDOM AGENDA

1. "A Lifetime of Fighting for Education for All, a Conversation with Virginia Walden Ford," *Catalyst*, George W. Bush Institute, no. 19 (Summer 2020).

2. "A Mayor Breakthrough," *Wall Street Journal*, May 6, 2003.

3. Juliet Eilperin, "House Advances Education Overhaul," *Washington Post*, May 24, 2001.

4. Spencer S. Hsu, "House Approves Vouchers for D.C.," *Washington Post*, December 9, 2003.

5. "Total and Current Expenditures Per Pupil in Public Elementary and Secondary Schools: Selected Years, 1919–20 through 2017–18," National Center for Education Statistics, Digest of Education Statistics, Table 236.55, 2020.

6. "Staff Employed in Public Elementary and Secondary School Systems, By Type of Assignment: Selected Years, 1949–50 through Fall 2018," National Center for Education Statistics, Digest of Education Statistics, Table 213.10, 2020.

7. "Department of Education Budget History Tables," Ed History spreadsheet, U.S. Department of Education, 2021.

8. Ibid., "NAEP Long Term Trend Results."

9. "Mathematics: Student Group Scores and Score Gaps, NAEP Long-Term Trend Assessment Results," *The Nation's Report Card*, 2020.

10. Eric A. Hanushek, Paul E. Peterson, Laura M. Talpey, and Ludger Woessmann, "The Achievement Gap Fails to Close," *Education Next* 19, no. 3 (Summer 2019).

11. Mark Dynarski and Kirsten Kainz, "Why Federal Spending on Disadvantaged Students (Title I) Doesn't Work," Brookings Institution, November 20, 2015.

12. "NAEP Report Card: 2019 NAEP Reading Assessment," *The Nation's Report Card*, 2019.

13. "National Achievement Level Results," *The Nation's Report Card*, 2019.

14. "What Are the NAEP Achievement Levels and How Are They Determined?" National Assessment Governing Board, accessed November 2021.

15. "How Did U.S. Students Perform on the Most Recent Assessments?" *The Nation's Report Card*, accessed November 2021.

16. Emma Brown, "Obama Administration Spent Billions to Fix Failing Schools, and It Didn't Work," *Washington Post*, January 19, 2017.

17. "PISA 2018 U.S. Results," National Center for Education Statistics, 2018.

18. *A Nation at Risk: The Imperative for Educational Reform*, National Commission on Excellence in Education, April 1983.

19. Martin Armstrong, "PISA 2018: The Top Rated Countries," *Statista*, December 3, 2019.

20. Sarah D. Sparks, "Young Adolescents' Scores Trended to Historic Lows on National Tests. And That's Before COVID Hit," *Education Week*, October 14, 2021.

21. "See How Eighth Grade Students Performed in Civics," *The Nation's Report Card*, 2018.

22. "See How Eighth Grade Students Performed in U.S. History," *The Nation's Report Card*, 2018.

23. Patrick J. Wolf, James P. Greene, Matthew Ladner, and James D. Paul, "Is More School Choice Associated with Higher State-Level Performance on the NAEP?" School Choice Demonstration Project, University of Arkansas, March 2021.

24. Ibid., Figure 1, p. 23.

25. Ibid., Figure 2, p. 25.

26. Ibid., Figure 3, p. 26.

27. "The 123s of School Choice," Slide 7.

28. Figlio, Hart, and Karbownik, "Effects of Scaling Up Private School Choice."

29. Martin F. Lueken, "School Choice Saves Money and Helps Kids," *Wall Street Journal*, December 12, 2021.

30. The other substantive campaign promises, by our calculation, were building a wall at the southern border and repealing Obamacare.

31. "As Gov. Wolf Attacks Charter Schools, We Have Questions About His Expensive, Ultra-Exclusive Education at the Hill School," National Coalition for Public School Options, accessed August 2021.

32. Liana Loewus, "Teaching Force Growing Faster Than Student Enrollment Once Again," *Education Week*, August 17, 2017.

33. "Staff Employed in Public Elementary and Secondary School Systems," Table 213.10.

34. Houston Keene, "AFT head Randi Weingarten makes over $560,000 per year, 9 times average teacher salary, records show," *Fox News*, July 9, 2021.

35. Michael Kranish, "Cory Booker Once Allied Himself with Betsy DeVos on School Choice. Not Anymore," *Washington Post*, September 20, 2019.

36. William Mattox, "'School Choice Moms' Tipped the Governor's Florida Race," *Wall Street Journal*, November 20, 2018.

37. Tanya Paperny, "How Lobsters Are Keeping Students in School," *Atlantic*, October 11, 2016.

38. Betsy DeVos, "Betsy DeVos' Back-to-School Letter to America's Parents," *Detroit News*, August 31, 2020.

CHAPTER NINE: THE GREAT PARENTAL AWAKENING

1. Laura Meckler, "Nearly Half of Schools Are Open Full-Time, Survey Finds," *Washington Post*, March 24, 2021.

2. Emma Dorn, Bryan Hancock, Jimmy Sarakatsannis, and Ellen Viruleg, "COVID-19 and Education: The Lingering Effects of Unfinished Learning," McKinsey & Company, July 27, 2021.

3. Hailly T.N. Korman, Bonnie O'Keefe, Matt Repka, "Missing in the Margins 2020: Estimating the Scale of the COVID-19 Attendance Crisis," Bellwether Education Partners, October 21, 2020.

4. Bianca Vásquez Toness, "One in five Boston public school children may be virtual dropouts," *The Boston Globe*, May 23, 2020.

5. Alyson Klein, "Children, Teens Are in a 'Mental Health State of Emergency,' Child Health-Care Groups Warn," *Education Week*, October 19, 2021.

6. Erica L. Green, "The Students Returned, but the Fallout from a Long Disruption Remained," *New York Times*, December 24, 2021.

7. Kevin Mahnken, "New Federal Data Confirms Pandemic's Blow to K-12 Enrollment, with Drop of 1.5 Million Students; Pre-K Experiences 22 Percent Decline," *The 74*, June 28, 2021.

8. Alex Spurrier, Juliet Squire, and Andrew J. Rotherham, "The Overlooked," Bellwether Education Partners, August 31, 2021.

9. Debbie Veney and Drew Jacobs, "Voting with Their Feet: A State-Level Analysis of Public Charter School and District Public School Enrollment Trends," National Alliance for Public Charter Schools, September 22, 2021.

10. Casey Eggleston and Jason Fields, "Census Bureau's Household Pulse Survey Shows Significant Increase in Homeschooling Rates in Fall 2020," U.S. Census Bureau, March 22, 2021.

11. "Tracking School Systems' Response to COVID-19," Center on Reinventing Public Education, accessed October 2021.

12. Alexandra Hutzler, "Everything We Know About Betsy DeVos' Microgrants for Students and Teachers Hit by the Coronavirus Crisis," *Newsweek*, March 31, 2020.

13. "COVID-19 Guidance for Safe Schools and Promotion of In-Person Learning," American Academy of Pediatrics, originally published June 24, 2020.

14. Hailly T. N. Korman, Bonnie O'Keefe, and Matt Repka, "Missing in the Margins 2020: Estimating the Scale of the COVID-19 Attendance Crisis," Bellwether Education Partners, October 21, 2020.

15. "Schools Should Prioritize Reopening in Fall 2020, Especially for Grades K–5, While Weighing Risks and Benefits," National Academies of Sciences, Engineering and Medicine, July 15, 2020.

16. Talia Kaplan, "Betsy DeVos Says Kids Need to Return to Classroom: 'There Are No Excuses for Sowing Fear,'" Fox News, July 9, 2020.

17. Alec MacGillis, "The Students Left Behind by Remote Learning," *New Yorker*, September 28, 2020.

18. Douglas N. Harris, Engy Ziedan, and Susan Hassig, "The Effects of School Reopenings on COVID-19 Hospitalizations," National Center for Research on Education Access and Choice, January 4, 2021.

19. Margaret Honein, Lisa C. Barrios, and John T. Brooks, "Data and Policy to Guide Opening Schools Safely to Limit the Spread of SARS-CoV-2 Infection," *JAMA Network*, January 26, 2021.

20. "Covid-19 in Children and the Role of School Settings in Transmission—Second Update," European Centre for Disease Prevention and Control, July 8, 2021.

21. Corey DeAngelis and Christos Makridis, "Are School Reopening Decisions Related to Union Influence?" Social Science Research Network, September 1, 2020.

22. Julia Martin, "'Stop harming kids.' Students, parents protest after union blocks Montclair school reopening," NorthJersey.com, January 25, 2021.

23. Zachary Evans, "Chicago Mayor Accuses Teachers Union of Holding Students 'Hostage,'" *National Review*, January 6, 2022.

24. Dana Goldstein and Eliza Shapiro, "'I Don't Want to Go Back': Many Teachers Are Fearful and Angry Over Pressure to Return," *New York Times*, July 11, 2020.

25. "The Same Storm, but Different Boats: The Safe and Equitable Conditions for Starting LAUSD in 2020–21," United Teachers Los Angeles, July 2020.

26. "Education Stabilization Fund," U.S. Department of Education, accessed September 2020.

27. Colin Binley, Geoff Mulvihill, Camille Fassett, and Larry Fenn, "Detroit Schools Got More COVID Aid Per Student Than Any Big District in the Country," *Cranes Detroit Business*, August 26, 2021.

28. "Covid 'Relief' Through 2028," *Wall Street Journal*, February 23, 2021.

29. Valerie Strauss, "Disability Rights Advocates Urge Education Secretary DeVos to Ensure Special Education Students Receive Equal Services," *Washington Post*, April 20, 2020.

30. Erica Green, "DeVos Weighs Waivers for Special Education. Parents Are Worried," *New York Times*, April 2, 2020.

31. "Secretary DeVos Reiterates Learning Must Continue for All Students, Declines to Seek Congressional Waivers to FAPE, LRE Requirements of IDEA," U.S. Department of Education press release, April 27, 2020.

32. Asher Lehrer-Small, "The Week in School Reopenings: Nearly 9 in 10 Youth Have Access to In-Person Learning, but Some Big City Districts Are Only Now Returning Students to Classrooms," *The 74*, April 12, 2021.

33. Associated Press, "Look Up How Much Covid Relief Aid Your School District Is Getting," *Education Week*, September 10, 2021.

34. "Introduction to Critical Race Theory," Equity Collaborative, May 7, 2020.

35. Stephanie Saul, "How a School District Got Caught in Virginia's Political Maelstrom," *New York Times*, November 4, 2021.

36. Zachery Evans, "McAuliffe: Critical Race Theory Controversies are 'Made Up' by GOP to 'Divide People,'" Yahoo News, October 10, 2020.

37. Christopher F. Rufo, "Woke Elementary," *City Journal*, January 13, 2021.

38. "K–12 Math Ethnic Studies Framework," Seattle Public Schools, August 20, 2019.

39. Michael Powell, "New York's Private Schools Tackle White Privilege. It Has Not Been Easy," *New York Times*, August 27, 2021.

40. Paul Rossi, "I Refuse to Stand By While My Students Are Indoctrinated," *Common Sense*, April 13, 2021.

41. Frederick M. Hess, "Oregon Democrats Resurrect the 'Soft Bigotry of Low Expectations,'" *The Dispatch*, August 12, 2021.

42. "Retiring 'Work Hard. Be Nice.' As KIPP's National Slogan," KIPP: Public Schools, July 1, 2020.

43. Leslie Harris, "I Helped Fact-Check the 1619 Project. The Times Ignored Me," *Politico*, March 6, 2020.

44. "POLL: Americans Overwhelmingly Reject 'Woke' Race and Gender Politics in K–12 Education," Parents Defending Education, May 10, 2021.

45. Hannah Natanson, "Amid Critical Race Theory Controversy, Teachers Union Chief Vows Legal Action to Defend Teaching of 'Honest History,'" *Washington Post*, July 6, 2021.

46. Madeline Will, "Teachers' Unions Vow to Defend Members in Critical Race Theory Fight," *Education Week*, July 6, 2021.

CHAPTER TEN: WHAT'S A PARENT TO DO?

1. Todd Rose, *The End of Average: How we Succeed in a World That Values Sameness* (New York: Harper One, 2016).

2. H. L. Mencken, "The Little Red Schoolhouse," *American Mercury*, April 4, 1924, p. 504.

3. "Average Class Size in Public Schools, by Class Type and State: 2017–18," National Center for Education Statistics, accessed December 2021.

4. Thomas Jefferson, *Notes on the State of Virginia*, (Chapel Hill: University of North Carolina Press for the Institute of Early American History and Culture, 1954).

5. "Every Student Succeeds Act (ESSA)," U.S. Department of Education, accessed November, 2021.

6. "What Is the Protection of Pupil Rights Amendment (PPRA)?" U.S. Department of Education, accessed December 2021.

7. "Family Educational Rights and Privacy Act (FERPA)," U.S. Department of Education, accessed December 2021.

8. Ashley Parker and Trip Gabriel, "Donald Trump Releases Education Proposal, Promoting School Choice," *New York Times*, September 8, 2016.

9. Betsy DeVos, Opening Statement Before the Senate Health, Education, Labor, and Pensions Committee, January 17, 2017.

EPILOGUE

1. Josh Mitchell, "DeVos Resigned After She Believed 25th Amendment Taken Off Table," *Wall Street Journal*, January 8, 2021.

2. The full text of the letter read:

Dear Mr. President:

For more than thirty years, I have fought on behalf of America's students to expand the options they have to pursue a world-class education. As you know, too many of them are denied an equal opportunity to a high-quality education simply because of where they grow up or how much money their family makes. You rightly have called this one of the most significant civil rights issues of our time.

Leading the U.S. Department of Education has given me an exceptional opportunity to advocate on behalf of the forgotten students the traditional system leaves behind. We have achieved much.

We have sparked a national conversation about putting students and parents in charge of education, leading to expanded school choice and education freedom in many states. We have restored the proper federal role by returning power to states, communities, educators, and parents. We have returned due process to our nation's schools and defended the First Amendment rights of students and teachers. We have dramatically improved the way students interact with Federal Student Aid. We have lifted up students by restoring year-round Pell, expanding Second Chance Pell, delivering unprecedented opportunities for students at HBCUs, and so much more.

Finally, Mr. President, I know with certainty that history will show we were correct in our repeated urging of and support for schools reopening this year and getting all of America's students back to learning. This remains the greatest challenge our nation's students face, particularly students of color and students with disabilities. Millions are being denied meaningful access to education right now, in no small part because of the union bosses who control so much of the traditional system.

We should be highlighting and celebrating your Administration's many accomplishments on behalf of the American people. Instead, we are left to clean up the mess caused by violent protestors overrunning the U.S. Capitol in an attempt to undermine the people's business. That behavior was unconscionable for our country. There is no mistaking the impact your rhetoric had on the situation, and it is the inflection point for me.

Impressionable children are watching all of this, and they are learning from us. I believe we each have a moral obligation to exercise good judgement and model the behavior we hope they would emulate. They must know from us that America is greater than what transpired yesterday. To that end, today I resign from my position, effective Friday, January 8, in support of the oath I took to our Constitution, our people, and our freedoms.

Holding this position has been the honor of a lifetime, and I will be forever grateful for the opportunity to serve America and her students.

Sincerely,

Betsy DeVos

ABOUT THE AUTHOR

Betsy DeVos is a leader, an innovator, a disruptor, and a champion for freedom. She is the nation's leading advocate for education freedom for students of all ages, having served as the eleventh U.S. secretary of education from 2017 to 2021. Betsy advocates for free people, free markets, free exchange of ideas, and most notably, freedom in education. As a champion for school choice and multiple education options for all students after high school, she believes in the unique potential of every student and that there is no one-size-fits-all pathway to success. For more than three decades, she has been tireless in her pursuit of public policy reforms that get government out of the way and allow all students the freedom, flexibility, resources, and support they need to choose where, when, and how they learn. Her advocacy has led to the creation of new educational choices for K–12 students in more than twenty-five states and the District of Columbia and expanded post–high school education options for students and adult learners alike.

DeVos is also an accomplished business leader. She served as chairman of The Windquest Group, a privately held investment and management firm based in Michigan with a diversified consumer product and service portfolio. She is the former chair of the American Federation for Children, the Philanthropy Roundtable, and the Michigan Republican Party, and has served on a number of other national boards, including the Kennedy Center and the American Enterprise Institute. DeVos is a graduate of Calvin College and is married to entrepreneur, philanthropist, and community activist Dick DeVos. Together they have four children and ten grandchildren.

INDEX